Queering Motherhood: Narrative and Theoretical Perspectives

Demeter Press logo based on the sculpture "Demeter" by Maria-Luise Bodirsky <www.keramik-atelier.bodirsky.de>

Printed and Bound in Canada.

Library and Archives Canada Cataloguing in Publication

Queering Motherhood / edited by Margaret F. Gibson

Cover photograph by Euphemia Redden

Cover Design & Typeset by Lyndsay Kirkham

Includes bibliographical references.

ISBN 978-1-927335-31-4 (pbk.)

Queering motherhood : narrative and theoretical perspectives / edited by Margaret F. Gibson.

1. Lesbian mothers. 2. Motherhood. 3. Queer theory. 4. Feminist theory. I. Gibson, Margaret F., 1974-, editor
HQ75.53.Q83 2014 306.874'308664 C2014-905461-0

Demeter Press
140 Holland Street West
P. O. Box 13022
Bradford, ON L3Z 2Y5
Tel: (905) 775-9089
Email: info@demeterpress.org
Website: www.demeterpress.org

Table of Contents

To Lauren, Lindsay, and Alistair.

Acknowledgements

It is fitting that this particular book has so many parents. First, I owe a debt of gratitude to Andrea O'Reilly and the staff at Demeter Press for seeing the need for this book and supporting its conception well before my own involvement. Thanks are also due to the anonymous reviewers for their time, encouragement, and suggestions. Next, the contributors to this book deserve a medal each for their unwavering commitment to this project throughout an extended editorial and production process. While the range of topics and styles represented in their chapters is vast, all of the authors brought generosity and rigour to their work. I hope they are as pleased with the final product as I am. Among the contributors, Joani Mortenson warrants special mention as the previous editor of the collection. I am indebted to her for her initial work on the collection and her subsequent encouragement as I took on this new role. I am particularly grateful for her work in finding the cover image.

I would also like to thank the people in my own life who have supported this endeavor. My thesis committee at the University of Toronto, including my supervisor, Izumi Sakamoto, has indulged me as I have divided my time between this book and my dissertation. Moving back in time, I am eternally grateful to the informal queer mothers' group I attended almost ten years ago, founded by Ilana Landsberg-Lewis and continued by many others. That group not only offered a child-proofed place to speak with other adults but also provided me with a much-needed queer community in a time of sleep deprivation. Reaching still further back, I would like to thank my mother, Sally Gibson, for leaving her feminist magazines lying around when I was learning to read, and my father, Douglas Gibson, for showing me that men could indeed get dinner on the table. Both have also passed along an interest in engaging, clear prose.

As any parent who has been consumed by a large project can testify, a small army of friends, colleagues, relatives, and caregivers has been indispensable. I can name only a few. To Alison MacKay, Hyacinth Bouchard, Zechariah Bouchard, and Jenna Rose, thank you all for taking such terrific care of my children. To Katie Gibson, Jane Gibson, Sandy Sergio, David Sergio, Carrie Costello, Pablo Felices-Luna, Carla Reynolds, and Michaela Hynie, thank you all for your unwavering encouragement over the years.

Finally, my understanding of queering motherhood would be hopelessly hypothetical without my wife, Lauren Sergio, and my children, Lindsay and Alistair. You have each supported the creation of this book. Thank you for everything you have taught me along the way.

Introduction

Queering Motherhood in Narrative, Theory, and the Everyday

MARGARET F. GIBSON

> Heterosexuality as a compulsory orientation reproduces more than "itself": it is a mechanism for the reproduction of culture, or even of the "attributes" that are assumed to pass along a family line, such as whiteness. It is for this reason that queer as a sexual orientation "queers" more than sex, just as other kinds of queer effects can in turn end up "queering" sex. It is important to make the oblique angle of queer do this work. (Ahmed 161-162)

Queering makes the things we otherwise take for granted suddenly unpredictable, uncooperative, and unexpected. As Sara Ahmed describes, the designation "queer" has something to do with sex, with gender, with race, with embodiment, and with disrupting the normative practices of kinship and culture. At the same time, queer is not reducible to any of these other terms, even as an antonym or a flip side. Queer eludes definition, but constantly asks that we define our terms. Queer questions any notion of faithful reproduction, of more of the same, or even of predictable notions of variation. Queer brings the political and the social into a self-conscious connection with the intimate.

What might "queering motherhood" then mean? Reproduction, sexuality, culture, kinship, race, embodiment — all have intimate and expected connections to motherhood. When any of these are pulled outside of expectation, are "queered," can any aspect of motherhood remain untouched? There are unstable boundaries to what can be queered, and how. What is seen as "not yet queer" is vulnerable from multiple oblique angles, as Ahmed observes. Michael Warner, almost twenty years earlier, expressed a similar insight: "Het[erosexual] culture thinks of itself as the elemental form of association, as the very model of intergender relations, as the indivisible basis of all community, and as the means of reproduction without which society wouldn't exist" (xxi). In this light, queering motherhood becomes a truly expansive project, an endeavor that might profoundly destabilize existing social relations, institutions, and discourses.

We are certainly experiencing an explosion in public discussions of different family forms, including but not limited to families with gay parents, transgender parents, lesbian parents, and bisexual parents. In Canada, where I live, it is difficult to find a week in which the mainstream media do not report on lesbian, gay, bisexual, or, less frequently, transgender/transsexual or queer people (LGBTQ people) and their families.[1] This is an astonishing shift in societal attention when compared with mainstream media reports from ten years ago, when such references to non-heterosexual and non-cisgender parents were rare and unrelentingly controversial.[2]

For example, I am writing during the build-up to the Olympic Games in Sochi, Russia. Almost every Canadian news report about the event also highlights the violent effects of anti-queer legislation in that country. Many have included accounts of queer parents who are fearful that their children will be taken from them. While there are certainly queer critiques that could be made of such media accounts (especially using Jasbir Puar's concept of "homonationalism"), their prevalence nonetheless represents a widespread and astonishingly rapid socio-cultural shift that has given at least some queer parents an unprecedented presence in the mainstream (Puar 4).

WRITING ABOUT QUEER PARENTS: IS IT KID STUFF?

The academic realm has also been the site of a growing and apparently unquenchable interest in research and writing about LGBTQ parents and their children. It has been less than twenty years since groundbreaking social science researchers such as Fiona Nelson, Charlotte Patterson, and Judith Stacey started writing large-scale studies of lesbian mothers and gay fathers. These authors explored the sociological and relational possibilities that such parents might experience, opening up space to explore how child-rearing might proceed outside of heteronormative scripts and in spite of institutional barriers. These earlier investigations often built upon Kath Weston's 1991 *Families We Choose: Lesbians, Gays, Kinship*, which explored practices of family among gays and lesbians in California (including some parents). As Weston described, gays and lesbians practiced "chosen family" in the face of widespread institutional erasure of queer kinship, erasure that was characterized by both a lack of legal protection for queer relationships and the common experience of being "disowned" by family of origin upon coming out as gay or lesbian. Thus Weston depicted such "choice" as already shaped and restricted by heteronormativity, even as chosen family was a creative and positive presence in many people's lives (Weston *Long Slow Burn* 83-93).

While some of this early research explored the potential alternatives to "nuclear" family models that could be found among LGBTQ people, a lot of research has since become more narrowly focused on proving that queer parents are not inherently harmful to children.[3] There has been good reason for this shift. Research has been urgently required to support queer parents' efforts to access reproductive and adoptive service systems, or to obtain custody of their children after divorce or separation. Researchers have been routinely summoned by lawyers and legislators to demonstrate the fitness of queer parents, thus putting considerable pressure on the types of research that were required (see Thompson 56-84; Stacey and Biblarz; Clarke). In this context, most social science researchers in the field have reported, over and over again, that children of queer parents scored within "normal" and "acceptable" ranges on various developmental measures, and that they are no more likely than children of heterosexual parents to develop queer identities themselves.

This research emphasis on "good outcomes" among the children of LGBTQ parents has had a profound impact on legislative and court proceedings, and continues to be necessary in jurisdictions where being LGBTQ can be used as a legal reason to deny parental custody, adoption, or foster caring. At the same time, it accepts the terms of existing systems that would view "normalcy," particularly regarding sexuality and gender, as a "good outcome." Indeed, the very possibility of "difference" to be found in queer parents and their families, when compared to their heterosexual counterparts, has been avoided and downplayed by researchers as legally and politically risky (Stacey and Biblarz).

Further, this focus on child outcomes has restricted what researchers, journalists, and parents themselves are able to say about LGBTQ parenting experiences. An emphasis on whether and how the children of queer parents "measure up" to a predetermined standard inevitably steers our attention away from any critiques of normative motherhood that queer parents might express. As a result, a lot of questions have been left unanswered about what queer parents might actually experience, or do, or want. What if queer parents have different objectives for their children than meeting the standard developmental outcomes? What if queer parents don't particularly care if their children demonstrate "normative" (i.e. heterosexual, cisgender) sexual and gender identities? What if queer parents parent "queerly," with different goals, values, and strategies than those found in dominant ideologies of motherhood? What if LGBTQ parents are "queer" to different degrees, or in different ways?

Simultaneously, and particularly when marriage rights have been politically prioritized, many queer parents have themselves been tempted by the lure of "normalcy."[4] Such parents may emphasize the ways that they are "just like" other couples and families, highlighting relational features (such as monogamy or marriage) or social practices (such as church attendance or "stay-at-home parenting") that make them seem more mainstream. Of course, not all queer parents want such normalcy and not everyone has equal access to it. In particular, people whose lives are more resolutely outside of the idealized norm have been left out of both political discourse and research literature. Transgender, transsexual, bisexual, and multiply marginalized queer parents, such as those living in poverty or experiencing racism, have been largely excluded from existing research and popular discourse (Downing; Ross and Dobinson; Moore and Brainer).[5] It is also important to note that strategies and practices of "queer respectability" or what Lisa Duggan calls "homonormativity" (50), extend beyond parenthood and are widespread in LGBTQ media representation, political strategizing, and even organizational development (see Ward).

As many jurisdictions have witnessed a decline in the urgency and prevalence of legal threats to LGBTQ parental rights, researchers have started turning (or indeed, returning) their attention toward other questions and goals regarding queer parents. Rachel Epstein's groundbreaking 2009 collection, *Who's Your Daddy? And Other Writings on Queer Parenting*, has simultaneously challenged homonormative scripts and provided an invaluable resource for parents, community members, researchers, and "queer spawn" as the first Canadian anthology on queer parenting. There is a growing critique of the way that social science has shaped emerging constructions of queer parenthood (see for example Malone and Cleary). A number of scholars, among them Julie M. Thompson, Laura Mamo, Damien Riggs, Jacquelyne Luce, Victoria Clarke, and Stephen Hicks, have re-centred their analyses on parents' experiences within existing institutions and discourses. Their research has investigated the institutional and sociocultural pressures that are imposed upon queer people who parent (or want to parent): these include biomedical notions of "risk" in family creation (Mamo, Luce), socio-legal constructs such as "the best interests of the children" (Clarke, Riggs, Thompson), and widespread concerns about children's presumed need for "gender role models" (Clarke, Hicks, Thompson).

Meanwhile, there has been an explosion of popular and literary writing about queer pregnancy, adoption, and parenting. These works showcase an impressive diversity of parental experiences, including a range of LGBTQ attitudes toward "fitting in" as a family. They have been met by a well-established LGBTQ market for the consumption of books related to reproduction and parenting (Esterberg 76).[6] Many of these works have crossed genre divides between academic, activist, literary, how-to, and humour writing. The Internet has only further expanded the accessibility of queer parents' voices—as well as offering a forum to their most virulent detractors. Across multiple fronts, the number of readily available representations of LGBTQ-identified parents has proliferated.

DOES QUEERING MOTHERHOOD EQUAL QUEER MOTHERS?

The project of queering motherhood certainly has a great deal to gain from listening to the perspectives of parents with "queer" sexual and gender identities, especially when it brings these experiences to the centre of the analysis. Through the voices of queer-identified parents we can hear stories and insights that might otherwise be drowned out by the din of cisnormative and heteronormative "tradition." Such stories expand our notions of the possible, and create connections between individuals across time and space. The perspectives of queer-identified parents allow us to see how our existing sociocultural scaffolding is constructed. They can point to the gaps or weakened joints that merit our attention as we build and dismantle identities and relations in the everyday.

But it is a mistake to think that queering motherhood is only and inevitably a matter of addition, of bringing parents who identify as "queer" and/or "trans" into existing, unyielding frameworks. Motherhood is such a closely monitored and prevalent identity, such a fundamental component of social ideology, that there is ample territory for "queering": academic concepts, political movements, cultural representations, and institutional arrangements, to name a few options. The parenting experiences and insights of those who do not identify as "queer" can also queer motherhood. In this volume, "queering" is understood to extend beyond individual identity and toward a consideration of how relationships, communities, genders, and sexualities might proceed otherwise. Queering motherhood can therefore start where any of the central gendered, sexual, relational, political, and/or symbolic components of "expected" motherhood are challenged. These challenges can be experiential, empirical, or theoretical.

A few words about motherhood are in order. As a foundational social construct, "motherhood" is invoked whenever we take parenting and reproduction seriously, regardless of whether or not the individuals involved are seen as, or believe themselves to be, "mothers." Even when we consider the practices and perspectives of queer fathers, transgender and transsexual parents, genderqueer parents, intersex parents, or even of queer people who did not ultimately become parents, we grapple with the institution of motherhood. Parenthood, fatherhood, family, and other social constructs may very well be simultaneously queered as we "queer motherhood." Indeed, such further queering is inextricable and inevitable. Further anthologies on queering fatherhood or queering kinship would be welcome contributions.

It is also worth noting that the power of "motherhood as an institution" (Rich 34) means that too often *any* alternative versions of motherhood are displaced or dismissed. Such re-assertions of patriarchal, restrictive, cisnormative and heteronormative motherhood can be seen in individual narratives: of a trans "Papa" being "mommed" (see Garner), or of an adoptive mother who knows she is "supposed" to feel like her child's saviour (see Jeske). They are also found in the narrow understandings of family, gender, and scholarly practice that prevail across academic disciplines. Some authors in this collection have explicitly discussed the ways that existing theories and methods in their respective fields do not allow motherhood to be easily "queered" (e.g. Sardadvar and Miko).

Any anthology can only achieve so much against the daily onslaught of what sociologist Dorothy Smith dubbed "SNAF" or the "Standard North American Family," wherein cisgender, middle-class, heterosexual, married, non-primary-breadwinner, "traditional" mothers are identified as the key to children's every success and the reproduction of patriarchal, capitalist society (Smith 159). Yet this collection exists in the hope that it will raise questions through a fuller exploration of the experiences and ideas that operate outside of, and in spite of, dominant institutional forms of motherhood. The effects of such questions may be difficult to contain.

NARRATIVE, THEORY, AND THE EVERYDAY

> We were a Black and a white lesbian in our forties, raising two Black children.... We had to learn and teach what works while we lived, always, with a cautionary awareness of the social forces aligned against us—at the same time, there was laundry to be done, dental appointments to be kept, and no you can't watch cartoons because we think they rot your feelings and we pay the electricity. (Lorde 76)

Scholarship on both motherhood and queerness falls outside of disciplinary boundaries, and the authors in this collection select from a wealth of theoretical and analytical approaches. At the same time, there is a vast textual, topical, and theoretical expanse that "queering" and "motherhood" can address. It is easy to get lost in such a world of untethered possibility.

Audre Lorde's quotation brings us back to the everyday ground that queering motherhood must also walk. In her 1986 essay on lesbian parenting, Lorde insists that we contend with the undeniable social structures of exclusion (racism, misogyny, homophobia), *as well as* the everyday demands and delights of raising young people to thrive, nevertheless. Her essay argues that we cannot afford to tune out the societal or the particular, the political or the personal, since each shapes the other.

Lorde's assertion resonates throughout this collection, whether in chapters geared primarily to "experience" or "representation" or "activism." Queering motherhood must attend, not only to motherhood as it occurs in overarching discourses and institutional restrictions, but also to everyday activities, material inequities, and embodied relationships. In other words, these authors grapple with the messiness of family, gender, scholarship, embodiment, representation, and policy. This is a multilayered and potentially complicated approach, and each chapter achieves it through different methods, topics, and formats.

What approaches might support such a combined attention to the discursive (or structural) with the everyday (or experiential) in the endeavor of queering motherhood? The subtitle of this collection "narrative and theoretical perspectives" offers a possible guidepost. And yet, these terms also require some clarification. Too often, "theory" is contrasted with "real life," and "narrative" (or even "anecdote") is contrasted with "evidence." Theory and narrative are here presented as scholarly, rigourous, and necessary.

While "narrative" is a central feature of this collection, it is defined broadly as stories, excerpts from stories, and storytelling devices (such as verbal images or metaphors). Narrative offers a way to bring "everyday experiences" into scholarly analysis, and also encourages us to see "texts" such as films or press releases as the products of particular people, in particular moments, with particular audiences. Some of the narratives included in this volume were collected from formal research studies (e.g. Epstein, Craven and Peel, Sardradvar and Miko). Most of the authors in this book (but not all) have also included some narrative information about their own relationship to the topic discussed. Sometimes these personal narratives are the focus of the chapter; sometimes they are combined with other people's narratives; often they are integrated with academic findings and theoretical reflections. A few chapters include narratives and texts found in films, websites, books, or other media. The exact use and form of narrative is left open to the authors' definitions and purposes. For some, the unit of analysis is an excerpt, a metaphor, or a story. In others, the method of analysis is also a story.

Similarly, "theory" appears in various guises. Most contributors, but not all, consider large-scale, academic forms of theory, citing well-known writers such as Cixous, Marx, or Butler. Particular theoretical concepts form the backbone of some chapters. In others, the theory being considered is more evident in unstated assumptions or troubling encounters. Theory in this sense is a way of explaining the world beyond one immediate moment, of addressing the "why" of experience (hooks *Teaching to Transgress* 59-75). Theory is thus an active and evolving entity with "real life" implications, not a fixed and distant object.

Bringing narrative and theory to the task of queering motherhood thus encourages us to draw connections between the experiential, the representational, and the analytical, although not in any prescribed way. The integration of narrative and theory is certainly not unusual in feminist, critical race, or queer scholarship, or in many academic disciplines such as cultural studies or anthropology. At the same time, such an approach goes against socially-dominant assumptions that large numbers, objective analyses, and *a priori* hypotheses are the only path to knowledge. In so doing, this collection does not intend or assert any methodological imperative, that the approaches listed are the only or best way to queer motherhood. Instead, *Queering Motherhood* brings forth stories often untold and explanations unexplored—because they are ignored, assumed, or unfathomable under dominant ways of interpreting the world.

CROSS-FERTILIZATION: MOTHERING QUEER THEORY, QUEERING MOTHERING THEORY

> Here we can think about *low theory* as a mode of accessibility, but we might also think about it as a theoretical model that flies below the radar, that is assembled from eccentric texts and examples and that refuses to confirm the hierarchies of knowing that maintain the *high* in high theory. (Halberstam 16, emphasis in the original)

Queer theory writer Judith Halberstam builds upon the work of Stuart Hall, among others, to consider what "low theory" might offer queer investigations. In *The Queer Art of Failure*, Halberstam pulls together unanticipated combinations of academic tools of analysis with children's television shows, popular movies, and other texts that usually escape the notice of "high theory." Halberstam describes "low theory" as a deliberate means to escape the limitations of disciplinarity, "the hierarchies of knowing" that restrict our thinking and our expression when we ask to be taken seriously.

Motherhood, and parenting practice more generally, is a domain that often "flies below the radar" of academic and theoretical seriousness. Patriarchal assumptions of motherhood's mindlessness, universality, "common sense," or "biological" inevitability have been consistent targets of feminist critique.[7] In taking motherhood seriously, scholars of mothering and motherhood have already challenged the very divisions between "high theory," "low theory," and real life. Further, many have drawn upon "popular" examples as a strategy to connect with a broader audience.

But, queer theorists such as Halberstam offer more than simply an argument for attending to broadly available texts, practices, and concepts. The emerging scholarly tradition of queer theorists is irrevocably interdisciplinary and unapologetically attentive to "popular" discourses or "stupid archives" (Halberstam, Berlant). What are the possible benefits of developing motherhood archives and mothering practices as "low theory"? That is, by taking notions of parenting, motherhood, and sexuality as our focus, can we be more playful? Can we "queer motherhood" by shaking off methodological and theoretical formulae in our own beliefs and practices of what constitutes academic writing on motherhood, or scholarship more generally? In this collection, several authors have departed from academic formulae of scholarship to include poems, journal entries, and emotional confessions. There is room for further considerations of the silly, the mundane, and the "stupid" in our work. As any parent knows, there is an abundance of material detritus, emotionally-charged but inarticulate and unresolved interactions, and tedious repetitions in caring for young people. How can these be accessed and used toward "scholarly" ends?

More generally, can the combined resources of queer theory and maternal theory provide fertile territory for developing new lines of inquiry and new tools of analysis? This collection certainly suggests as much. While maternal theory is a well-developed field in many respects[8], its central texts do not fundamentally challenge heteronormative and cisnormative assumptions. While most recent writers on motherhood have incorporated some LGBTQ content in their work, this has largely occurred as an add-on rather than a central refashioning of existing scholarship. For example, classics such as Nancy Chodorow's *The Reproduction of Mothering* have accepted the heteronormative family structure as the basis of psychic development, wherein the "problem" to be solved becomes the division of caring work done by mothers and fathers. Further, gender is usually analyzed as a constant, completed "fact" in such scholarship, a starting place from which individual women strive to meet unobtainable standards of "motherhood" (e.g. Griffith and Smith). Even Adrienne Rich, well-known as a lesbian mother and motherhood theorist, did not discuss the relevance of her lesbian perspective in *Of Woman Born* until the preface of the second edition (xxx-xxxii).

Yet, scholars of queer kinship must not ignore maternal theory. Motherhood scholarship offers excellent examples of how to bring material and economic considerations together with symbolic and representational concerns. For example, analyses of motherhood as both a refuge from and a site of racist oppression and cultural imperialism are fundamental to any consideration of reproduction and parenting. These important investigations can be seen in the work of Patricia Hill Collins, Cherrie Moraga, Dorothy Roberts, bell hooks, and Audre Lorde, among others. "Mothering discourses" and their near-saturation of institutional relations, texts, and daily experiences have been usefully explored by scholars such as Allison Griffith and Dorothy E. Smith, as well as in Adrienne Rich's influential treatise. Analyses of the legal definitions, policy implications, and economic costs/ contributions of mothering—and of caring labour more generally—are also indispensable contributors to a more material understanding of child-rearing labour and family structures (see e.g. Cornell, Crittenden, Neysmith et al.). Critiques of "intensive mothering" practices as apparently elective, largely middle-class practices in the Global North that reinforce economic and gender hierarchies, offer crucial considerations for queer examinations of parenting work and identity (see Hays 412-414, O'Reilly "Feminist Mothering" 815-819).

Meanwhile, the classic cannon of queer theory—if such a thing exists—has largely operated outside of the realm of the parental. For example, while many contributors in this collection cite pivotal work by Judith Butler on performativity, gender, and social intelligibility, Butler's own reliance on psychoanalytic traditions has meant she has considered "subjectfication" almost exclusively from the perspective of the infant/ child rather than from that of the parent/caregiver (e.g. *The Psychic Life of Power* 132-150).[9] This is a focus retained by many other queer theorists, particularly those who have used psychoanalytic resources; such approaches relegate mothers and other caregivers to the background of subjectification. Further, in contrast with the largely relational focus of maternal theorists (e.g. Diquinzio; Kinser 123-140; Chandler 529-541), queer theorists and others from post-structuralist lineages have often relied on "individuated" subjects (Smith 104-109), who seem to operate free from explicit social ties and processes.

Further, a central critique of queer theory is that too many of its acolytes stay safely in the realms of "discourse," at a remove from the immediate legal, social, or emotional concerns of everyday life. This focus on the textual, symbolic, and representational at the expense of the material, relational, and embodied leads many queer scholars to ignore material concerns such as poverty, violence, and labour. Such matters are particularly crucial to understanding everyday experiences of parenting (see Kinsman and Gibson, this volume). As a result of this flight to discourse, otherwise provocative notions such as Lee Edelman's objection to "reproductive futurity"—in which the symbolic Child is invoked as a futuristic rationale for existing subjugation—remain distantly removed from questions of how the reproduction and parenting of actual children might take place. Finally, and of particular concern in this volume, Viviane Namaste and others have convincingly argued that queer theory has contributed to the conceptual "erasure" of transgender and transsexual people; its writers may attend to and even celebrate the theory of gender transgressions, but they often ignore the experiences of exclusion and violence faced by trans people (Namaste 9-23).

Despite the need to address these failings, queer theorists' willingness to take risks in both their choice of content and their theoretical flexibility offer exciting possibilities to scholars of parenting ideologies and practices. Furthermore, more writers are addressing these critiques and absences, both through modifying queer investigations and through integrating other theoretical resources. The work of writers such as Sara Ahmed, Lauren Berlant, Judith Butler, Jasbir Puar, Eve Kosofsky Sedgwick, Dean Spade, Michael Warner, and Kath Weston all identify important connections between political economy, cultural rhetoric, and everyday violence in the (re)production of cisnormative and heteronormative institutions, including motherhood.

Bringing together the most productive strands of queer theory and maternal theory promises new resources for scholars of sexuality, gender, and motherhood. Even as they share common theoretical allegiances with feminist traditions, these conceptual and analytical resources have seldom been pooled or recombined in scholarly practice. *Queering Motherhood: Narrative and Theoretical Perspectives* can be seen as one part of such a larger project. At the same time, the contributors draw upon a wide variety of other theoretical resources that extend beyond queer theory or motherhood studies. The reader is invited to consider other "playful" and promising combinations within and across chapters.

QUEERING MOTHERHOOD AS A COLLECTIVE AND ECLECTIC ENDEAVOR

The authors in this volume have all considered what it might mean to rethink, re-shape, and re-establish notions and practices of motherhood from queer perspectives. Some of them have focused on the experiences of mothers who identify as queer due to lesbian, bisexual, transgender, or other non-heterosexual/ non-cisgender identities. Others have explored the experiences of people who may identify as parents but not mothers, or as mothers but not women. Two chapters have examined the experiences of people who may or may not be parents, but who have attempted to bring children into their lives from queer social locations. Several chapters have moved away from experiential accounts to explore the cultural, political, and historical meanings of parenting and motherhood using queer theories and perspectives. Finally, a number of chapters have examined how mothering practices may be "queered" when they do not follow normative scripts, even if the individuals themselves may not identify as queer.

As an aid to the reader, I have grouped the chapters under three sections.

QUEER CONCEPTIONS: WHERE TO BEGIN?

Queering motherhood invites questions that precede the birth, or even the conception, of a child. In this section are five chapters that consider different aspects of conception, pregnancy, and birth. First, Rachel Epstein examines the ways that institutional restrictions shape the experiences of lesbian, gay, bisexual, and transgender prospective parents in fertility/ assisted reproduction clinics. In particular, Epstein highlights the experiences of prospective parents who plan to use "known sperm donors"; many are encouraged or even coached to lie about their relationships by clinic staff. By identifying the relationship with the known sperm donor as both legally fraught and experientially significant, Epstein asks that we attend to how particularly "queer" forms of kinship are unrecognizable in institutional settings.

Tanya M. Cassidy considers historical records about 17th and 18th-century European midwifery practices using a multi-layered, queer perspective. She examines the professional rivalry between midwives and doctors as rife with sexual fears and accusations and considers their present-day implications. Cassidy's exploration of "touch" as a domain with few archival records relies on other "oblique" sources—such as a journalist's account of a drag pantomime at a "mollyhouse"—to illustrate the sensual and relational role of the midwife.

Cary Gabriel Costello blends an analysis of medical texts and practices with his own experiences of intersex pregnancy and birth. He argues that medical and gender ideologies have infringed, often violently, on the bodies and choices of intersex individuals. Costello asks that we re-examine how "fertility" and "intersex" are defined by medical texts and practices, and that we critique the ways that such categorization practices are reinforced by gender dualism and unquestioned medical authority.

Alisa Grigorovich examines social media responses to the widely publicized "pregnant man," trans parent Thomas Beatie, who was the centre of a media whirlwind. Grigorovich analyses online comments that individuals made in response to news stories about Beatie, and identifies three main categories of transphobic objection to his pregnancy: gender essentialism, disgust, and concern "for the child." More generally, Grigorovich considers the reasons Beatie's pregnancy became so sensationalized and its possible impact on public discourse.

In the final chapter of this section, Christa Craven and Elizabeth Peel consider queer people's experiences of reproductive loss, whether through miscarriages, stillbirths, or failed adoptions. They bring findings from two of their own studies to explore what might be specifically "queer" about people's experiences of these types of losses, and note particular struggles for intended parents often termed "non-biological". They call for greater attention to this topic throughout the research literature on miscarriage, stillbirth, adoption, and queer parenting.

QUEERING PRACTICES, PRACTICING QUEERS

In the next section, the authors examine the experiences and practices of parenting in more detail. They consider not only how queer individuals parent, but what might be "queer" in the practices of parenting and forming families.

Barbara Gurr, for example, uses autoethnography to explore what is "queer" in her mothering experience as a heterosexual, cisgender mother to a transgender daughter. She describes the ways that she and then others scrutinize her parenting differently when her child asserts her own gender identity, and how the feared spectre of "Bad Feminist Mom" rears its head in such moments. Gurr also considers how her family as a whole has a "coming out" experience, both in facing hostile responses and in developing new identities and communities.

Raine Dozier challenges the absence of transgender experiences in "queer parenting" research, in which sexual identities have received the primary focus. Dozier draws on her own experiences as a genderqueer parent, and brings in some of her children's thoughts on the fears and freedoms associated with having a "guy mom." Dozier describes how institutional definitions of motherhood continue to influence everyday experiences, as seen in legal systems where Dozier is viewed as a "single mother," and suggests that doing "ordinary" mothering/ parenting practices as a queer, trans person can itself be seen as "queer."

Karin Sardadvar and Katharina Miko also challenge notions of what "queer" might include by revisiting how their field of sociology understands families. They identify rigidly gendered, heterocentric, and sexually-restrictive assumptions in family research and consider how case studies from their own studies with Austrian families highlight the inadequacies of existing categories. Sardadvar and Miko argue that queer family research and queer theory help us to understand these often "heterosexual" families in a way that dominant sociological frameworks do not.

Kelly Jeske takes a different approach and offers a deeply personal narrative of her experiences as a queer, adoptive mother. She describes her desire to voice the emotions that have been silenced in most narratives of motherhood, and of adoptive motherhood in particular—fear, desperation, longing, grief, doubt, depression, shame, suicidality. Speaking these truths, Jeske suggests, is another way of queering motherhood, as is finding new forms of family when parental relationships change.

T. Garner also delves into hir own experiences of transgender parenting, identity, and embodiment in "Becoming Papa: From Daughter to Dad." By considering narratives of hir relationships with hir children, father, and father-in-law, Garner brings a multi-generational consideration of what parenting and fatherhood can look like in everyday life. Garner incorporates theories of embodiment into understanding hir role of "Papa" as an ongoing, embodied, social practice in which storytelling matters.

QUEER FUTURES? YEARNINGS, ALLIANCES, AND STRUGGLES

In this final section, the authors address questions about the symbolism, meaning, and potential of queering motherhood. While some continue to draw upon intensely personal narratives, all include questions about the activist and symbolic possibilities of queering forms, representations, and practices of motherhood.

Joani Mortenson, working with contributions from her son, Luke Mortenson, begins this section by combining poems, reflections on a conference presentation, a photograph, and academic analyses to explore maternal eroticism. Mortenson proposes that we widen our recognition of the embodied possibilities of sensory, emotional connection between mother and child, and argues that "maternal eroticism" can provide life-giving possibilities that contrast with heteronormative idealizations of motherhood. In its varied, non-linear format, this chapter also urges us to widen the forms of meaning-making we value as mothers, parents, and scholars.

I wrote the next chapter, based largely on my experiences as a queer mother learning to navigate disability service systems alongside my daughter. In it, I discuss the ways that rage and resistance can be seen in mothers' experiences, and how these connect with larger beliefs about disability and professional expertise. I argue that queer communities are not immune to ableist and mother-blaming ideologies, nor are we exempt from the institutional influence of "experts," yet there are possibilities for us to nurture resistance in our own lives, and in those of our children.

Damien W. Riggs and Sujay Kentlyn offer a chapter on the under-examined topic of trans women's ageing in the context of kinship relations—or lack thereof. While they draw on a range of research findings and narratives, they focus the chapter on the story of KrysAnne from the American documentary *Gen Silent.* Riggs and Kentlyn use KrysAnne's story to illustrate how the combination of inadequate housing and health-care for older people, widespread transphobia, and older trans parents' frequent estrangement from their children and other family can have dire consequences when an older trans woman becomes unwell or frail.

Mary Jo Klinker considers queer possibilities by exploring how American antimilitarist movements have used maternal imagery. She describes both the history of maternal symbolism in anti-war mobilizations and its recent invocations in protests against the Iraq war. Drawing upon concepts used in queer theory such as "queer time" and "fetal personhood," Klinker argues that the symbolic abundance of maternal meanings—with "mothers" often championing contradictory causes—can make the use of maternal imagery a fraught choice for activists.

The final chapter in this section, and in the collection, takes another format entirely. In it, I interview Gary Kinsman, longtime queer activist and sociologist. Kinsman discusses the ways that queer movements have inadequately attended to parenting and the needs of young people. He argues that legalistic strategies, trends in queer theory, and the emergence of "the neo-liberal queer" have shifted activist and scholarly focus away from more radical revisions of kinship and child-rearing. Kinsman suggests ways that we can move toward a more collective approach to queer parenting, and challenge the material inequities that are imposed through classism, racism, sexism, and capitalist imperialism.

CONCLUSION

The greatest asset of *Queering Motherhood: Narrative and Theoretical Perspectives* is the abundant knowledge that the contributors have generously brought to this volume: conceptual tools, empirical data, life-changing stories, reflections, creative projects, questions, theories, strategies, models, excerpts from treasured or newly-discovered texts. Readers have an opportunity to engage with prominent and emerging scholars from different countries, identities, political commitments, and disciplines as they grapple with notions of queerness and motherhood. The richness of the chapters means that each resists an easy summary or typology, and many could have easily moved into other thematic sections.

I am under no illusion that these other authors would agree with my definition of "queering motherhood." Indeed, I hope they would not. Instead, I encourage readers to read each chapter in search of additional definitions and applications of what "queering motherhood" is or could be. Even with the range of topics, disciplines, geographic locales, topics, and approaches evident in this volume, there are inevitable gaps. For example, with contributors currently living in Australia, Canada, the United States, Ireland, and Austria, *Queering Motherhood* has an undeniable international reach; it is also limited by a focus on Eurocentric cultures and traditions. As readers encounter the ideas and words of each author, I encourage them to bring their own experiences, questions, and commitments into the conversation. There is much to be added, much to be expanded upon, much to be challenged. Queering motherhood is a long-term, open-ended, evolving undertaking. Let us begin.

NOTES

[1]Sexual and gender identifiers are slippery and inadequate, and many people do not easily identify with any of the "LGBTQ" labels (or cisgender or heterosexual). I use "lesbian," "gay," "bisexual," and "heterosexual" to mean people who identify their sexuality in these ways. I use "cisgender" to describe people for whom the sex and gender they were assigned at birth aligns neatly with their subsequent sex or gender identities. "Trans" and "transgender" are used to describe people who do not (or do not exclusively) identify with the sex and gender they were assigned at birth. "Intersex" is used to describe people whose reproductive anatomy has been categorized as falling between "male" and "female" in dualistic gender systems, usually at birth. "Heteronormative" describes beliefs and systems that presume heterosexual identities and relationships to be the "norm." "Cisnormative" describes beliefs and systems that presume cisgender identities and relationships to be the "norm." "Queer" is used as the most general catch-all available for people who have sexual or gender identities and relationships that fall outside of heteronormative and cisnormative categories.

[2]I would hasten to add that reports on trans, intersex, and genderqueer parents continue to be met with particular vitriol. See Grigorovich's chapter in this collection.
[3]See the collection edited by Abbie E. Goldberg and Katherine R. Allen for detailed summaries of social science research with LGBTQ families. See also the American Psychological Association's reports and annotated bibliography, and the summary of existing research trends in Gibson "Queer Mothering and the Question of Normalcy."
[4]See Epstein "Queer Parenting in the New Millennium" and Gibson "Queer Mothering and the Question of Normalcy" for more detailed considerations of this point.
[5]Vivianne Namaste's investigation of the "erasure" of transgender people's concerns in social science is particularly relevant to both parenting practices and parenting research.
[6]For examples, see works listed by Bergman, Brill, Epstein (ed. *Who's Your Daddy*), Flacks, Lorde, Moraga, Pepper, and Savage.
[7]See cited works by Rich, Ruddick, and O'Reilly.
[8]See *Maternal Theory* (edited by Andrea O'Reilly) for examples of central texts in this scholarship.
[9]Judith Butler does address issues of queer parenting in "Is Kinship Always Already Heterosexual?" in *Undoing Gender* (102-130). Throughout this volume she also invokes more relational notions of subjectivity than are found in her earlier work.

WORKS CITED

Ahmed, Sara. *Queer Phenomenology: Orientations, Objects, Others.* Durham: Duke University Press, 2006. Print.

American Psychological Association. *Lesbian and Gay Parenting.* Washington, DC: APA, 2005. Print.

Bergman, S. Bear. *Blood, Marriage, Wine and Glitter.* Vancouver: Arsenal Pulp Press, 2013. Print.

Berlant, Lauren. *The Queen of America Goes to Washington City: Essays on Sex and Citizenship.* Durham: Duke University Press, 1997. Print.

Bos, Henny. "Lesbian-Mother Families Formed Through Donor Insemination." *LGBT-Parent Families: Innovations in Research and Implications for Practice.* Ed. Abbie E. Goldberg and Katherine R. Allen. New York: Springer, 2013. 21-37. Print.

Brill, Stephanie A. *The Queer Parent's Primer: A Lesbian and Gay Families' Guide to Navigating the Straight World.* Oakland: New Harbinger, 2001. Print.

Butler, Judith. *Gender Trouble: Feminism and the Subversion of Identity.* London: Routledge, 1990. Print.

—. *The Psychic Life of Power: Theories in Subjection.* Stanford: Stanford University Press, 1997. Print.

—. *Undoing Gender.* London; Routledge, 2004. Print.

Chandler, Mielle. "Emancipated Subjectivities and the Subjugation of Mothering Practices." *Maternal Theory: Essential Readings.* Toronto: Demeter Press, 2007. 529-541. Print.

Chodorow, Nancy. *The Reproduction of Mothering.* University of California Press, 1978. Print.

Clarke, Victoria. "What About the Children? Arguments Against Lesbian and Gay Parenting." *Women's Studies International Forum* 24.5 (2001): 555-570. Print.

Collins, Patricia Hill. *Black Feminist Thought.* New York: Routledge, [2000] 2009. Print.

Cornell, Drucilla. "Adoption and Its Progeny: Rethinking Family Law, Gender, and Sexual Difference." *Adoption Matters: Philosophical and Feminist Essays.* Ed. Sally Haslanger and Charlotte Witt. Ithaca NY: University Press, 2005. 19-46.

Crittenden, Anne. *The Price of Motherhood: Why the Most Important Job in the World Is Still the Least Valued.* New York: Henry Holt and Company, 2000. Print.

DiQuinzio, Patrice. *The Impossibility of Motherhood: Feminism, Individualism and the Problem of Mothering.* New York: Routledge, 1999. Print.

Doucet, Andrea. *Do Men Mother?* Toronto: University of Toronto Press, 2006. Print.

Downing, Jordan B. "Transgender-Parent Families." *LGBT-Parent Families: Innovations in Research and Implications for Practice.* Ed. Abbie E. Goldberg and Katherine R. Allen. New York: Springer, 2013. 105-116. Print.

Duggan, Lisa. *The Twilight of Equality? Neoliberalism, Cultural Politics, and the Attack on Democracy.* Boston: Beacon, 2003. Print.

Edelman, Lee. *No Future: Queer Theory and the Death Drive*. Durham, NC: Duke University Press, 2004. Print.

Epstein, Rachel. "Queer Parenting in the New Millennium: Resisting Normal." *Canadian Woman Studies* 24.2/3 (2005):7-14. Print.

—, ed. *Who's Your Daddy? And Other Writings on Queer Parenting*. Toronto: Sumach Press, 2009. Print.

Esterberg, Kristin G. "Planned Parenthood: The Construction of Motherhood in Lesbian Mother Advice Books." *Feminist Mothering*. Ed. Andrea O'Reilly. Albany: SUNY Press, 2008. 75-88. Print.

Flacks, Diane. *Bear With Me: What They Don't Tell You about Pregnancy and New Motherhood*. Toronto: McClelland and Stewart, 2005. Print.

Gibson, Margaret F. "Adopting Difference: Thinking Through Adoption by Gay Men in Ontario, Canada." *Signs: Journal of Women in Culture and Society* 39. 2 (2014): 407-432. Print.

—. "Intersecting Deviance: Social Work, Difference, and the Legacy of Eugenics." *British Journal of Social Work* (2013). Web. 30 Sept. 2013.

—. "Queer Mothering and the Question of Normalcy." *Mothering Across Difference*. Ed. Andrea O'Reilly. Toronto: Demeter, 2014. 347-366. Print.

Goldberg, Abbie and Katherine Allen, eds. *LGBT-Parent Families: Innovations in Research and Implications for Practice*. New York: Springer, 2013. Print.

Griffith, Alison I. and Dorothy E. Smith. *Mothering for Schooling*. New York: RoutledgeFalmer, 2005. Print.

Halberstam, Judith (Jack). *In a Queer Time and Place: Transgender Bodies, Sexual Subcultures*. New York: New York University Press, 2005. Print.

—. *The Queer Art of Failure*. Durham: Duke University Press, 2011. Print.

Hays, Sharon. "Why Can't a Mother Be More Like a Businessman?" *Maternal Theory: Essential Readings*. Ed. Andrea O'Reilly. Toronto: Demeter Press, 2007. 408-430. Print.

Hequembourg, Amy. *Lesbian Motherhood: Stories of Becoming*. New York: Harrington Park Press, 2007. Print.

Hicks, Stephen. "Gender Role Models… Who Needs 'Em?!" *Qualitative Social Work* 7.1 (2008): 43-59.

—. "Is Gay Parenting Bad for Kids? Responding to the Very Idea of 'Difference' in Research on Lesbian and Gay Parents." *Sexualities* 8.2 (2005):

153-169.
—. *Lesbian, Gay, and Queer Parenting: Families, Intimacies, Genealogies.* Basingstoke, UK: Palgrave Macmillan, 2011. Print.
hooks, bell. "Revolutionary Parenting." *Maternal Theory: Essential Readings.* Ed. Andrea O'Reilly. Toronto: Demeter Press, 2007. 145-156. Print.
—. *Teaching to Transgress: Education as the Practice of Freedom.* New York: Routledge, 1994. Print.
Kinser, Amber E. "Mothering as Relational Consciousness." *Feminist Mothering.* Ed. Andrea O'Reilly. Syracuse: SUNY Press, 2008. 123-140. Print.
Lorde, Audre. "Turning the Beat Around: Lesbian Parenting 1986." *I Am Your Sister: Collected and Unpublished Writings of Audre Lorde.* Ed. Rudolph P. Byrd, Johnnetta Betsch Cole, and Beverly Guy-Sheftall. New York: Oxford University Press, 2009. 73-80. Print.
Luce, Jacquelyne. *Beyond Expectation: Lesbian/ Bi/ Queer Women and Assisted Conception.* Toronto: University of Toronto Press, 2010. Print.
Malone, Kareen and Rose Cleary. "(De)Sexing the Family: Theorizing the Social Science of Lesbian Families." *Feminist Theory* 3.3 (2002): 271-293. Web. 22 Oct. 2010.
Mamo, Laura. *Queering Reproduction: Achieving Pregnancy in the Age of Technoscience.* Durham, NC: Duke University Press, 2007. Print.
Moore, Mignon R. and Amy Brainer. "Race and Ethnicity in the Lives of Sexual Minority Parents and Their Children." *LGBT-Parent Families: Innovations in Research and Implications for Practice.* Ed. Abbie E. Goldberg and Katherine R. Allen. New York: Springer, 2013. 133-148. Print.
Moraga, Cherrie. *Waiting in the Wings: Portrait of a Queer Motherhood.* Ann Arbor MI: Firebrand, 1997. Print.
Namaste, Viviane. *Invisible Lives: The Erasure of Transgendered and Transsexual People.* Chicago: University of Chicago Press, 2000. Print.
Nelson, Fiona. *Lesbian Motherhood: An Exploration of Canadian Lesbian Families.* Toronto: University of Toronto Press, 1996. Print.
Neysmith, Sheila M., Marge Reitsma-Street, Stephanie Baker Collins and Elaine Porter. *Beyond Caring Labour to Provisioning Work.* Toronto: University of Toronto Press, 2012. Print.
O'Reilly, Andrea. "Feminist Mothering." *Maternal Theory: Essential Readings.* Toronto: Demeter Press, 2007. 792-821. Print.

—, ed. *Maternal Theory: Essential Readings.* Toronto: Demeter Press, 2007. Print.

Pepper, Rachel. *The Ultimate Guide to Pregnancy for Lesbians: How to Stay Sane and Care for Yourself from Pre-conception Through Birth.* San Francisco: Cleis Press, 1999. Print.

Puar, Jasbir. *Terrorist Assemblages: Homonationalism in Queer Times.* Durham: Duke University Press, 2007. Print.

Rich, Adrienne. *Of Woman Born: Motherhood as Experience and Institution.* New York: W. W. Norton, 1986 [1976]. Print.

Riggs, Damien W. "Developmentalism and the Rhetoric of Best Interests of the Child: Challenging Heteronormative Constructions of Families and Parenting in Foster Care." *Journal of GLBT Family Studies* 2.2 (2006): 57-73.

Roberts, Dorothy. *Killing the Black Body: Race, Reproduction, and the Meaning of Liberty.* New York: Vintage, 1998. Print.

Ross, Lori E. and Cheryl Dobinson. "Where is the 'B' in LGBT Parenting? A Call for Research on Bisexual Parenting." *LGBT-Parent Families: Innovations in Research and Implications for Practice.* Ed. Abbie E. Goldberg and Katherine R. Allen. New York: Springer, 2013. 87-104. Print.

Ruddick, Sara. *Maternal Thinking: Toward a Politics of Peace.* Boston: Beacon Press, 1995 [1985]. Print.

Savage, Dan. *The Kid: What Happened After My Boyfriend and I Decided to Go Get Pregnant.* New York: Penguin, 1999. Print.

Sedgwick, Eve Kosofsky. "How to Bring Your Kids Up Gay." *Social Text* 9.2 (1991): 18-27. Print.

Smith, Dorothy E. *Writing the Social: Critique, Theory, and Investigations.* Toronto: University of Toronto Press, 1999. Print.

Spade, Dean. *Normal Life: Administrative Violence, Critical Trans Politics, and the Limits of Law.* Brooklyn, NY: South End Press, 2011. Print.

Stacey, Judith. "Gay Parenthood and the Decline of Paternity As We Knew It." *Sexualities* 9. 1 (2006), 27-55. Print.

Stacey, Judith and Timothy J. Biblarz. "(How) Does the Sexual Orientation of Parents Matter?" *American Sociological Review* 66. 2 (2001): 159-183. Print.

Thompson, Julie M. *Mommy Queerest: Contemporary Rhetorics of Lesbian Maternal Identity.* Amherst and Boston: University of Massachusetts

Press, 2002. Print.

Ward, Jane. *Respectably Queer: Diversity Culture in LGBT Activist Organizations.* Nashville. Vanderbilt University Press, 2008. Print.

Warner, Michael. "Introduction." *Fear of a Queer Planet: Queer Politics and Social Theory*. Ed. Michael Warner. Minneapolis: University of Minnesota Press, 1993. Print.

Weston, Kath. *Families We Choose: Lesbians, Gays, and Kinship*. New York: Columbia University Press, 1991. Print.

—. *Long Slow Burn: Sexuality and Social Science*. New York: Routledge, 1998. Print.

I. Queer Conceptions: Where to Begin?

1.

The Relationship That Has No Name

Known Sperm Donors, the Canadian *Semen Regulations*, and LGBTQ People

RACHEL EPSTEIN

INTRODUCTION

Sara Ahmed describes the processes by which some people 'flow' through institutions, while others, i.e. those who are outside institutional norms, are seen to block, get in the way of, or go against the flow (181). She suggests that it is those who do not inhabit the norms of an institution that produce significant knowledge about the blockages, restrictions and stoppages within institutional worlds.

This chapter is about one such blockage, an administrative blockage that lesbian, gay, bisexual, transgender/ transsexual, and queer (LGBTQ) people experience in relation to a set of government regulations known as the *Processing and Distribution of Semen for Assisted Conception Regulations* (referred to from here on in as the *Semen Regulations*). These regulations, which came into effect in 1996 under the *Food and Drugs Act*, set out the health and safety requirements for processing and distributing third-party donor semen used or intended for use in assisted conception. The *Semen Regulations* define assisted conception as "a reproductive technique performed on a woman for the purpose of conception, using semen from a donor who is not her spouse or sexual partner." Sperm being used for assisted conception is required to be frozen and quarantined for six months, while the donor must test negatively for HIV and hepatitis at the start and the end of this time period.

Meanwhile, people seeking insemination with the semen of their spouse or sexual partner are excluded from the freezing and sexually transmitted infection (STI) testing requirements. The rationale for this quarantine exemption for 'sexual partners' relates to the risk of contracting STIs. If you are having sex with someone, you are assumed to be already taking the risk of contracting whatever diseases they might have. Insemination with their fresh, unquarantined sperm is not perceived as an additional risk to the health of the person being inseminated.

What this regulation means in practice is that a heterosexual couple, having tried to conceive for a period of time at home through sexual intercourse, can approach a clinic for assistance in getting pregnant and can request insemination with fresh sperm from the male partner. Other individuals and couples (including single, queer female and trans-masculine people) who have also tried to conceive for a period of time at home through home insemination with a known sperm donor, cannot make the same request. Although sexual intercourse and home insemination entail the same health risk, those using a known sperm donor will be required to have the donor tested and the sperm frozen; they must then wait out the six month quarantine period before beginning inseminations. This involves added medicalization, a hefty financial burden (for testing, freezing and storage of sperm), a significant time delay, and the use of frozen rather than fresh sperm, which decreases the chances of conception.[1]

As a way around these regulations, some single and LGBTQ people represent a known sperm donor as a 'sexual partner' in the fertility clinic. This typically involves actively participating in the misrepresentation and misrecognition of one's sexual orientation, sometimes gender identity, and kinship relations. There are also potential legal and emotional consequences of having the donor listed as 'sexual partner' on official medical forms.

This chapter explores the implications of the strategies deployed by LGBTQ people in relation to the *Semen Regulations*, drawing on interviews from a research study on LGBTQ people's experiences with reproductive services in the province of Ontario, Canada. In 2010-11, the Creating Our Families (COF) project interviewed 66 LGBTQ people across Ontario about their experiences, since 2007, with Assisted Human Reproduction

(AHR) services.[2] Here, I use the experience of five COF participants (or participant couples) to explore the impact of the *Semen Regulations*' prohibition of the use of fresh sperm from anyone other than a 'sexual partner' on LGBTQ people.

Charis Thompson suggests that ethicality in fertility clinic practices might be evaluated based on whether or not violations to the personhood of clients takes place (201). As I consider some of the strategies deployed by queer and trans people in relation in relation to the *Semen Regulations*, I also reflect on whether these strategies involve ruptures or violation to the personhood of those involved. In so doing, I use Pfefer's concepts of 'normative resistance' and 'inventive pragmatism' to differentiate strategies that rely on, versus those that resist, concepts of normalization. I suggest that normalization strategies, or "inventive pragmatism," such as those that involve deception or lying about sexual relations and identity, can be costly and/or violating to the self. The act of lying about one's sexual orientation and/or family configuration and relationships means not just being misrecognized, as is common in LGBTQ fertility clinic experiences (See Ross, et al; Epstein) but being asked to *actively participate in one's own misrecognition*. I also argue that at the root of the struggles that participants describe is the fact that "known sperm donor" is not intelligible as a kinship category within the institutional framework of reproductive services and legislation, or indeed within mainstream social discourses.

LYING IN WAITING ROOMS

The people

Antoinette and Donna Antoinette and Donna are two queer-identified women in a relationship. Antoinette identifies as white, and Donna as black. They are particular focused on issues of race in their decision-making regarding a sperm donor and eventually decide that rather than sifting through information about 'race' on sperm bank websites, they prefer to use a known sperm donor. They explore insemination through a clinic, but eventually get pregnant at home.

Tonya and Jacqueline Tonya and Jacqueline are two women in a relationship. Tonya identifies as white and lesbian and Jacqueline as mixed race and bisexual. They have decided to use Tonya's brother as their sperm donor and assumed they could get assistance for this process from a fertility clinic.

When they discover that this is not the case, they eventually successfully inseminate at home.

Lucy and Clare Lucy and Clare are two white women in a relationship. Lucy identifies as queer, and Clare as bisexual. They have decided to use a known sperm donor and make phone calls to clinics all over Ontario, asking about assistance with insemination.

Dan Dan is a white, trans man, partnered with another trans man who is not present for the interview. Dan has not yet achieved pregnancy and is still actively involved in the process. He represents his sperm donor as his sexual partner in the fertility clinic, where he is assumed to be a cisgender female lesbian.

Joe and Charlie Joe and Charlie are two white trans men in a relationship. Charlie wants to get pregnant. For reasons related to their experience as trans men in the health care system, as well as their preference for a known donor, they ultimately choose to inseminate at home with sperm from a known donor. However, they do utilize the services of a clinic to test Charlie's fertility, and they explore the options open to them for clinic insemination.

FRUSTRATIONS WITH THE *SEMEN REGULATIONS*

Because AHR services are, in general, becoming more open to LGBTQ clients, there are growing expectations amongst LGBTQ people that they can be assisted by clinics in their reproductive journeys, including assistance with insemination with a known donor. People express shock and surprise when they discover that there are administrative barriers, or *blockages* to refer back to Ahmed's concept, to receiving assistance. Participants describe the stress and confusion this adds to their experience:

> *Jacqueline:* We thought it was going to be pretty standard, we thought we were going to go in and tell them what we wanted to do and they'd tell us the process and it would be easy. We figured it was just a money issue that we had to figure out, we were never expecting that we would be told that we weren't able to do that.

> *Lucy*:...finding out that there were some barriers to fertility-like type services was *really* stressful. Like, highly stressful.

Joe and Charlie summarize their frustrations with the *Semen Regulations* and the barriers they encounter to using the known donor of their choice. They express concerns about time delays, financial burden, the use of frozen (versus fresh) sperm, and legal issues:

> *Joe:* What they were willing to allow was that we could have our donor come up and he could give a sample and they would test it and freeze and test it again six months later and he could keep coming up and giving samples which they would freeze and store at you know a substantial cost and then, once the embargo was lifted, they were willing to let us use it but it was going to be a six month wait, it was going to be using frozen sperm and it was going to be a crap ton of money.
>
> *Charlie*: And they would have linked the donor and I on the paper work and seen the donor and I as the parents...
>
> *Joe*: Which then would have been a further crap ton of money because we would have had to have a second parent adoption and all three of us would have had to have our separate lawyers and la la la.

In addition to these practical barriers, people encounter a policy that seems contradictory and discriminatory:

> *Tonya*: And I said right there, "Well, hang on a second, people come in here every day to become inseminated with their partner's sperm. Just because we know this guy, he's my brother, he's a family member, he's got to qualify to be a donor? Do you make these people qualify to be donors?" And they said, "Well, no, but they're married or they're in a relationship," they didn't even have to be married, they just had to be consenting adults in a relationship. And we were like, "OK, we're consenting adults in a relationship just not an intimate one, so how does that differ in definition to you?"

Participants point out the contradiction in requiring testing, freezing and quarantining for sperm from a known donor, when a sexual partner could just as likely be putting them at risk:

> *Antoinette*: But what makes the husband so trustworthy?! That's what I want to know. The assumption, you know, that relationships between the two are truthful and that no one's lying to each other and, you know, everyone's monogamous.

> *Lucy*: As near as I understood it— it was a liability issue for a medical doctor, or clinician, or whoever it would be, to do an insemination with a known donor, who hadn't had the sperm banked and frozen for something like six months...which seemed like a funny double-standard when really, you could go to any old bar on Saturday night and be like "Okay, I'm going to sleep with this person." Versus, you know, our plan was we asked our friend to have STI tests done. And he did.

People also challenged the concept of 'risk,' suggesting that the risk of choosing a donor from a sperm bank catalogue, i.e. choosing someone one does not know based on a list of characteristics and reported history, is perhaps greater than the risks involved in using a donor that is known.

> *Clare*: It [using an anonymous donor] feels like more risk to me...you know, this person I know and care about and have chosen to be my kid's father...I mean you have to have a lot of respect for someone to ask them to be the biological father of your child. It's like, that is a huge thing. And so, psychologically and emotionally it feels less risky to me to go with a known donor than some anonymous guy that, you know, who knows why they donated sperm? Like... probably for the most part it's for good reasons. But, you know, it just felt more risky.

Some AHR practitioners and others working in the field recognize the discriminatory nature of the *Semen Regulations*, and collaborate with patients to find ways to circumvent the restrictions. In most instances, this meant practitioners or clinic staff suggested that people misrepresent identity(ies) and/or family configurations. Interviewees reported that they had been advised by receptionists, students, and doctors to lie in order to access service. In most instances it was recommended that people represent the sperm donor as a 'sexual partner' to the person getting pregnant. In one instance, it was suggested that the person getting pregnant, his partner and the donor could present as a 'threesome.'

Below I consider these options and their implications in light of Thompson's concepts of 'violations to personhood' (179-204), as well as Pfeffer's 'normative resistance' and 'inventive pragmatism' (578). While nobody in the sample *did* present as a threesome and only one person (Dan) actually presented his donor as a 'sexual partner,' participants' contemplation of these strategies, as well as their decisions *not* to deploy them, can throw light on the potential costs of having to lie and collaborate in one's own misrecognition in order to access a desired service.

INVENTIVE PRAGMATISM/ NORMATIVE RESISTANCE

Carla Pfeffer explores the strategies deployed by couples composed of trans men and cisgender women in negotiating institutional contexts (574-602). She suggests that at times these couples can and do choose to manipulate existing social structures to their benefit, while at other times they might choose to actively resist normative structures and assumptions. She uses the analytic constructs "normative resistance" and "inventive pragmatism":

> *Normative resistance*: conscious and active strategies and actions for making life choices distinct from those considered most socially expected, celebrated, and sanctioned;
>
> *Inventive pragmatism*: active strategies and actions that might be considered clever manipulation of an existing social structure in order to access social and material resources on behalf of oneself or one's family. (Pfefer 578)

'Normative resistance' might include resisting traditional marriage, parenthood, and monogamy, and insisting on being visibly 'queer.' 'Inventive pragmatism,' what one might call instrumental work-arounds, might involve choosing to access marriage and legal parenthood when these can benefit oneself or one's family.

Pfefer's 'inventive pragmatism' is a process in which people make use of identified weaknesses and/or fissures in institutional power in order to derive social or economic benefits. One might argue that the decision to misrepresent one's sexual orientation, gender identity or family configuration in the fertility clinic is an example of 'inventive pragmatism,' the identification of a way through a barrier, a work-around that involves "manipulation of an existing social structure." The question I raise below is, 'inventive pragmatism' at what cost? What are the consequences of actively participating in one's own misrecognition?

TO LIE OR NOT TO LIE, THAT IS THE QUESTION

People's emotional responses to being advised to lie, to present their sperm donor as a 'sexual partner,' are complex and multi-layered, and include surprise, relief, gratitude, worry, anxiety, fear, discomfort, and, often, anger.

> *Jacqueline*: The medical professional left the room, I can't remember what they were doing, they left and there was only a student in the room with us and she said, "Well, if I were you I would just come back with your donor and pretend that you're a couple and there'd be no issue and you'd get it done."
>
> *Tonya*: I just looked at her as if she had two heads.

Clare called all the reproductive clinics she could find on line and asked about using a known donor. All of them, except one, said "We just can't do that" or "We just don't do that," until someone from a clinic in a major Ontario city made a suggestion:

> *Clare*: [She said] "Oh yes. There's a legal issue. We can't do that but just come in and tell us he's your sexual partner." Whoever answered the phone told me that. She was super-kind and really nice. And was like, "Oh yes...well, I'll tell you a secret," kind of thing, you know?
>
> I wasn't feeling like, "I can't believe that you're telling us to lie!" I was feeling like "Thank you, for, you know, telling me how this works."

Charlie and Joe received similar coaching on how they could circumvent the *Semen Regulations*, in their case from a doctor.

> *Joe*: Our meeting with the doctor was also very friendly and warm and I really got the sense that he was familiar with the Human Reproduction Act and how it is often unfair to queer couples. So he said things like, "If you have a known donor, we are willing to do cycle monitoring here, send you home

> with sample jars and syringes. We'll give you a bag of those things. If that doesn't work for you and you're looking at inseminating here, you just need to tell me you're sexually active with the donor as well as with your spouse and we can do that here. Like it really felt like he got it and was willing to work with us.
>
> *Charlie*: And [he] cheerfully suggested that threesomes (his language), were, you know, a common way for people with no sperm in their relationships to get pregnant. So even that conversation felt like, 'We know what the law says, he knows what the law says, we'll be able to dance around the law in terms of what we need, in terms of our language here and, let's get going.' And to go home with a bag of sample jars and large size syringes also felt like OK, they really are going to help as far as they can help us without legally putting us or them at risk.

Although most people express some form of gratitude, thankfulness or relief at being offered a potential way through the barrier of the *Semen Regulations*, they often also describe anger. Participants identify different sources of this anger. For instance, Tonya describes feeling angry at the assumption that she would put her partner's health at risk, in addition to anger at the institutional barriers they faced as a queer couple:

> *Tonya*: I was angry. First of all I was upset that we had to go through some different kind of process than a couple that's in a consensual relationship. In this case it's the same thing, *you have a consensual relationship*. If you think that I'm going to let my partner put sperm in her body that hasn't been tested for STDs, you're wrong. Like, no way. And he (the donor) wouldn't either! You know. And those kinds of test are covered by OHIP, you can get them done and we did, for our own purposes, they were done.

Clare also expresses anger at being put in a position where she was asked to lie about her queer identity after many years of being 'out':

> Angry that we had to lie again, you know? I spent a couple of years of my life lying already about who I was, and, you know,

> I hadn't been there in over ten...twelve years...I don't want to be lying anymore. Why do we have to lie? So I was angry about that. But also, you know, thankful for this woman and that there was an option. But... yeah, I was angry.

Participants also express anxiety, worry and ethical concerns about lying on an official medical record. They worry about the implications for the donor, as well as for themselves.

> *Clare*: I felt relieved, like, we finally figured this out. It took a long time. But I also felt like I'm not sure I can do that. I'm not sure I can walk in there. What kind of implications does this have for him and his family...if he lies on a medical record and says he's our sexual partner? ...even though his partner *knew*, we didn't feel comfortable with that scenario. But pleased to have found it out.

In general, LGBTQ people are concerned about what it means to misrepresent who the intended parents are on an official record. Again, this occurs in the context of historical vulnerability and present day concerns about parental recognition for LGBTQ people.

> *Jacqueline*: We don't want that anywhere on record that we're coming in pretending that... you know what I mean? Like even legally we would never want that to be on record that he would be the parent or anything, so...

The vulnerability of the non-biological parent is particularly salient when the donor's name, and not hers/his, is put on the record. Tonya expresses the legal vulnerability she experiences as the non-biological parent and, ultimately, the fear that she could lose her child.

> *Tonya*: I'm not going to lie about my relationship to my child, you know what I mean? For me to be put on record as ever lying in order to do something for my benefit, it's just not who I am. And...so if it came to a point where something fell through with my brother for example, having an example of a point and time where I lie doesn't work in my best interest and I'm not willing to lose my children over it, so that's where that sits. I was worried legally, I didn't want that.

Dan describes his 'husband' (i.e. donor) being asked to sign forms giving him the right to decide, in the case of Dan's death, what happens to any existing embryos. Dan goes on to describe how having his partner's name on the medical record caused problems when it comes time to inseminate:

> At one point it went badly...my chart had my real-life partner's name on it, which was not the source of the sperm. And the sperm lab looked at the sticker and said "This is no good. You must need quarantined sperm. There's been a mistake." And so we were saying 'No, there's no mistake. We're inseminating today, I'm ovulating today. This is our first time. We're doing it today.' And they said, 'No, no, no there's a problem. We can't proceed.' So that was bad. My partner took care of it and I thought, 'Oh, it's just a misunderstanding, it'll be fine.' I don't think I really realized that they could've just said 'No. This is against the rules, this is not the procedure. I'm not endangering my own lab-tech license or whatever is on the line, I'm not going to do it.'

As a result of this near miss, Dan and his partner remove the partner's name from the medical record with the result that his partner's name is completely absent as an intended parent:

> I think we peeled the sticker off because it was just too complicated. It was sad, because it was nice to have his name there. Because it felt good...because he *is* my partner and this is our child that we're trying to make together.

Dan experiences the exclusion of his partner through his erasure on the medical record. Clare, the non-genetic, intended parent with her partner Lucy, describes an additional, and significant, implication of presenting their donor as Lucy's 'sexual partner': Clare would be left out of the conception process itself.

> *Clare*: My role, as the other mom, would be not to go. I couldn't...I wouldn't show up. I remember talking to you [Lucy] about how I would feel about that...in the end, you know, sure I'd like to be there. But maybe in the end, you would just do it. I remember feeling kind of angry. But relieved. But confused. I don't...I don't know...And feeling

> excluded. I remember— actually I *did*, remember I did feel excluded?
>
> *Lucy*: You did at the beginning. Now you don't because there's just so many dirty diapers...there's more than enough of everything to go around.
>
> *Clare*: I did feel excluded. That's right...I'd forgot. I did feel excluded from it. And that was a concern that I had at the time...was feeling part of it... the whole thing — part of creating a family and...you know. Yeah. I didn't have any legal worries. Like, that wasn't it. It was more on an emotional level... not wanting to feel excluded.

Dan is the only person we interviewed who actually did misrepresent his donor as a 'sexual partner' in the clinic. He talks about how it feels to participate in a process in which he is so dramatically misrecognized. Although he identifies as a trans man and is partnered with another trans man, in the clinic he is presenting as a heterosexual woman with a cisgender male 'sexual partner' who is providing sperm. However, while the clinic assumes he *is* a woman, at times they also assume he is a lesbian, and that he is using an anonymous sperm donor. So a gay trans man, pretending to be a cisgender heterosexual woman, is misread as a lesbian. His gender identity, sexual orientation and route to parenthood are distorted and misconstrued, and his partner is left out of the process.

> *Dan*: And the doctor would be saying 'Oh, well, father's sample at this time. Don't worry; we'll take care of the timing.' And I'd say 'No, I'm talking about a person. It's not a...a sample.' And then I'd get all uptight. How do I talk about, like... 'I mean my husband, I mean my boyfriend.' I didn't know what to say but there were a couple of times that I burst out laughing because it was clear that he was assuming that I was a lesbian and I was thawing out a sperm sample. And I didn't know how to say without myself getting in trouble, 'No, he's...a...a live person coming to the clinic and ejaculating in a cup'. So there were moments where I panicked that I've said the wrong thing, but for the most part I forgot... I blocked it out.

Another consequence of Dan's 'deception' in the clinic is that he hesitates to complain about unsatisfactory treatment he is getting from this doctor, because he ia grateful that he is being allowed to use the donor of his choice:

> We [the doctor and I] were not a good fit. And I'm stubborn and I didn't want to make changes. Partly because I was so grateful that she was letting me use my known donor and pretending he was my partner...I put up with it for a long time.

Finally, although he describes often 'blocking out' the fact that he is lying, Dan articulates his underlying fears and anxieties about the potential consequences of lying:

> The doctor did explain that this person would be my partner in the clinic. That on my records he's my partner. On my chart, he's my partner. When I speak of him to the other staff I refer to him as my partner. I think at the moment she said it, it all seemed kind of heavy and serious and I worried, 'What if I slip up?' But I definitely completely forgot for most of the time I was at the clinic because I used inappropriate language and I was reminded a few times, 'who's the partner and who's the supportive friend.' And then I thought, 'Are the police going to come? Is the Ministry of Labour going to investigate me, the Ministry of Health going to investigate me? How serious is it if I say the wrong thing?

LYING AS VIOLATION

If ethicality, as Thompson (179-204) suggests, can be evaluated by ruptures or violations to personhood, the above narratives are rife with such violations. Consider the following: To be put in a position of having to actively collaborate in the misrepresentation and misrecognition of one's sexual orientation, gender identity and/or family configuration. To be potentially perceived as an irresponsible or "bad partner" by putting one's partner's health at risk. To be forced to (re)hide an aspect of one's identity that has been historically challenging to disclose. To have one's partner administratively erased from an official medical record and to have instead an inaccurate record that potentially gives significant decision-making power to someone who should not have it. To have one's partner or co-parent left out of the process of conceiving a child that you intend to parent together. To be reluctant to advocate for good health care because one is feeling grateful for having access at all. To experience underlying fears and anxiety about the implications of all of the above, including, whether based in reality or not, the fear that one's child will be taken away. All of these practices constitute violations or ruptures to personhood.

The participants above were offered two options: the option of presenting one's sperm donor as a 'sexual partner,' and the option of presenting themselves and the sperm donor as a 'threesome.' While both strategies fit Pfeffer's definition of inventive pragmatism, i.e. "making use of identified weaknesses and/or fissures in institutional power in order to derive social and material resources on behalf of oneself or one's family," the former (presenting a donor as a sexual partner and representing oneself as heterosexual) deploys conventional social structures and assumptions, while the latter (presenting as a threesome that includes the donor) overlaps with what Pfeffer calls "normative resistance." In other words, the "threesome" option can be seen to offer a choice to present as a family configuration "distinct from those considered most socially accepted, celebrated and sanctioned" (Pfeffer 578). This hybrid strategy does not necessitate the denial of sexual or gender identities, nor does it exclude an intended parent from the conception process (as the 'sexual partner' scenario often does). But, unless it actually reflects reality, presenting as a threesome still involves a deception or a misrepresentation.

In both scenarios of misrepresentation LGBTQ people might find themselves on "shaky legal ground," (Pfeffer 594) when, for example, donors are put on medical records as intended parents. Embirbayer and Mische identify "potentially frightening and destabilizing consequences" (cited in Pfeffer 594) should one be externally challenged after having pragmatically made use of institutional conventions. Dan describes how "it went badly" when his real-life partner's name was on the file; Clare and Tonya describe their fears of the implications of lying on an official record, including their fears of somehow losing their children. Central to these fears is the fact that only certain kinship relations are legally, socially, and institutionally recognized and supported.

THE RELATIONSHIP THAT HAS NO NAME

The decision to conceive by way of a known sperm donor is complex. For some LGBTQ people, the decision is purely economical, in that the costs of accessing AHR services and donor sperm are prohibitive. Others grapple with the relational and emotional implications of using an anonymous donor:

> *Dan*: I definitely wanted somebody who could answer questions when my kid said, 'Why do I look like this? How did I come to be? Why was he donating his sperm?' I very much wanted to say, 'There he is, go ask him! Here's his phone number, here's his e-mail address, go ask him. I don't want to speak 'for him'."

Some struggle with the "eugenics" involved in donor selection, with the ways that donors are characterized in sperm catalogues and the complexities of deciding what one is really looking for in a donor and how this can be "measured":

> *Lucy*: And it was a really weird sense of being, like, "Oh now we have to choose, like, from a group of men who have chosen to donate sperm...which is great...but it's like... I just felt, what a bizarre way to make a choice... actually I don't know what it's like. I'm assuming it's a catalogue like you see on TV.

> *Charlie*: And I would say for me the eugenics side of it felt kind of gross, and it's not that you don't pick a partner for qualities you like, you certainly do pick a partner for qualities you like but you don't have the same sort of totally theoretical, totally abstract, no real human being in the room sort of weighing of what are my absolute priorities about a person? How do I quantify that and compare them? As we talked about it, we eventually came down to, we would like a donor that is smart and kind and that those felt like the values we really wanted. And 'kind' isn't represented in those catalogues.

Those who have been historically mistreated by institutionalized medicine might steer away from extensive medical involvement in the conception process. Additionally many recognize the fertility advantages of "fresh sperm" and a DIY approach.

> *Joe*: We sort of thought, let's see if we can go with the formula that we know has a high likelihood of success. Fresh sperm,

> you know really fresh, like thanks for the cup, see you in ten minutes. And I think also as trans people who have been in a lot of ways kind of at the mercy of the medical system, staying away from it to whatever degree possible felt like a good idea.

While the use of an anonymous donor assumes and guarantees no involvement of the donor in the child's life or the parenting process, the use of a known donor can involve an enormous range of involvement, from absolutely none to full integration as a caregiver or parent. The negotiated, flexible and sometimes ambiguous relations that a known sperm donor might have, both with a child and with the child's parents or primary caregivers, make this a kinship configuration that lies outside of convention and, most often, outside of language. Susan Goldberg describes struggling with what to call a sperm donor and how to render a family of more than two people as parental (or something else) units, intelligible to others. "Is Rob a father? A dad? An uncle? A parent? A very good friend? Something in between all of these? Is it that we don't know, or that language fails us when it comes to the words to describe our relationship?" (29). Sometimes donors are "dads," sometimes they are not, and sometimes they are something in between: "Chip was more than a sperm donor, but less than a daddy" (Goldberg 21). Robert Leckey attempts to summarize what this looks like in practice:

> Donors may be known or involved without being considered to be "fathers" or co-parents with the mothers. Some lesbians prefer that their child's donor be seen not as a "father" or a "parent" but, rather, as an "uncle" who will not take part in decision making... Conversely, referring to the donor as a "father" need not imply involvement. (Leckey 596)

Fiona Kelly divides donors into three categories:

> - A "flexibly defined male figure" with whom their children have a relationship but to whom no parental status is imputed
> - Donors as symbolic "fathers" with almost no relationship with their progeny
> - Donor as an active, practicing parent with all the rights and responsibilities implied by that status, though without legal custody. (Kelly 102)

What becomes clear in this discussion is that, within North American kinship discourse, the known sperm donor is a largely unintelligible category. How does one conceive of a person who is in some cases a father, in some cases NOT a father, sometimes sort of a father, sometimes like an uncle, and sometimes a complete stranger? Perhaps the known sperm donor is a hybrid kinship category, one that exists as what Judith Butler might call "the not-yet-subject and the nearly recognizable":

> Indeed, there are middle regions, hybrid regions of legitimacy and illegitimacy that have no clear names, and where nomination itself falls into a crisis produced by the variable, sometimes violent boundaries of legitimating practices that come into uneasy and sometimes conflictual contact with one another. These are not precisely places where one can choose to hang out, subject positions one might opt to occupy. These are nonplaces in which one finds oneself in spite of oneself; indeed, these are nonplaces where recognition, including self-recognition, proves precarious if not elusive, in spite of one's best efforts to be a subject in some recognizable sense...the claim of the not-yet-subject and the nearly recognizable (Butler *Undoing Gender* 108).

When we asked the COF participants who had involved a known sperm donor in their procreative planning what kind of changes they would like to see in the AHR system, a primary concern was the desire to have their ties with their known donor recognized *as a relationship*. People framed their discontent within a framework of discrimination, equity, rights and/or choice. Many perceive the root of the problem lying in the lack of recognition of the known donor and the consensual *relationship* that is involved:

> *Tonya*: In the case of known donors they need to acknowledge that...*having a known donor is a relationship*. They need to understand that the people who are establishing that relationship are in a consensual relationship and that they are taking the risks that are inherent in having a relationship because of that consent...
>
> *Dan*: Straight people choose their partners and have kids and queer people should be able to choose their partners...donors...source of donor-egg...whatever...and accept the risk of what they're doing.

> *Clare*: I feel like I have a right to decide who is going to be the father of my child. And it seems completely absurd to me that you're denying me that right. And I do understand that it's for a good reason. But I think there needs to be a loophole here. And I always kept thinking to myself, "Why can't we just sign a waiver?...you know...we did an STI check. Why can't we show you that paper with the date that was yesterday and sign a waiver so that you're no longer liable? And it's our choice. Is this not our choice? Like, this should be our choice, you know?...Everyone else seems to have this right. It just seems crazy to me...we should be able to sign something. So...that's what I would say to the Minister: Create a form. Find some lawyers. Figure this out.

RECOGNIZING LGBTQ PEOPLE IN AHR SERVICES: A TWO-STEP PROCESS

A first step in the recognition of LGBTQ in the context of AHR services is a dismantling of the heterosexual matrix (Butler *Gender Trouble* 151): a taking apart of the assumptions that gendered body parts (ovaries, uterus, testicles, penis) produce gendered gametes (sperm, eggs), are tied to sexed bodies (male/female), with binary gender identities (man/woman), normative gender expression (femininity/masculinity), normative sexual orientation (heterosexual) and normative sexual practice (heterosexual intercourse – which is called 'sex'). However, once the assumptive links of the heterosexual matrix have been disentangled or separated, a second step involves putting things back together in a way that recognizes LGBTQ kinship relations.

People need space to define their identities and to create narratives separate from the heteronormative assumptions currently embedded in clinic practice. Clinic and sperm bank practices currently serve to separate the sperm donor from his gametes, a separation that assists to negate the intimacies of sperm donation (Nordqvist 1661-1668). However the people quoted in this chapter, all of whom chose known sperm donors, *want recognition of the relationship* with their donor, in most cases not as 'father,' but as something else.

In a broader sense, the LGBTQ participants in this study are asking for the space to define their own families and kinship relations. The dismantling and re-constituting of the pieces of the heterosexual matrix might be conceptualized as taking apart and putting back together the pieces of a puzzle. However, the puzzle can be reassembled in a multitude of ways. LGBTQ people (and others) who are making use of AHR services to have children, require legal, social, and linguistic space to allow them to assemble their particular puzzles in the pattern—and involving the body parts, gametes, identities and kinship relations—they choose.

NOTES

[1]The *Semen Regulations* were unsuccessfully challenged constitutionally in 2007 (Susan Doe v. Canada).

[2]The COF project team consisted of co-principal investigators Dr. Lori Ross (Social and Epidemiological Research Department, Centre for Addiction and Mental Health) and Dr. Leah Steele, co-investigators Rachel Epstein (LGBTQ Parenting Network, Sherbourne Health Centre), and Stu Marvel (Osgoode Hall Law School), and project staff datejie green,Lesley Tarasoff and Scott Anderson. The Creating Our Families project was funded by the Canadian Institutes for Health Research.

WORKS CITED

Ahmed, Sara. *On Being Included: Racism and Diversity in Institutional Life.* Durham and London: Duke University Press, 2012. Print.

Attorney General of Canada. Susan Doe v. Canada. 84 O.R. (3d) 81 (2007). Print.

Butler, Judith. *Gender Trouble: Feminism and the Subversion of Identity.* New York: Routledge, 1990. Print.

— *Undoing Gender.* New York & London: Routledge, 2004. Print.

Epstein, Rachel. "Married, Single or Gay?: Queerying and Trans-forming the Practices of Assisted Human Reproduction Services." Doctoral dissertation, Faculty of Education, York University, 2014.

Goldberg, Susan & Chloe Brushwood Rose. *And Baby Makes More: Known Donors, Queer Parents, and Our Unexpected Families.* London, Ontario: Insomniac Press, 2009. Print.

Government of Canada. *Processing and Distribution of Semen for Assisted Conception Regulations.* Ottawa: Government of Canada, SOR/96-254 (1996): 1-17. Print.

Kelly, Fiona. *Transforming Law's Family: The Legal Recognition of Planned Lesbian Motherhood.* Vancouver, Toronto: UBC Press, 2011. Print.

Leckey, Robert. "The Practices Of Lesbian Mothers and Quebec's Reforms." *Canadian Journal of Women and the Law* 23 (2011): 579-599. Print.

Nordqvist, Petra. Choreographies of Sperm Donations: Dilemmas of Intimacy in Lesbian Couple Donor Conception. *Social Science & Medicine* 73 (2011): 1661-1668. Print.

Pfefer, Carla. "Normative Resistance and Inventive Pragmatism: Negotiating Structure and Agency in Transgender Families." *Gender & Society* 26 (2012): 574-602. Print.

Ross, Lori E., Lesley A Tarasoff, Scott Anderson, datejie green, Rachel Epstein, Stu Marvel, Leah Steele. "Sexual and Gender Minority People's Recommendations for Assisted Human Reproduction Services." *Journal of Obstetrics and Gynaecology Canada* 36.2 (2014): 146-153. Print.

Thompson, Charis. *Making Parents: The Ontological Choreography of Reproductive Technology.* Cambridge, Mass: MIT Press, 2005. Print.

2.

The Secrets of Touch and the Sexualities of Birth

A Queer Consideration of Early Modern European Midwifery

TANYA M. CASSIDY

In December 2008, the American television program 20/20 publicized a documentary by Debra Pascali-Bonaro which sensationally reported the phenomenon of "orgasmic childbirth" as a long-forgotten phenomenon. Pascali-Bonaro's documentary features Ina May Gaskin, a so-called "grandmother midwife" operating as a home-birth advocate outside the nursing profession. Using her own experience, and featuring the filmed experience of eleven women, she argues that the possibility of reaching a state of strangely relaxed orgasm at the point of delivery has been occluded and ignored by traditional obstetrics. Specifically to achieve an orgasmic birth we are told a mother needs water, a doula, massage, privacy, darkness and touch. These women feel that mothers have been robbed of the chance of experiencing something they never knew was possible, something Pascali-Bonaro has titled "the best kept secret."

This documentary provoked heated debate and controversy, but its revelations came as less of a surprise to this researcher, since I have studied the literature of European midwifery in the early modern period. Midwives have long been associated with "mysteries" and "secrets" of intimate touching, and the fear and fascination which midwives have often attracted is, I believe, connected with traditions of how they "touch" pregnant women, traditions which make Pascali-Bonaro's assertions all the more credible. In this chapter, I will seek to destabilise the presumed equivalence between compulsory heterosexuality and reproduction, arguing that reproductive health has a long-standing relationship with same-sex intimacy.

This chapter applies classic Simmelian sociological theories of the senses to historical gendered interactions surrounding European childbirth in the later part of the seventeenth century through the eighteenth century (see for example the following essays by Simmel: "Sociology of the Senses" and "The Sociology of Secrecy and of Secret Societies"). During this time period "secrets of the female sex," as Sarah Stone labelled them in her 1737 discussion of childbirth, were changing as the male midwife was becoming increasingly visible and the intimacy of touch was a key feature. The historical study of the senses is a comparatively new area, with the sense of "touch" taking a prominent historical and cross-cultural place. Key to the historical study of the sense of touch is the linkage between childbirth and/or pregnancy and the touching performed by mothers themselves and their midwives. The interplay between physical pleasure and pain provides a choreography for the erotics of a procedure that initiates every human existence.

In this chapter I follow some classical Chicago sociological traditions, such as Erving Goffman's work, in committing to the theorization of a multiplicity of selves based on interaction, in order to account for the detailed dynamics of everyday exchange. More recently many of these interactional ideas have been applied to the study of sexuality by the philosopher Judith Butler (*Gender Trouble, Bodies That Matter*). My own introduction to queer studies was from medical sociology, concentrating on issues such as medicalization and social control, as well as the sociological study of the boundaries of what is regarded as the domain of the medical. Midwifery has always been a contested space, fighting to distinguish itself from medicine while recognizing the claims of medicine to intervene where necessary. Although these changes began in the seventeenth century, it is in the eighteenth century that historians have long discussed medicine's usurpation of childbirth practice in Europe. However, these historians of childbirth have not generally addressed the role of same-sex intimacies.

Why do we *not* think about birth or reproduction in relation to issues of sexuality? Is it because we have a contemporary vision that this process is a quintessentially heterosexual one in which once the sperm has "infected" the egg the only thing left is time before, as Boucé reminds us that many seventeenth and eighteenth century authors envisioned, the "monster" emerges? The gametes needed are not in dispute, but the behaviours surrounding this process have been far more dependent on intimate same-sex contact than has been commonly understood.

Thomas Laqueur argued that the study of seventeenth- and eighteenth-century midwifery manuals, from France and England in particular, can help illustrate changing ideas of sex and the body. Other historians such as Porter and Wilson have discussed the making of the male midwife. Although both discussed this topic in relationship to sexuality, they did not consider same-sex issues, nor did they concentrate on the few manuals that were written by female midwives (e.g. Sharp, Stone). The knowledge available from such midwifery manuals, written by both male and female midwives, helps to frame my discussion of the lost knowledge regarding same-sex sexuality and birth.

Porter and Wilson, as well as van Teijlingen and colleagues argue the eighteenth century saw a conflict between the new male obstetricians (so-called "man midwives") who published texts and used scientific instruments, and the old female midwives who rarely published and who used their hands. However, an examination of the history of midwifery literature shows that this conflict was more prolonged and more complicated than this simple summary might imply. For example, midwifery manuals, normally but not always written by men, were designed for a female readership: female midwives, women who might be pregnant themselves, or female friends of pregnant and labouring women.

Many historians have written about the animosity between the traditional female practitioners versus the belated arrival and eventual domination of men. Male obstetricians, the social historian Roy Porter reminds us, were not portrayed as predatory toward their counterparts, female midwives, but were frequently viewed as sexually dangerous toward their pregnant clients. On the other hand, historians have rarely discussed how sexuality figured in the representation and the work of the *female* midwife. The historical study of whether men should touch labouring women has occluded the study of how women already touched other women.

PANTOMIMES OF BIRTH: LAYERED HOMOEROTICS AND TRADITIONS OF WOMEN'S TOUCH

Exactly what was touched, and why and for how long in the context of early modern midwifery is something that we can never know for certain, at least where it departs from material and textual evidence such as written documents and birthing supplies. Intuitive touch is learned with experience rather than something prescriptively dictated.

Perhaps surprisingly, one of the most explicit discussions of the midwife's touch and the ritual of birth comes from a non-medical, all-male, homo-erotic interpretation as narrated by a disapproving outsider. An anonymous writer, likely Edward or "Ned" Ward, a popular journalist of the early eighteenth century in England, wrote a 1709 pamphlet that described a pantomime of a midwife and a labouring woman in a Mollie or Molly house. "Molly house" is the preferred term for English eighteenth-century drinking establishments known to be frequented by men seeking same-sex sexual intimacies. Although various Molly-midwife descriptions are found throughout the century and even into the early part of the nineteenth century, the 1709 account attributed to Ward is certainly one of the earliest.

Ward's particular take on midwifery tropes illuminates not only midwifery as a familiar paradigm of same-sex intimate contact, but also the wider anxiety that surrounded an ancient professional compact that had generally excluded men, all filtered through a distanced, anti-queer narrative format:

> Not long since, upon one of their Festival Nights, they had cusheon'd up the Belly of one of their *Sodomitical* Brethren, or rather Sisters, as they commonly call'd themselves, disguising him in a Womans Night-Gown, Sarsnet-Hod, and Nightrale, who, when the Company were met, was to mimick the wry Faces of a groaning Woman, to be deliver'd of a joynted Babie they had provided for that Purpose, and to undergo all the Formalities of a Lying in. … One in a high Crown'd Hat, and an old Beldams Pinner representing a Country Midwife, another busy Ape, dizen'd up in a Hussife's Cof, taking upon himself the Duty of a very officious Nurse, and the rest, as Gossips, apply'd themselves to the Travelling Woman, according to the Midwife's Direction, all being as intent upon the Business in hand, as if they had been Women, the Occasion real, and their Attendance necessary. After Abundance of Bussle and that they had ridiculously counterfeited all the Difficulties that they fancy'd were accustomary in such Cases, their Buffoonary Maukin was at length Disburthen'd of her little Jointed Bastard, and then putting their Shotten Impos-

> tor to Bed upon a double Row of Chairs; the Baby was drest by the midwife; the Father brought to Compliment his New-born Son; the Parson sent for; the Gossips appointed; the Child Christen'd, and then the Cloth was spread; the Table furnish'd with cold Tongues and Chickens; the Guests Invited to sit down, and much Joy express'd that my Gammar *Molly* had brought her honest Gaffer a Son and Heir to Town, so very like him, that as soon as Born, had the eyes, Nose, and Mouth of its own credulous Daddy. (Anonymous Chapter 25)

Republished several times, this account appears in the middle of a decription of thirty one clubs in thirty two chapters (Cassidy, 99-113). This narrative has been recuperated by a number of historians of sexuality, and Davidson has linked it to an imagined form of male reproduction. In addition, as the eighteenth century literary historian Terry Castle has argued, in the eighteenth century pantomimes, such as described in this passage, are continuous with masquerades and masquerades were linked to polymorphic sexual dynamics.

The above Molly club description affords us interesting details of an interpretation of birth as a homo-erotic realm. For example, we witness the role of the gossips who perform the role of godparents. According to the online OED, the noun "gossip" originally referred to "one who has contracted spiritual affinity with another by acting as a sponsor at a baptism," and could originally apply to either sex ("gossip, n," def 1). Another more familiar definition, and one of the earliest nearly exclusive female uses, refers to someone who "delights in idle talk; a newsmonger, a tattler" ("gossip, n," def 3). But we should also remember that the female gendering of this term refers to it being used to describe a "familiar acquaintance, friend, chum" which later became exclusively associated with women, especially those female "friends" present at the birth ritual ("gossip, n" def 2). It is also important to note that early modern midwives were often given license by the church to to perform baptisms on dying babies.

The lying-in rituals of the seventeenth century and later lasted for approximately a month from the time of quickening, which historians such as Scott, Cresssy and Coster, have argued in the seventeenth and eighteenth centuries was often not recognized to occur until after the fifth month, which would mean it would last longer than a month. At the end of the lying-in there was a "churching" of the mother, formally known as the thanksgiving of women after childbirth. This ceremony formally acknowledges the woman's reentry into social and religious life after her birthing experience. Although similar ceremonies are common in many cultures, Cressy (106-146) has argued that in post-reformation England that this was a celebratory occasion for the woman herself, rather than for her husband or her child, a female-centred occasion which culminated in the new mother feasting with her gossips.

The term midwife has an interesting history: literally the compound of "mid"after the fifteenth century was replaced by "with," so we might see this as a term which means being with a wife (OED "midwife, n," def 1). Rather than viewing the term wife as a correlative to the term husband, some late sixteenth early seventeenth century texts use the term as one of affection of a female friend. The use of the term midwife as a verb, "to midwife," is also informative. Again according to the OED from the 1630s onwards, the verb midwife can be translated as "to help or be instrumental in bringing (something hidden) to light, or (a piece of work, esp. a work of art) into being or public view" ("midwife, v," def 2). The key to midwifery therefore is to bring the secret to view, revealing the mystery. Secret friendships between women are revealed, at least to other women.

Radcliffe argues that the revelation of secrets is a reoccurring trope of the seventeenth and eighteenth century discussions of midwifery, and a staple part of male midwifery dating back to the Chamberlen family in France and their "secret instrument" (forceps), kept secret by the practice of using a sheet tied around the male-midwife's neck, ostensibly to keep the mother calm when the instrument was being used. Thus a secret male midwifery body of knowledge is created based on technology, rather than on experiences that female midwives were allowed to share.

Ward's excerpt shows a pantomime of a woman's birthing experience, attended to primarily by midwives and other women, as central to the entertainment and communal identity of molly houses. This was apparently a widespread and long-lived ritual performance at molly houses, and its significance and impact warrant further consideration by historians of both sexuality and childbirth. Even as the rituals of midwifery were being increasingly truncated for women with the advent of male obstetrics, homo-erotic men were keen to keep them going, at least in pantomime. Almost fifty years after Ward's description, an anonymous and outraged 1757 pamphleteer describes the ongoing popularity of this performance in molly houses:

> ...what appears the most horrible and detestable to human

> Nature is the Sham Lying-in, where the Lady-looking Gentleman is brought to Bed with all the Formality of a real Labour; the Spouse of a fair-faced Incubus affects as great Care and Concern at the feigned Pangs of his Beloved, as if it was the real Wife of his Bosom; the He-Midwife is no less assiduous in his Part, the Male Nurse is likewise making great Preparations, while the Gentleman Gossps are all in full Employ, and lending their Assistance to the screaming Minion. (Anonymous 10-12)

How do we understand both the enduring prevalence of Lying In performances in molly houses, and the author's disgusted, if fascinated, response? Can these performances be seen as a celebration or a mockery of both gender norms and childbirth—or possibly both? Was there an awareness in these texts, largely lost in more recent cultural symbolics of childbirth in the west, that the women's realm of "lying in" might offer a homoerotic template of same-sex touch? Might this performance of same-sex contact and intimacy have reached for a historic legacy of midwifery in order to confer a social place and legitimacy for other homoerotic and homosocial practices? Biological sex and gender are simultaneously shifting and delineated in the context of a this all-male cast. The line between parody and tribute can be similarly difficult to affix.

I call upon historians of medicine and sexuality to "queer" their own practice and revisit the layered meanings of such accounts of midwifery as forms of same-sex touch and homosocial legitimacy. The so-called "facts" of biology are always interpreted through a cultured and politicised prism. The sociological complexity and theoretical import of historical practices can also be seen in other seventeenth and eighteenth-century European sources. In the next section I consider what can be gleaned from midwifery treatises and manuals.

MIDWIFERY MANUALS: ANATOMY, DESIRE, AND GENDERED DIVIDES

The secrets of midwives' touch were revealed in print by the seventeenth-century female midwife Jane Sharp. *The Midwives Book: or, the Whole Art of Midwifry Discovered*, 1671 was specifically written to counter the male vision of the female body and the birthing process. Sharp, operating within the confines of humerial Galenic medical knowledge, presents a female vision of birth, which includes, as did most male-authored manuals of the time, a detailed discussion of both male and female reproductive anatomy. As Elaine Hobby has pointed out, many of Sharp's male alternatives described the female body in very negative terms, whereas Sharp said "we women have no more cause to be angry, or be ashamed of what Nature hath given us than men have" (Hobby 201). Many such anatomical discussions were to disappear from the manuals over the next century, perhaps to keep them within the carefully policed confines of professional medical training.

Lacqueur points to Sharp, who he considers to be "well-informed," regarding the logical inconsistencies of her time concerning reproductive anatomy. He offers the concern that women can not at one and the same time have a full inside penis—what we now refer to as the vagina, and what Sharp says "the passage for the yard, resembleth it turned inward" (Sharp 40)—and a small outside penis—what we call the clitoris, what Sharp said "will stand and fall as the yard doth and makes women lusful and take delight in copulation" (Sharp 42)—without some departure from a male template of anatomy. Lacqueur concedes that perhaps Sharp is not ultimately inconsistent, especially when we consider her description that the vagina only resembles the penis whereas the clitoris functions as one (Lacqueur 65).

Instead of dwelling on cliteral hypertrophy like many of her male colleagues, Sharp merely mentions this possibility, and then almost immediately she returns to a discussion of the clitoris' contribution to sexual desire:

> ...Commonly it is but a small sprout, lying close hid under the Wings, and not easily felt, yet sometime it grows so long that it hangs forth at the slit like a yard, and will swell and stand stiff if it be provoked, and some lewd women have endeavoured to use it as men do theirs. In the Indies, and Egypt they are frequent, but I never heard but of one in this Country, if there be any they will do what they can for shame to keep it close. (Sharp 38)

Key to Jane Sharp's "secrets of the female sex" is, as both Hobby and Lacqueur recognise, the humoral theory that orgasm is necessary for pregnancy. Sharp gives details regarding the important organ that "makes women lustful and take delight in Copulation, and were it not for this they would have no desire nor delight, nor would they ever conceive."[1]

In male-authored manuals, such as Chamelen's 1657 manual, the clitoris is also discussed but male authors tend to ignore any clitoral role in conception and female pleasure; they instead concentrated on the clitoris' contribution to "excessive female sexuality," including homoerotic practices. Again as Elaine Hobby, the literary scholar who recently edited a modern edition of Sharp's text, has said,

> The slide made here, from sexual pleasure, to its excessiveness (especially in foreigners), to stories of women pursuing such joys with one another rather than with men, seems to have been seen as an almost inevitable sequence, judging by the frequency with which such narratives appear. (Hobby 204)

Some of these narratives, as Toulalan points out, include discussions of men dressing as women primarily to be able to have intimate sleeping arrangements with women. So common was the depiction of homoeroticism between women, historians such as Jennings and Aldrich, have argued that it was broadly acceptable.

Toulalan argues that historians' concentration on the mostly highly visible representations of erotic desire between women, "the chaste female friend and the 'masculinised' tribade," "ignores the representation of women in erotic literature who engage in sexual acts with each other, and who, while referring to tribady, do not themselves either embody the culturally imagined firgure of the the tribade or identify themselves as such" (Toulalan 50). Time spent together in intimate settings involves the use of touch, often in the form of the hand, and resulting in at least one of the partners having an orgasm. The private, but widely accepted intimacy between women during this time period should be considered in any analysis of intimate touch between women during childbirth.

But these manuals also show the changes in public attitudes towards female same-sex intimate touch. Since the mid seventeenth century the formalities of the lying-in ritual were undergoing a transformation. Not only was the time spent lying in being shortened, but also the same sex intimacy surrounding the process was being eroded. Moreover, medical visions of body and sex were being transformed in key respects. Knowledge regarding the role of orgasms with birth were being displaced. By the end of the century not only would midwifery be dominated by males, but the clitoris would be considered a completely irrelevant body part with regard to the entire birthing process.

CONCLUSION: GENDER, SEX, AND THE MEANING OF BIRTH

As the eighteenth century is drawing to a close, the frontispiece to John Blunt's 1793 *Man-Midwifery Dissected or the Obstetric Family Instructor, for the Use of Married Couples and Single Adults of Both Sexes* captures the sexual divisiveness of midwifery as a profession in crisis. From the seventeenth through the eighteenth century birthing increasingly became not only more medicalized but also more masculine. This image splits the biological sex of the midwife, half male, half female. Blunt's discussion is unusual in the fact that it presents an argument against male midwifery from the perspective of a male narrator. Primarily it is a treatise against the overuse of birthing tools by male practitioners. Blunt does not advocate that males should instead use their hands, but instead the entire profession should be returned to women. Blunt thereby dissents from a confidently masculinist modernity's assumption of hegemonic birthing authority suggesting that time honoured same sex feminine intimacies framed an invaluable collective body of knowledge.

It can be argued that the meaning of birth was different for male practitioners than it was for female, and that these differences contributed to the establishment of the discipline of obstetrics as separate and distinct from midwifery, differences in perspective that can be seen today. Female midwives have generally viewed birth as a natural part of life while many obstetricians have emphasised that every birth is a potential medical emergency.

This contrast in the meanings attributed to birth was particularly evident when it came to the establishment of medical institutions for childbirth. For example, Bartholomew Mosse established the first lying-in hospital in 1745 in Dublin which was staffed by male midwives exclusively. There had been dedicated birthing wards in London since 1739, and prior to that in Paris, all of which were staffed by male midwives. Fielding Ould who had written *A Treatise of Midwifery in Three Parts* in 1742 , argued that birth is always a "life and death situation" especially when the expectant mother is attended by "ignorant women." Birth was frequently portrayed as a fundamentally dangerous medical procedure. Traditional midwifery, on the other hand, argued that most births are not problematic, and that the need for tools and male midwives was extremely limited. For example, Sarah Stone argued that with proper training, female midwives could learn how to use their hands in even some of the most difficult cases.

> I am well assured, unless the women-midwives give themselves more to the study of the art, and learn the difficult part of their business, that the modesty of sex will be in greater danger of being lost, for want of good women-midwives, by being so much exposed to the men professing this art: for 'tis arrived to that height already, that almost every young man, who hath served his apprentiship to a barber-surgeon, immediately sets up for a man-midwife; althou' as ignorant, and, indeed, much ignoranter, than the meanest woman of the profession. (Stone x-xi)

The complex scandals thrown up by discussions of midwives, man midwives and the occasional female-man midwife (as Stone has been called because she advocated that female midwives should use some of the knowledge and techniques of male midwives) concern issues of touch, gender, and sexuality.

The eighteenth century saw the triumph of a masculinised medical gaze that claimed a kind of de-sexualised 'objectivity' in order to legitimate its own truth claims. Anxieties were caused by the idea that man midwives might "touch" women in the same way that traditional midwives had used touch. Politically therefore, from Chambelen onwards it became important for man midwives to argue that they intended to (literally) keep women at arm's length by means of specialist instruments. Forceps created a sense of scientific 'distance' that denied 'man-midwives' the intimacies shared for generations by the sisterhood of midwives. The triumph of the man midwife was continuous with the elimination of both touch and any notion of pleasure associated with what had once been a lengthy, intimate, and social birthing procedure.

Thus when twenty first-century viewers encounter televised testimonials that link sexually pleasurable childbirth to non-profssionalized midwifery practice, such as those in "Orgasmic Childbirth," they also encounter a hidden legacy. Similarly, viewers' surprise at sexual and social connectedness between women to the birth experience is not coincidental, but illuminates shifts in professional power and social customs. While contemporary discourse stresses the non-procreative, non-productive nature of same-sex intimacy, such an approach suppresses a rich heritage of belief and practice that regards homosocial forms of intimacy as crucial to the slow process of birthing.

The exploration of such histories can contradict common assumptions that "queering motherhood" is a necessarily recent phenomenon. In "queering" our own scholarly perspectives on both historical and contemporary texts, we can (re)trace how birth, sexuality, power, and touch between women have been integrated in other social contexts, and question our established practices and beliefs that surround birth, gender, and pleasure.

NOTES

[1] Sharpe, 1691: 36. In recent decades according to Buckley, Sharp's defence of the female orgasm has been supported by modern understandings of the release of the hormone oxytocin during orgasm, a hormone that helps both direct sperm to its target and also eases and helps anaesthetise the birth itself.

WORKS CITED

ABC 20/20. *Orgasmic Birth.* New York: ABC Television, 2008. Web.

Adam, Barry D. "The Construction of a Sociological 'Homosexual' in Canadian Textbooks" *Canadian Review of Sociology and Anthropology* 23.3: 399-411. 1986. Print.

Aldrich, Robert, ed. *Gay Life and Culture: A World History.* London: Thames & Hudson, 2006. Print.

Anonymous [believed to be Ward, Edward]. *The Secret History of Clubs: Particularly the Kit Cat, Beef-Stake, Virtuosos, Quacks, Knights of the Golden-Fleece, Florists, Beans, etc.* London, 1709. Print.

Bouce, Paul-Gabriel. "Imagination, Pregnant Women, and Monsters in Eighteenth-Century England and France," *Sexual Underworlds of the Enlightenment.* Ed. G.S. Rouseau and Roy Porter. Manchester: Manchester University Press, 1987. 86-100. Print.

Buckley, Sarah. "Ecstatic Birth: The Hormonal Blueprint of Labor." *Mothering Magazine.* 111, March/April 2002. Web.

Butler, Judith. *Bodies That Matter: On the Discursive Limits of "Sex".* New York: Routledge, 1993. Print.

——. *Gender Trouble: Feminism and the Subversion of Identity.* New York: Routledge, 1990. Print.

Cassidy, Tanya M. "People, Performance and Place: Theoretically Revisiting Mother Clap's Molly House." *Queer People: Negotiations and Expressions of Homosexuality 1600-1800.* Ed. Chris Mounsey and Caroline Gonda. Lewisburg, PA: Bucknell University Press, 2007. 99-113. Print.

Castle, Terry. *Masquerade and Civlization: The Carnivalesque in Eighteenth-Century Culture and Fiction.* Stanford: Stanford University Press, 1986. Print.

Chamberlen, Hugh and F. Mauriceau ed. and trans. *The Accomplisht Midwife.* [Fr. orig., Traité des maladies des femmes grosses (1668)]. 1673. Print.

Classen, Constance (ed.). *The Book of Touch.* Oxford: Berg, 2005. Print.

Conrad, Peter, and Joseph Schneider. *Deviance and Medicalization: From Badness to Sickness*. Philadelphia: Temple University Press, 1992. Print.

Coster, William. "Purity, Profanity and Puritanism. The Churching of Women 1500-1700." *Women in the Church*. Ed. W.J. Sheils and Diana Wood. Oxford: Blackwell, 1990. 377-387. Print.

Cressy, David. "Purification, Thanksgiving and the Churching of Women in Post-Reformation England." *Past and Present* 141: 106-146. 1993. Print.

Davis, Elisabeth and Pascali-Bonaro, Debra. *Orgasmic Birth: Your Guide to a Safe, Satisfying, and Pleasurable Birth Experience*. New York: Rodale, 2010. Print.

Davison, Michael. "Pregnant Men: Modernism, Disability and Biofuturity in Djuna Barnes." *Novel: A Forum on Fiction*. 43.2: 207-226. 2010. Print.

Dunn, Peter M. "Bartholomew Mosse (1712-59), Sir Fielding Ould (1710-89), and the Rotunda Hospital, Dublin. *Archives of Diseases of Child Fetal Neonatal*. 81: F74-F76. 1999. Print.

Goffman, Erving. *Presentation of Self in Everyday Life*. New York: Doubleday Anchor Books, 1959. Print.

Hastings, Donnan, and Fiona Magowan. *The Anthropology of Sex*. New York: Berg, 2010. Print.

Hobby. Elaine. 2001. ""Secrets of the Female sex": Jane Sharp, the reproductive female body, and early modern midwifery manuals." *Women's Writing* 8.2: 201-212. 2001. Print.

Jennings, Rebecca. *A Lesbian History of Britain*. Oxford: Greenwood World Publishing, 2007. Print.

Laqueur, Thomas. *Making Sex: Body and Gender from the Greeks to Freud*. Cambridge, Mass: Harvard, 1990. Print.

Mounsey, Chris. *Christopher Smart: Clown of God*. Lewisburg, PA: Bucknell Unviersity Press, 2001. Print.

Norton, Rictor. *Mother Clap's Molly House: The Gay Subculture in England, 1700-1830*. London: Gay Men's Press, 1992. Print.

Ould Fielding. *A Treatise on Midwifery. In Three Parts*. Dublin: Nelson and Conno, 1742r. Print.

Oxford English Dictionary. *Oxford English Dictionary Online*. 2005. Web.

Pascali-Bonaro, Debra (Dir.). *Orgasmic Birth: The Best Kept Secret*. 2008. Film.

Plummer, Ken. *Intimate Citizenship: Personal Decisions and Public Dialogues*. Seattle, WA: University of Washington Press, 2003. Print.

Porter, Roy. "A Touch of Danger: the Man Midwife as Sexual Predator." *Sexual Underworlds of the Enlightenment.* Ed. G. S. Rousseau and Roy Porter. Manchester: Manchester University Press, 1987. 206-233. Print.

Radcliffe, Walter. The Secret Instrument: (the Birth of the Midwifery Forceps). London: Heinemann Medical Books, 1947. Print.

Ragan, Bryant T. 'The Enlightenment Confronts Homosexuality' *Homosexuality in Modern France.* Ed. Jeffrey Merrick and Bryant T. Ragan. New York: Oxford University Press, 1996. 8-29. Print.

Rey, Michel. 'Police and Sodomy in 18th Century Paris: From Sin to Disorder.' *Journal of Homosexuality* Vol. 16.1/2: 129-146. 1988. Print.

Scott, Caitlin. "Birth Control and Conceptions of Pregnancy in Seventeenth-Century England." *Retrospectives.* 2.1: 73-85. 2013.Print.

Seidman, Steven. (ed.) *Queer Theory/Sociology*. Cambridge, MA: Blackwell, 1996. Print.

Sharp, Jane. *The Midwives Book or the Whole Art of Midwifery Discovered.* edited by Elaine Hobby. Oxford, UK: Oxford University Press, [1671] 1999. Print.

Simmel, Georg. "Sociology of the Senses." In Robert E. Park and W.W. Burgess. eds. *Introduction to the Science of Sociology.* Chicago: Chicago University Press, 1921. 356-360. Print.

—-."The Sociology of Secrecy and of Secret Societies," translated from the German by Albion W. Small, *American Journal of Sociology.* XI: 441-98. 1905-6. Print.

Smith, Mark Michael. *Sensing the Past: Seeing, Hearing, Smelling, Tasting, and Touching in History.* Berkeley: University of California Press, 2007. Print.

Stone, Sarah. A Complete Practice of Midwifery. London: T. Cooper, 1737. Print.

Toulalan, Sarah. "Extraordinary Satisfaction: Lesbian Visibility in Seventeenth-Century Pornography in England." *Gender and History.* 15.1: 50-68. 2003. Print.

van Teijlingen E. R., Lowis G.W., McCaffery P.G, and Porter M. (eds). *Midwifery and the Medicalization of Childbirth: Comparative Perspectives.* New York: Nova Science, 2000. Print.

Wilson, Adrian. *The Making of Man-Midwifery: Childbirth in England, 1660-1770*. Boston: Harvard Press, 1995. Print

3.

Not a "Medical Miracle"

Intersex Reproduction and the Medical Enforcement of Binary Sex and Gender

CARY GABRIEL COSTELLO

INTRODUCTION

My daughter was not of woman born. This concept has fascinated people throughout the ages.[1]

My daughter's gestation was perfectly "natural," I should point out—but I carried her, and I was never of the female sex. I was diagnosed as "true gonadal intersex," having been born with an intermediate ovotestis and variant reproductive anatomy. I was assigned female at birth, and was living as such when I gave birth to my daughter, but I never identified as a woman, and I am now legally male.

A lot of myths circulate around the topic of intersex fertility, and many of them are perpetuated by doctors. They all relate to the current Western ideological insistence on binary or dyadic sex (See Carrera, DePalma and Lameiras; Davidson; Dreger *Hermaphrodites and the Medicalization of Sex*; Elliot; Hird; Kessler, *Lessons from the Intersexed*). This ideology holds that there are two and only two sexes, and that this dichotomy is required by "nature" in order to perpetuate the human species. In biological fact, sex is a spectrum. Intersexuality is found in all animals, and has always been part of the human condition (See Fausto-Sterling; Greenberg; Moore and Persaud; Preeves; Roughgarden). In utero, all people start out with an intermediate phalloclitoris and undistinguished ovotestes, and these distinguish to a greater or lesser extent depending on our genotype, hormonal exposure, and other factors. As many as one in 50 people has some intersex characteristic (Blackless et al. 9; Fausto-Sterling 51-54); however, in contemporary Western society we are hidden away, medically "corrected," erased (See Hausman; Karkazis, Reis, *Bodies in Doubt*). And often this erasure is bound up in rhetoric about fertility.

INTERSEXUALITY INTRODUCED

Before I can discuss the topic of intersex fertility, I must give some background on intersexuality generally. There is a lot of variation in how assorted elements of the reproductive organs develop from person to person in all of us. For example, people acknowledge with a lot of rib-elbowing the variation in penile size. Variation in the size and shape of genitalia, and in other parts of the body, is part of human diversity. Doctors are well aware that livers and lungs and blood vessels vary between individuals, and may look quite different from an iconic anatomical diagram. But we rarely care about having an unusually shaped liver. The shape of genitals, however, is given huge cultural weight, because we pin our commitment to binary gender roles on them.

As members of Western society, we look at the shape of a newborn's genitalia and project for that child a future of dresses and diets and talking about emotions, or sports and strength and getting under the hood of a car. We do know that people are complicated. Most people want to be more than walking gender stereotypes. Still, in the contemporary West, we understand people through the lens of dyadic gender difference; intersex people call that framing into question. When we see a baby born with intermediate genitalia, and can't project a future for them based on our well-known binary gender narratives, people in our society—including doctors—treat the situation as shocking and deeply problematic.

It's important to point out that revulsion towards sex variation is only one possible response among many. In every society, some physical variations are devalued, some considered neutral, and others esteemed. In the U.S. today, for example, while intersex variations are considered "disorders," not being able to curl one's tongue (a recessive trait) is accepted with a shrug, while having green eyes (which is about as common in the U.S. as being intersex) is celebrated. And in some societies, intersex status has been celebrated. The term "hermpahrodite," for example, comes directly from the name of the ancient Greek god Hermphrodite, child of Hermes and Aphrodite, whose intersex form was deemed divinely perfect by the ancient Greeks. Many cultures, in fact, have treated being neither male nor female as a sacred characteristic. Consider angels in Judeo-Christian tradition, the ancient Egyptian god/dess of the Nile Hapi, whose breasts and phallus were depicted as constantly flowing with fertility, the Norse trickster god Loki, who enjoyed a male pregnancy, and the Hindu deity Ardhanarishvara, whose body unites Shiva and Shakti into intersex perfection.

A number of societies have divided the sex spectrum socially into more than two sexes, and have assigned visibly intersex individuals to additional categories. Some sex systems are trinary, as in those Native American systems that acknowledge male, females, and two-spirit individuals (such as the Zapotec muxe and Navajo nadleehe), or the Polynesian societies that recognize a third sex (such as the Hawai'ian mahu and Samoan fa'afafine) (See Driskill et al.; Herdt; Matzner). In my own Jewish tradition, four sexes have been halachically recognized: male, female, tumtum (neither) and androgyne (both). A person designated an androgyne must fulfill the religious requirements proscribed for both men and women; a tumtum individual is required to fulfill neither (Fonrobert n. pag.). Still other societies have quintic sex systems, such as the Bugis of Indonesia, whose five sex categories we might render in English as "woman with vulva/woman with penis/man with vulva/ man with penis/intersex" (Davies 1 [quotation marks mine]).

Contemporary Western society is deeply immersed in a dyadic framing of sex, and deals with children who are born visibly intersex by assigning the child to the male or female sex category. Western doctors' contemporary "solution" to intersexuality is not only to designate each individual legally either male or female, but to "correct" what doctors call "Disorders of Sex Development" via medical procedures (surgery, administration or suppression of hormones, the prescription of vaginal dilating exercise devices, etc.) (Davis 168; Feder 225; Reis 538-9).

The practice of surgical sex assignment has been the norm for about fifty years, but Western medicine has been working to erase most intersex bodies for far longer. Before surgical intervention became common, doctors devised a method of classifying intersex conditions that defined the vast majority of intersex people as "pseudohermaphrodites." This system classifies intersex people by their gonads: an intersex person with testes is a "male pseudohermaphrodite," an intersex person with ovaries is a "female pseudohermaphrodite," and only that small percentage of us with ovotestes or an ovary and a testis are deemed "true hermaphrodites." (Dreger et al. 729; Fausto-Sterling 37; Preeves 26-28) This classificatory scheme frames an intersex person with testes as "really male"–even if she has breasts, labia, clitoris, and vagina, even if she was raised female, wears dresses, and identifies as a woman. A person with with ovaries is framed as "really female," even if he has a penis, scrotum, and just won the Mr. Olympus bodybuilding contest.

The system of classifying intersex people that defines most of us as not "really" intersex did two things for the medical profession. First, it allowed doctors to present themselves as penetrating nature's mysteries, and as having knowledge beyond the supposedly "naive" impressions of laypeople who looked at someone with intermediate genitalia and saw the person as truly neither male nor female (Costello 25). Secondly, in an era before sex assignment surgery, it gave doctors the ability to claim to have taxonomically "eliminated" most intersex individuals by assigning us to a dyadic sex category.

The medical system of classification has nothing to do with the lived experience of intersex people. One could look at a person with breasts, a menstrual period, and a penis and come up with any number of arbitrary rules for assigning zim[2] to a binary sex category—by genital appearance, by genotype, by the size of the uterus/prostatic utricle. Each such scheme would be internally consistent, but again, have no relation to the experienced sex or gender of intersex people. Intersex people do not experience ourselves as defined by our gonads. Gender identity, physical appearance, and social input are much more potent influences on anyone's experience of their sex—whether intersex or not—than is any one component of physical sexual makeup.

Think about this: if you asked the people you know who identify as female what being a woman means to them, how many do you think would answer, "It means I have ovaries"? Would you not expect instead to hear complex and thoughtful responses about self-identification, relating to culture, dress and deportment, emotional and communicative styles, beauty ideals and demands, experiences shared with other women, concerns about marginalization, and many other topics? If you then asked, "If you had ovaries and they were removed, would you no longer consider yourself a woman?" would you expect to hear them say, "of course"? Not likely. Gender identity and gendered culture are much more important to the experience of living as female than any particular element of biological makeup—a breast, a testis, a chromosome.

Yet doctors make life-altering binary sex-assignment decisions based upon such physical characteristics. When doctors' only interventions into the lives of intersex people were classificatory, intersex individuals' embodied experiences were not deeply impacted. But then doctors initiated the practice of infant sex assignment surgery, believing that if they applied a set of physical evaluative rules, they could determine a "true" or "best" binary sex and then assign genitally-variant infants to that sex, "curing" us. The problem was, as children so "cured" grew up, they began expressing unhappiness with their treatment. A substantial proportion of intersex people do not ultimately identify with the sex to which they were assigned, and if surgically altered, often mourn the loss of exactly those parts of their genitalia and reproductive systems with which they identify (Meyer-Bahlberg 29). Others, while growing up to identify with their assigned sex, are nevertheless distressed by the loss of sexual sensation and other persistent problems such as fistulas and infections that often result from invasive genital surgery; many disagree that such surgery was ever "necessary" (Davis 177; Karkazis ch. 7).

Today, advocates for the intersex community argue against infant genital surgery, saying that no one should be forced to have what is in essence sex change surgery without their fully informed consent (See Wilson). They suggest that parents choose a provisional dyadic sex since one is currently legally required on the birth certificate. But these advocates urge that no surgery be performed unless and until the intersex individual requests it, once ze is mature enough to do so, and ze has been given sufficient support and information to make a true fully informed, uncoerced decision (See Dreger Tamar-Mattis et al.).

Advocates for intersex people's human rights have made substantial progress in many places around the globe. In February of 2013, the Special Rapporteur on Torture (SRT) to the United Nation's Human Rights Council declared that genital "normalizing" surgery forced upon intersex children constituted torture and must be denounced (18-19). In autumn of 2013, the Parliamentary Assembly of the Council of Europe adopted a resolution entitled "Children's Right to Physical Integrity," which also declared that sex assignment surgery imposed upon intersex children violated their human rights (1). Soon thereafter, the Australian Senate released a report on "Involuntary or Coerced Sterilisation of Intersex People in Australia" condemning not only genital surgeries performed on infants without their consent, but the presumption that binary sex is necessary or normal. This report stated that no genital normalizing surgery should be performed without the approval of a tribunal, and public funds should be used to ensure that families of intersex children get adequate counseling (73-75).

Despite these medical policy changes elsewhere, doctors in North

America continue to perform infant sex assignment surgery routinely. They continue to dismiss the complaints of dissatisfied intersex patients as those of an unfortunate fringe. As campaigns against infant genital surgery have gotten more media attention, however, doctors have been forced to justify their practices, especially to parents of intersex infants. And they do this by presenting the lives of intersex people as tragic, putting us at risk for suicide without medical intervention to "correct" our bodies (Karkazis 193-4). We are said to face a crippling incapacity to use locker rooms, public rest rooms, showers, and the like. We are presented as never being able to find a partner or marry; we are framed as doomed to lives of isolation and shame. The observation that these all issues are social, rather than medical—and could be addressed socially through counseling, anti-bullying campaigns, the provision of gender-neutral bathrooms, and the like—is never raised.

INTERSEX FERTILITY

One way in which North American medical textbooks frame intersex people as "tragic" is by presenting us as usually infertile. Theorists and activists of many stripes have critiqued the idea that a person must procreate to be a fully mature and valid adult, and I will not recapitulate their arguments. What I want to address from an intersex perspective is the fact that many of us are capable of reproducing. In fact, ironically, doctors often take surgical steps to "normalize" intersex bodies that render us infertile.

For example, children born with external testes but absent or very small external phalli are often surgically assigned female (See Donahoe; Hendren, Lee et al.). The removal of their testes of course renders them infertile. Doctors frame these children as being incapable of reproduction because of their small or absent external phallic structures, justifying reassignment to female, but this claim is laughable. Size really is irrelevant to the delivery of sperm. Indeed, the availability of in vitro fertilization means that intercourse itself is unnecessary. What doctors are doing is conflating having a large penis with fertility and with male identity. It's magical thinking—but it is used by supposedly rational scientists to justify surgical castration of children with variant genitalia.

Further, consider those children who are born with external testes and intermediate genitalia that doctors usually reconstruct to appear fairly typically male, a status doctors term "hypospadias." A diagnosis of hypospadias is given to about 1% of American infants listed as "male" on their birth certificates (Paoluzzi, Erikson and Jackson 832), making it the most common diagnosis given to intersex people. Yet the fact that individuals diagnosed as having hypospadias are usually fertile does not challenge the claim made in medical textbooks that most intersex people are infertile. This is because hypospadias is medically classified as a "penile malformation" in a "male" rather than as an intersex condition. This is a very odd act of taxonomic prestidigitation, since individuals with hypospadias often have uteri, and may be born with substantial vaginae, which are not considered male anatomic structures (Fausto-Sterling I, Ikoma et al. 423-4, Kojima et al. 1151).

Doctors involved in the treatment of intersex children seem preoccupied with associating males with large phalli. Yet they remove a great number of average-sized, average-looking phalli, in the cases of children born with 46, XX Congenital Adrenal Hyperplasia (CAH)—and they justify their actions in the name of fertility (Karkazis 111-112). Intersex children with CAH may have intermediate genitalia, or have a phallus and scrotum, with no testes in the scrotum, instead having ovaries and a uterus, but no vaginal opening. Since they have ovaries, they are classified by doctors as "female pseudohermaphrodites," despite their often quite typical male genital appearance. Historically, most such children have been reared as males based on their having penises, but today North American doctors surgically assign them female. While doctors may have no qualms about removing the phallus from a baby whom they're been trained to see as "really female," parents are understandably quite taken aback when doctors propose to cut off their child's perfectly normal penis. So doctors assure them that that penis is really an "enlarged clitoris," and that with testosterone suppression medications and surgery to "reduce the clitoris" and construct vulva, their CAH baby can be a normal, fertile girl, and make them grandparents some day (See Diamond).

INTERSEX REPRODUCTION

In framing intersex individuals as usually infertile, doctors present procreation by intersex people as a medical curiosity. This justifies the publication of medical journal articles about a "case," should the doctor have an interest in enhancing his or her professional reputation. Doctors frame facilitating such a procreative act as a sort of "medical miracle," in which the doctor treating the patient is the hero. Wishing to be seen in such a light, doctors wind up putting a lot of pressure on those of us whom they know to be intersex and potentially fertile to reproduce. This sort of external pressure is uncomfortable and almost coercive, as I myself experienced. I was told by doctors that my questionable fertility would probably decline over time, that my atypical uterus would eventually "have to come out," and I was regularly urged not to postpone trying to have a baby.

While I love my daughter very much, I see the pressure that was put on me to conceive as unethical. My road to parenthood was painful, involving a series of miscarriages, a difficult pregnancy, and a labor, with my atypical uterus, that lasted 53 hours and left me with injuries that took several years to fully heal. Furthermore, the medical pressure placed on me to have a child was understood by doctors as confirming a female identity, and by me at the time at least to be incompatible with gender transitioning, which prolonged my gender dysphoria for many distressing years. Like many intersex people, I am left with negative feelings toward medical professionals because of my experiences, and do not trust them to act in my best interests. Yet medical doctors frame themselves in their own writing regarding intersex patients as "heroes."

In facilitating an intersex conception or gestation, doctors frame themselves as heroic in two ways. First, they are heroes for making this new life possible. Consider the patient advice given to intersex individuals with 46, XX genotype CAH regarding fertility:

> Once a woman with CAH decides she wants to conceive, she should seek out the supervision of a medical endocrinologist and an obstetrician who are experienced in the management of CAH during pregnancy. The endocrinologist will help with regularization of the steroid dose to achieve optimal ovulation and then will work with the obstetrician during pregnancy on medication adjustment. Occasionally, an Ob-Gyn trained in reproductive endocrinology and infertility may need to help if pregnancy does not occur with regularization of menses. .
>
> Once ovulation is occurring, sexual intercourse with a fertile partner is usually the next step in achieving a pregnancy. However, some women with CAH have discomfort during sexual intercourse, as their vagina may be shortened due to the androgen exposure in utero. In this situation, some women may choose surgery to enlarge the vagina or to have sperm injected directly into the vagina by an obstetrician.

(Seely and Bentley-Lewis: 1)

Note that the doctors speak here as if medical practitioners were the active figures doing the procreating, and the potentially pregnant person with CAH were just a consumer of numerous medical services. Reproduction is often presented as impossible without medical assistance in articles about reproduction by intersex individuals, and their offspring as medical miracles (See, e.g. Sugawara et al.; Younis et al.).

Doctors present themselves as the heroic actors in all sorts of infertility treatments, not just in the case of intersex patients. But the second way that doctors are framed as heroic in the case of intersex procreation is unique: doctors present a successful fertilization as validating the intersex person's sex assignment. This is evident in the above excerpt addressed to individuals with CAH which refers to individual seeking to become pregnant as a "woman." If an intersex person assigned female becomes pregnant, or an intersex person assigned male successfully inseminates, then doctors presume they made the "right choice" in the sex assignment. If an intersex patient expresses unhappiness with their sex of assignment, doctors may put even more pressure on them to procreate in a manner consistent with their assigned sex.

Unhappiness with one's assigned sex implies a critique of the medical professionals who made it. Rather than questioning the practice of surgical sex assignment in infancy, doctors use claims of potential fertility to seek to undermine the critique of professional practice. My own wife's experience provides an illustration. She was born with an intermediately-sized phalloclitoris, vagina, uterus, and external testes, diagnosed with "perineal hypospadias," and assigned male in infancy. Her external genitalia were reconstructed to look more phallic, with her vagina closed and her urethra meatus moved to the tip of the phalloclitoris. Doctors declared the surgery a complete success (though it robbed her of her capacity for phalloclitoral sexual sensation) and told her parents she was now a normal boy. However, when she grew old enough to consider herself and to speak, it became clear that she identified as a girl. Rather than recognize that an inappropriate sex had been assigned to her, doctors declared that the male assignment was obviously the correct one, as she would have no trouble "fathering" children in the future with her testes and reconstructed genitals. Her medical treatment then progressed to years of treatment by "gender therapists" intended to "correct" her gender identity by making her play sports, do pushups as punishment for feminine behavior, and be physically punished if she cried. (None of these "treatments" had any influence on her gender identity, although they did make her simultaneously miserable and more "butch" in her presentation.) Had she not gender transitioned as soon as she became an adult and could make her own medical decisions, chances are good that she too would have faced pressure to procreate to prove that the doctors' decision had in fact been "correct," as promised.

The pressure placed on unhappy intersex individuals to procreate in order to validate the medical sex assignment that is causing the person unhappiness builds upon a more general tendency of doctors to designate a sex assignment as "correct" when an intersex individual demonstrates heteronormative sexual activity according to zir assigned gender (Dreger *Hermaphrodites and the Medicalization of Sex* 8-9, 119-121; Hausman 74). If a person is assigned "female," then all is well if they are able to "accept a penis" in vaginal intercourse—and if they can actually become pregnant through this, doctors preen at having facilitated a "medical miracle" (See, e.g. Klingensmith et al.; Mayou, Armon and Lindenbaum; Swyer and Bonham). As someone who was assigned female and did eventually have a successful pregnancy, I can tell you that the assumption that functional sexual capacity proves a successful sex assignment did not work for me. For me, as for many, what mattered most in my sex assignment was gender identity. I did not identify as female, and thus I was uncomfortable in my assigned sex. Experiencing a pregnancy did not relieve my discomfort. Carrying a child did not "cure" my gender dysphoria. It didn't make me "feel like a real woman." It just made me feel pregnant.

I'm glad that I was able to become a parent, but the belief that procreating should have "cured" me of my distress with my sex assignment is magical thinking along the lines of the belief that procreating will "cure" a lesbian or gay man and make them heterosexual. Gender identity, sexual orientation, and procreative status are independent characteristics. Lesbians and trans men and intersex individuals aren't mystically "converted" by pregnancies. Gay men and trans women and intersex individuals who inseminate someone aren't thereby made straight or cis or dyadically-male-sexed.

CASE STUDY: PREGNANCY IN AN "APPARENTLY MALE PATIENT"

Sometimes intersex people assigned to the female sex inseminate a partner, or male-assigned intersex people become pregnant. Prior to the mid 20th century, when doctors wrote about "cases of hermaphroditism" they encountered as unaltered adults rather than surgically-altered children, this was a popular topic in Western medical journal articles. Such is not the case today, when reports are few and originate outside the West.

As an example, let us consider a 2006 report by Indian doctors Jha and Chy entitled "Pregnancy in a True Hermaphrodite." In a pattern set in Western medical journal articles a century earlier (Costello 20-22), it presents in a callous and prurient way a medical encounter with an individual assigned to one dyadic sex but involved in procreation in the manner deemed appropriate for the other:

> A unmarried apparently male patient, aged 17 years, attired in a shirt and waistcloth was seen on 13th September, 1997 with his hair clipped. . . He was having sex as a male and also as a female. On examination his skin was smooth, there was no moustache or beard, breasts were well developed and a suprapubic lump of about 12 weeks [pregnancy] size was felt. On examining the genitals a well developed penis with well formed scrotum united in the midline was seen. The urethra was under the scrotal folds and a long narrow vagina admitting one finger was present. . . Sonography showed a 17 weeks macerated fetus in the uterus. . . (Jha and Chy 350)

Accompanying this narrative is a photograph of the patient, presumably taken while he was undergoing a D & C procedure to remove the dead fetus. His legs are spread widely in stirrups, and the hands of two doctors display his blood-smeared genitalia for the camera, pulling up his penis, and pointing out the features in the caption: "Testis in the right gooin [sic], penis, catheter in the urethra, and finger in the vagina" (351). Having found their patient capable of pregnancy, the doctors apparently attempted to convince him to accept surgical reassignment to female: "[t]he patient refused corrective plastic surgery, karyotyping and even removal of the right testicle" (351). The patient left with his intermediate anatomy intact (350).

Articles like Jha and Chy's report of an Indian patient were once regularly published reporting the cases of North American and European intersex individuals, but that is no longer common. There is no obvious reason why intersex people should be born in Western nations with less capacity for fertility that in the past, but there are two other possible explanations. Either western medical interventions are rendering more intersex individuals infertile, or doctors have no remaining incentive to publish cases that might indicate "sex assignment failure." A person a doctor has assigned female is not "supposed" to impregnate anyone, thereby providing embarrassing proof they should have been assigned male, according to dyadic gender ideology. The idea that someone might actually be *happy* with a male sex assignment and also pleased to be able to reproduce by carrying a child does not enter the picture at all.

The framing of sex as dyadic also contributes to the omnipresent popular question about fertility and "hermaphrodites": can we impregnate ourselves? The answer is that the possibility of this happening is virtually nil, but I believe the reason this tired old query nevertheless comes up again and again is due to how most people, having no idea at all of what intersex bodies are actually like, have to use their imaginations. Given binary sex ideology, they figure that if a "hermphrodite" is both male and female, they must have both sets of "organs," meaning a penis, a vagina and uterus and ovaries, and a scrotum with testes. This is not at all the case: intersex bodies are sexually intermediate bodies, not two binary-sexed bodies pasted together. Even in those cases where an individual has an ovary and a testis, we have but one hormonal balance each, and a level of testosterone that would support sperm production would be incompatible with pregnancy. In Jha and Chy's report, the doctors even address this topic of popular fascination, concluding their article by stating, "Autofertilisation could not have been possible in this case as there was maturation arrest [of the sperm in the testis] at the spermatid stage," a result of the sex steroid balance that permitted the pregnancy (351).

CONCLUSION

I can't really blame people on the street for the depth of their ignorance about intersex fertility. People don't know about intersex bodies and experiences because we are hidden from them. Our sex status is erased by the legal requirement that we be declared male or female at birth. Our bodies are redacted by doctors trying to remove the evidence of our physical "deviance." Information about intersex statuses is not taught in high school biology classes. The large majority of intersex people are well-schooled to keep our "disorders" in the closet. So I'm less bothered by the tedious "if you're a hermaphrodite, could you get yourself pregnant?" question than I am by binary-gender-enforcing ideologies and actions of medical practitioners, who are supposed to act to improve patients' well-being.

Intersex people are not tragic figures due to infertility. Some of us don't want children, and some of us adopt. Some of us are made infertile by "normalizing" sex-assignment surgery that has been performed without our consent. And some of us do indeed produce children ourselves. We've done this throughout all of human history, not just recently due to "medical miracles." Most of us do so in private, with no medical journal articles trumpeting a fanfare.

It's time for some more sophisticated thinking about intersex fertility and reproduction.

NOTES

[1]The phrase "of woman born" has been seen as definitive of human nature in Western nations since Shakespeare in the 17th century made it central to the plot of Macbeth. It was also a phrase central to second wave feminism, and the title of Andrienne Rich's classic book on maternity and patriarchy(*Of Woman Born: Motherhood as Experience and Institution*).

[2]I use the gender neutral pronoun ze/zir/zim to refer to a person whose gender identity and pronoun preference are not known. As an intersex person, I am aware that one of the factors that leads to hasty sex-assignment decisions for newborns is our typical practice in English of using gendered pronouns to refer to people. The wider use of gender neutral pronouns, such as ze or the singular they, would reduce this vector of pressure.

WORKS CITED

Blackless, Melanie, Anthony Charuvastra, Amanda Derryck, Anne Fausto-Sterling, Karl Lauzanne, and Ellen Lee. "How Sexually Dimorphic Are We? Review and Synthesis." *American Journal of Human Biology* 12.2 (2000): 151-66. Web.

Carrera, Maria V., Renee Depalma, and Maria Lameiras. "Sex/Gender Identity: Moving Beyond Fixed and 'Natural' Categories." *Sexualities* 15.8 (2012): 995-1016. Print.

Costello, Cary G. (published as Costello, Carrie Yang) "Teratology: "Monsters" and the Professionalization of Obstetrics." *Journal of Historical Sociology* 19.1 (2006): 1-33. Print.

Council of Europe. Parliamentary Assembly. *Children's Right to Physical Integrity*. 2013. Web.

Davidson, Megan. "Natural Facts?" *Transgender Tapestry* 2002: 41-44. Print.

D Davies, Sharyn Graham. *Challenging Gender Norms: Five Genders among Bugis in Indonesia.* Belmont, CA: Wadsworth Pub, 2007. Print.

Davis, Georgiann. "'DSD is a Perfectly Fine Term': Reasserting Medical Authority through a Shift in Intersex Terminology." *Advances in Medical Sociology* 12 (2002): 155-182. Print.

Diamond, David A. "Gender Assignment Survey of AAP Urology Section Fellows." American Academy of Pediatrics Annual Meeting, San Francisco, October 11, 2004.

Donahoe, Patricia. K, David. M. Powell & Mary. M. Lee. "Clinical Management of Intersex Abnormalities." *Current Problems in Surgery* 28.8 (1991): 513-579. Print.

Dreger, Alice. D. "What to Expect When You Have the Child You Weren't Expecting." *Surgically Shaping Children: Technology, Ethics, and the Pursuit of Normality* (2006): 253-265. Print.

Dreger, Alice D., et al. "Changing the Nomenclature/Taxonomy for Intersex: A Scientific and Clinical Rationale." *Journal of Pediatric Endocrinology & Metabolism* 18.8 (2005): 729-734. Print.

Dreger, Alice D. *Hermaphrodites and the Medicalization of Sex.* Cambridge, MA: Harvard University Press. 1998. Print.

Driskill, Quo-li, Chris Finley, Brian Joseph Gilley, and Scott Lauria Morgensen, *Queer Indigenous Studies: Critical Interventions in Theory, Politics, and Literature.* Tucson: University of Arizona Press. 2011. Print.

Elliot, P. "Engaging Trans Debates on Gender Variance: A Feminist Analysis." *Sexualities* 12.1 (2009): 5-32. Print.

Fausto-Sterling, Anne. *Sexing the Body: Gender Politics and the Construction of Sexuality.* NY: Basic Books. 2000. Print.

Feder, Ellen K. "Imperatives of Normality: From 'Intersex' to 'Disorders of Sex Development.'" *GLQ: A Journal of Lesbian and Gay Studies* 15.2 (2009): 225-247. Print.

Fonrobert, Charlotte E. "Gender Identity in Halakhic Discourse." The Jewish Women's Archive, 1 Mar. 2009. Web. 10 Sept. 2011.

Greenberg, Julie A. "Defining Male and Female: Intersexuality and the Collision Between Law and Biology." *Arizona Law Review* 41 (1999): 265. Print.

Hausman, Bernice L. *Changing Sex: Transsexualism, Technology, and the Idea of Gender*. Durham, NIC: Duke UP. 1995. Print.

Hendren, W. Hardy. “The Genetic Male with Absent Penis and Urethrorectal Communication: Experience with 5 Patients.” *The Journal of Urology* 157.4 (1997): 1469-1474. Print.

Herdt, Gilbert, ed.. *Third Sex, Third Gender: Beyond Sexual Dimorphism in Culture and History*. Brooklyn, NY: Zone, 1996. Print.

Hird, Myra J. “Gender’s Nature: Intersexuality, Transsexualism and the ‘Sex’/’Gender’Binary.” *Feminist Theory* 1.3 (2000): 347-364. Print.

Ikoma, F., H. Shima, and H. Yabumoto. “Classification of Enlarged Prostatic Utricle in Patients with Hypospadias.” *British Journal of Urology* 57.3 (1985): 334-337. Print.

Jha, Kumudina and Ajit Kumar Chy. “Pregnancy in a True Hermaphrodite,” *The Journal of Obstetrics and Gynecology of India* 56.4 (2006): 350-351. Print.

Karkazis, Katrina Alicia. *Fixing Sex: Intersex, Medical Authority, and Lived Experience*. Durham: Duke UP, 2008. Print.

Kessler, Suzanne J. “The Medical Construction of Gender: Case Management of Intersexed Infants.” *Signs* (1990): 3-26. Print.

Kessler, Suzanne J. *Lessons from the Intersexed*. New Brunswick, NJ: Rutgers UP, 1998. Print.

Klingensmith, Georgeanna Jones, et al. “Glucocorticoid Treatment of Girls with Congenital Adrenal Hyperplasia: Effects on Height, Sexual Maturation, and Fertility.” *The Journal of Pediatrics* 90.6 (1977): 996-1004. Print.

Kojima, Yoshiyuki, Yutaro Hayashi, Tetsuji Maruyama, Shoichi Sasaki, and Kenjiro Kohri. “Comparison between Ultrasonography and Retrograde Urethrography for Detection of Prostatic Utricle Associated with Hypospadias.” *Urology*. 57.6 (2001): 11511-1155. Print.

Kuhnle, Ursula and Wolfgang Krahl. “The Impact of Culture on Sex Assignment and Gender Development in Intersex Patients.” *Perspectives in Biology and Medicine* 45.1 (2002): 85-103. Print.

Lambert, Sarah M., Eric JN Vilain, and Thomas F. Kolon. “A Practical Approach to Ambiguous Genitalia in the Newborn Period.” *Urologic Clinics of North America* 37.2 (2010): 195-205. Print.

Lee, Peter A., et al. “Micropenis. I. Criteria, etiologies and classification.” *The Johns Hopkins Medical Journal* 146.4 (1980): 156. Print.

Matzner, Andrew. *'O Au No Keia: Voices from Hawai'i's Mahu and Transgender Communities.* Xlibris, 2001. Print.

Mayou, B. J., P. Armon, and R. H. Lindenbaum. "Pregnancy and Childbirth in a True Hermaphrodite following Reconstructive Surgery." *BJOG: An International Journal of Obstetrics & Gynaecology* 85.4 (1978): 314-316. Print.

Méndez, Juan E. "Report of the Special Rapporteur on Torture and Other Cruel, Inhuman or Degrading Treatment or Punishment." UN Doc. A/HRC/22 53.1 (2013): 22. Print.

Meyer-Bahlburg, Heino FL. "Intersexuality and the Diagnosis of Gender Identity Disorder." *Archives of Sexual Behavior* 23.1 (1994): 21-40. Print.

Moore, Keith L., and T. V. N. Persaud. *The Developing Human: Clinically Oriented Embryology.* 8th ed. Philadelphia, PA: Saunders, 2007. Print.

Paulozzi, Leonard J., J. David Erickson, and Richard J. Jackson. "Hypospadias Trends in Two US Surveillance Systems." *Pediatrics* 100.5 (1997): 831-834. Print.

Preves, Sharon E. *Intersex and Identity: The Contested Self.* New Brunswick, NJ: Rutgers UP, 2003. Print.

Reis, Elizabeth. "Divergence or Disorder?: The Politics of Naming Intersex." *Perspectives in Biology and Medicine* 50.4 (2007): 535-543. Print.

Reis, Elizabeth. *Bodies in Doubt: An American History of Intersex.* Baltimore: Johns Hopkins UP, 2009. Print.

Rich, Adrienne. *Of Woman Born: Motherhood as Experience and Institution.* New York: Norton, 1995. Print.

Rosario, Vernon A. "'Is It a Boy or a Girl?' Introduction to Special Issue on Intersex." *Journal of Gay Lesbian Psychotherapy* 10.2 (2006): 1-7. Print.

Roughgarden, Joan. *Evolution's Rainbow: Diversity, Gender, and Sexuality in Nature and People.* Berkeley, CA: U of California P, 2009. Print.

Seeley, Ellen, and Rhonda Bentley-Lewis. "Pregnancy and CAH: What Every Woman with Classical CAH Should Know." *CARES Foundation.* CARES Foundation Newsletter, 2005. Web. 26 Sept. 2011.

Siewert, Rachel. *Involuntary or Coerced Sterilization of Intersex People in Australia.* Canberra: Community Affairs References Committee, 2013. Print.

Swyer, G. I. M., and D. G. Bonham. "Successful Pregnancy in a Female Pseudohermaphrodite." *British Medical Journal* 1.5231 (1961): 1005.

Print.

Sugawara, Nobuo, et al. "A Successful Pregnancy Outcome Using Frozen Testicular Sperm from a Chimeric Infertile Male with a 46, XX/46, XY Karyotype: Case Report." *Human Reproduction* 20.1 (2005): 147-148. Print.

Tamar-Mattis, Anne, et al. "Emotionally and Cognitively Informed Consent for Clinical Care for Sifferences of Sex Development." *Psychology & Sexuality* (2013): 1-12. Print.

Vidal, Isabelle, et al. "Surgical Options in Disorders of Sex Development (DSD) with Ambiguous Genitalia." *Best Practice & Research Clinical Endocrinology & Metabolism* 24.2 (2010): 311-324. Print.

Wilson, Gina. "Intersex Genital Mutilation – IGM: The Fourteen Days of Intersex" OII Intersex Network, 2012. Web. 11 Oct. 2013.

Younis, Johnny S., et al. "Successful Monozygotic Twin Pregnancy Fathered by a Male 46, XY True Hermaphrodite." *Reproductive Biomedicine Online* 22.1 (2011): 80-82. Print.

4.

'Pregnant with Meaning'

An Analysis of Online Media Response to Thomas Beatie and his Pregnancy

ALISA GRIGOROVICH

INTRODUCTION

Thomas Beatie first came out as transgender and pregnant in an online March 2008 article in *The Advocate*. Within a week of the article's publication, the Beatie family appeared on the *Barbara Walters Show* and the *Oprah Winfrey Show* and their story was circulated on all major television networks, print media outlets and throughout the internet. In November 2008 Beatie published an autobiography titled *A Labor of Love* in which he discussed his life and decision to transition as well as the reasons for his decision to carry his own child. In the same month a documentary about his story was also aired on *The Discovery Channel*. Beatie's daughter was born June 29, 2008 and following her birth, Beatie gave birth to two more children. Despite the existence of earlier media reports of male pregnancy (Califia; More), Beatie quickly became known as "the pregnant man"; reactions to his story have ranged from curiosity to outright hatred to dismissal of his male gender.

While Beatie is not the first transgender man to become pregnant, he is the first to incite such a sensationalist, and often transphobic, public response (Califia; More). What is it about Beatie's story that has elicited such public interest and debate? In this paper I will argue that media response to Beatie's story reveals that male pregnancy disrupts the 'naturalness' of the heterosexual matrix and threatens the hegemonic construction of the mythical 'Family.' Furthermore, I will show that media response can be divided into three specific normalizing discourses: gender essentialism, charges of obscenity, and a 'concern' for the unborn child.

Halberstam argues that it is important for scholars to interrogate mainstream representations of transgender people and their lives in order to reveal underlying hegemonic and transphobic discourses (47-75). Halberstam identifies three types of motivations for representing transgender lives by non-transgender people that are highly problematic: stabilization, rationalization and trivialization (54-55). The first of these seeks to stabilize 'normal' identity by presenting transgender people as the 'strange others.' The second project is interested in providing 'reasonable' explanations for 'dangerous' and 'outrageous' transgender behaviours. The final problematic representation, trivialization, attempts to contain the threat to gender stability that transgender people pose by presenting transgender people's lives as inconsequential and non-representative.

Media representations of transgender families, such as Thomas Beatie's story, thus demand a critical analysis. In this paper I will be drawing on queer theory, and in particular the work of Judith Butler (1990), to examine English language online media accounts (i.e. newspapers, magazines, television websites) of Beatie's first pregnancy, appearing online from the years 2008 to 2009. Although, I recognize that both queer theory and Butler's work on gender performativity have been critiqued by transgender and transsexual scholars (Jones; Namaste; Prosser), I nonetheless argue that both queer theory and Butler's work can be useful to an examination of the entrenched nature of essentialist and cissexist discourses with respect to pregnancy and parenting.

TRANSGENDER, TRANSSEXUAL(ISM) AND TRANSPHOBIA

There is some disagreement in both transgender studies and mainstream culture about the boundaries and distinctions between the terms transgender and transsexual. Typically, transgender is used in the broadest sense to refer to people who transgress gender norms in some way (Betcher; Whittle). The term transsexual, on the other hand, is used to refer to people who, through a variety of hormonal and surgical means, "alter their body in ways that may be constructed as at odds with the sex assignment of birth or which may not be readily intelligible in terms of traditional conceptions of sexed bodies" (Betcher 46). Although 'transgender' and 'transsexual' are terms that are sometimes used interchangeably in the literature, since Beatie has identified himself as a being 'transgender' (Beatie 2008b 34), this is how I will refer to him throughout this paper.

Transgender people in society are often subject to violence and discrimination due to transphobia and cissexism (Betcher; Feinberg; Namaste; Wilchins). Transphobia can be defined as fear and the expression of hatred, loathing, rage and/or moral indignation towards transgender people because of how they live or 'do' their gender (Betcher). Cissexism refers to the belief that transgender and transsexual genders are less authentic than or inferior to cisgendered[1] genders (Serano). As a consequence of these two social prejudices, transgender people experience discrimination, physical and psychological violence, and exclusion within social institutions and all areas of social life including healthcare, employment, education, marriage and parenting.

DUELLING ESSENTIALISMS

The overwhelming majority of the online material concerning Beatie and his pregnancy reflects a transphobic and essentialist understanding of sexuality and gender. In such an understanding of human gender and sexuality, it is assumed that there are only two sexes (male/female) and two genders (masculine/feminine) and that all individuals are both heterosexual and cisgendered.

Such essentialist accounts predominately focus on Beatie's existing and previous genitalia and secondary sex characteristics when reporting on his pregnancy and sexual behaviours. This can be seen in the following quotes from Beatie's televised interviews[2] with Larry King, on the *Larry King Show*, and Oprah Winfrey, on the *Oprah Winfrey Show*:

> [Transcript of Oprah narrating] Over the years, testosterone injections helped Thomas look and sound more masculine. His voice dropped a few octaves, and he began growing facial hair. These hormone treatments also altered his sexual organs. Thomas says his clitoris grew to the size of a small penis. "It looks like a penis," he says. "I can have intercourse with my wife."

> [Transcript of King speaking] Where did you learn how to do this (artificial insemination)? From the Internet, you said,

> right. You can't have the normal kind of intercourse, right? That's fascinating to me. I didn't know that. So you have a clitoris that looks like a penis so it can fit into having love relations? (King)

Butler has argued that there exists a:

> ...hegemonic discursive/epistemic model of gender intelligibility that assumes that for bodies to cohere and make sense there must be a stable sex expressed through a stable gender (masculine expresses male, feminine expresses female) that is appositionally and hierarchically defined through the practice of compulsory heterosexuality. (*Gender Trouble* 151)

Within such an understanding of gender, 'women' and 'men' are defined as such not only via their 'gendered characteristics,' but also via their relationships and differences to each other; thus to desire a man makes one a woman and vice versa. All other kinds of relations are excluded within this framework. The dominant understanding of gender in our society is thus an essentialist one, where gender is taken to be an immutable, biological 'fact,' evidenced by the differences in genitals and secondary sex characteristics between some bodies.

Kessler and McKenna have further proposed that "genitals are the essential insignia of gender" in Western society (173). Furthermore, these do not have to be 'real' genitals, as the identification of a body as either male or female is done through ideas about which gender has what kind of external body parts and appearance. Thus, bodies are determined to be male or female based on their appearance and the belief that this appearance reflects a certain kind of anatomical configuration. Alongside this, there is a cultural understanding that there are only two genders, male and female, that the male is always the sperm carrier while the female is the egg carrier, and that the two are engaged in a biological imperative to reproduce; Kessler and McKenna called this the 'natural attitude' of gender. These 'naturalized' beliefs are evidenced in the media obsession with Beatie's genitals and in the interest in his sexual behaviour patterns. Overwhelmingly, news reports of Beatie's pregnancy focus on his genitals and his masculinized appearance such as his beard and/or voice. This essentialism can also be seen at work in the denial that Beatie is a 'man' who is pregnant, such as in the following quotes from online media coverage of the story in a *UK Telegraph* and *LiveScience*:

> She [author quoting Margaret Somerville, a contributor for the National and McGill Law professor] said Mr. Beatie had "artificially" made himself a man and she would say to him: "You're not a man, you're a woman and you're having a baby and you're actually having your own baby." Just because you put on a clown suit, doesn't mean that you don't still exist underneath." (Elseworth)

> The inescapable biological fact is that men cannot become pregnant [...] if Beatie has retained his babymaking equipment, then he is in fact still biologically a woman, not a man. (Radford)

Within an essentialist discourse of gender and sex, Beatie's male identity is discredited through reference to his reproductive organs and his decision to become pregnant. Such reactions reflect not only an essentialist view of gender, but also an investment in the heterosexual matrix. According to Butler, the heterosexual matrix is a "grid of cultural intelligibility through which bodies, genders, and desires are naturalized" (*Gender Trouble* 17). This framework recognizes only two discrete sexes, male and female, and two genders which follow from these, masculine and feminine. Butler argues that it is precisely through the exclusion of other kinds of gender identities that this framework is maintained. Within such a framework, gender identities that do not conform to these norms are read as "developmental failures or logical impossibilities" (*Gender Trouble* 17).

Pregnancy in our society is thought to be one of the most salient characteristics that separate males from females and is proof of the 'naturalness' of heterosexual relations. As Hird elaborates, "[w]hatever social, political and economic changes might take place to alter women's position in society, sexual reproduction is seen as both immutable 'fact' and cause of structural differences between women and men" (Hird 1). Within such an understanding of pregnancy, Beatie's identity as a 'pregnant man' is unintelligible, and his identity as a male subsequently deemed a failure. This can be seen in the following transphobic quotes from online newspaper articles:

> In fact, Thomas Beatie is not a "pregnant man" but a woman who wanted to be a man, had surgery to remove her breasts, and took male hormones but kept female reproductive organs. He has a beard, but in the characteristic that most defines the physical difference between a man and a woman,

> Thomas Beatie is a woman. Legally, he's a he. Biologically, he's a she. (Cramer, par 4)

> But it takes more than a mastectomy and hormone treatments to overturn biology. Thomas may be a man in the eyes of the law, but she remains physically a woman, with a woman's reproductive system, a woman's genitals, and a woman's chromosomes. (Jacoby, par 3)

Essentialist discourses are present not only in the denial of Beatie as a 'real' man but also in the questioning of his heterosexual sexual identity and his relationship with his wife. Rubin writes that sexual essentialism is the idea that one's sexuality, like one's gender, is a 'natural force' that is unchanging and the idea that there are only three kinds of sexual relations possible: homosexual, heterosexual and bisexual (Rubin). The questioning and the denial of Beatie's marriage reflect the hegemonic view that marriage is a relation that is only possible between two 'biologically opposite' individuals. Thus, Beatie cannot be a heterosexual male and married to a woman if he possesses 'female parts,' which is evidenced by his ability to become pregnant. The questioning of the validity of the decision by Beatie to 'become' a man rather than 'remain' a lesbian also reflects the common collapse of the distinction between sex and gender identity that results from the centrality of the heterosexual matrix in social consciousness. The assertion that Beatie is a 'lesbian' rather than a heterosexual man by virtue of his pregnancy therefore reflects the essentialist belief in the discrete and unchanging nature of gender and sexuality, and the relationship between the two. In the discrediting of his gender and sexuality, the heterosexual matrix remains intact and the threat that Beatie's pregnancy poses to it is nullified. Such essentialist denial can be seen in the following quotes from Beatie's interview on Larry King and an online article about Beatie's appearance on Oprah:

> When you met, were you—what kind of couple were you? What I meant was did you consider yourself gay? [Transcript of King speaking to Beatie's wife, Nancy] So you feel you're married to a man? (King)

> 'Sexuality is completely different than your gender,' he [Beatie] said, responding to a question about why he did not

> remain a lesbian woman. 'I felt more comfortable being the male gender.' (Goldman)

The discrediting of Beatie's gender identity and sexual identity is often done on the basis of the uncovering of his 'biological truth' and presented in terms of deception or duplicity. As Halberstam notes, transgender people are often accused of being "eccentric, duplicitous, deceptive, odd, self-hating" and are presented in contrast to normative, non-transgender people, which are judged to be more 'honest' and 'true' (57-58). As Bettcher adds, this attribution of deception often plays a role in the transphobic responses that have everyday consequences for transpeople (47-50). Fundamental to this rhetoric is the belief that in transgender people there is a contrast between the 'appearance' and 'reality' of genitals, which are taken as the essential determinants of sex. Therefore, when the deception is 'discovered,' transphobic violence and discrimination is justified on the grounds that the transgender person deceived the perpetrator. As Bettcher points out, this rhetoric of deception puts transpeople in a "dangerous double bind" - to reveal one's transgender status and be subjected to immediate violence/hatred or to hide it and run the risk of being exposed as a 'deceiver' and punished for it. It is important to note that often this is not a choice over which a transgender person has much control. For instance, Beatie has argued that one of the reasons he came out was the fact that he did not want to be misrepresented and discriminated against if his pregnancy was found out later (*A Labor of Love* 263-276).

Within such an understanding of transgender, Beatie's decision to become pregnant 'exposes' his 'true' gender and renders him an impostor. The media coverage of his story reflects this rhetoric of deception in two ways. First, stories of his pregnancy often include a discussion of his life prior to transitioning and focus on how well he performed femininity through dating men and modeling. These types of stories attempt to discredit Beatie's present male identity, thus keeping intact essentialist sex/gender frameworks. Second, many stories of Beatie's pregnancy present themselves as 'revealing the truth' behind the pregnancy by uncovering Beatie's 'true sex,' by referencing the fact that he was assigned female at birth and/or qualifying that he is a 'transgender' man. These discussions of his transitioning and/or transition status also emphasize that he chose to keep his 'female' organs, or uterus, after transitioning. The use of a deception narrative as a way to translate the pregnancy to readers and viewers exists despite the fact that Beatie has come out himself as a transgendered and was quite candid about his life prior to transitioning. This manufacturing of deception also reflects the social investment in gender and sex essentialist frameworks and the cultural belief in the 'bodily truth' of gender (Fausto-Sterling 1-29). This can be seen in the following excerpts from online newspaper article and an online editorial article:

> Mr. Beatie *reveals* that, as a female called Tracy Lagondino, he used to date men in his teens. Before having gender reassignment surgery, Miss Lagondino was encouraged to model by her dad and even became a Miss Hawaii Teen USA finalist." (Emphasis my own, Paris)

> Their physical bodies show the *facts* [...] No shot of hormones or plastic surgery alters their sexual gender; they only help to *masquerade* their *true* sex [...] what more biological *proof* do you need than Tracy becoming pregnant? (Emphasis my own, Winslow)

OBSCENE GESTURES

A second type of transphobic response to Beatie's pregnancy is that of fear and disgust. This response arises from the fact that Beatie's pregnancy, and male pregnancy in general, is seen as violating social taboos and is thus obscene and dangerous. Mary Douglas has argued that cultural beliefs and rituals with respect to bodily taboos reflect the desire to enforce order on what is "an inherently untidy experience" (4). She has proposed that *proper* bodies and behaviours are established through the exaggeration of difference and the repulsion and demarcation of improper bodies. These taboos are then used to justify punishment and power over individuals and their behaviours.

Drawing on the work of Douglas, Butler adds that in contemporary Western society there is a particular understanding, or discourse, of what constitutes a (proper) body. This discourse establishes what is a body using specific codes and markings that reflect the appropriate and possible limits and contours of a gendered body (1990 131). Furthermore, Butler proposes that the *gendered* body only becomes a coherent body through the exaggeration of bodily differences between *female* and *male* bodies. One such difference is established through dichotomous genital differentiation which reflects the belief that there are only two kinds of bodies possible (Butler).

Consequently, male pregnancy and the idea that one can be male and have a vagina disrupts the very contours of what is thought to be a (gendered) body, generating a repulsion of it. Given that culturally and historically pregnancy has been associated with female bodies, the pregnant male body exceeds the established limits of what constitutes a *proper* body.

Beatie's pregnancy is thus not only judged to be 'wrong' but also as threatening to society in general. This hysterical fear of the male pregnant body can be seen in the following online newspaper account:

> Medically, it's do-able. Morally, it's debatable. But on a purely emotional level, the very idea of male pregnancy is difficult to accept [...] Male pregnancy does not feel like progress. It feels threatening, and horrifying, and appalling. (Leith)

Kipnis suggests that the human body has a particular symbolic function in our society and that the control over bodies is a symbol of social control. She argues that the need to control individual bodies arises out of the social need to create and maintain a 'proper' work force and passive law abiding citizens. As a result, "the out-of-control, unmannerly body is precisely what threatens the orderly operation of the status quo" (134). A male pregnant body is judged to be 'out-of-control' because it violates socially sanctioned norms of gender and reproduction, which state that only female bodies may become pregnant. As a result, within such a symbolic framework, the pregnant male body becomes unintelligible as a legitimate body and thus needs to be controlled and disavowed. This transphobic disavowal can be seen in this excerpt from an online article about Beatie's pregnancy in the *Boston Globe*:

> Those of us for whom gender is not a spectrum of possibilities but a matter of either/or are more likely to regard the whole situation (male pregnancy) as profoundly aberrant and detrimental - especially for the baby about to be brought into the world. [...] These are only the latest in an endless series of reminders that sexual urges and appetites can be powerful and perverse and lead to harmful consequences. That is why human societies have always constrained sexual behavior with equally powerful taboos and moral standards. (Jacoby par. 7)

According to Kipnis, disgust is a key mechanism of the regulation of bodies and she argues that the distinctions between proper and improper bodies "are maintained through the expressions of taste, disgust and exclusion" (135). Through the expression of disgust, bodies that are judged to be obscene because they violate social norms are repulsed and expelled from society. In maintaining the distinctions between what is a normal or abnormal body, a society is thus able to maintain control over the particular functions and roles of specific bodies and thus the status quo. This mechanism of disgust is evident in responses to Beatie's pregnancy that judge it to be 'improper' because it violates reproductive and gendered norms which are thought to be necessary for the 'greater social order.' In particular, in these responses Beatie's pregnancy is seen as a 'threat' and is thought to be the reflection of some sort of general social 'degeneracy.' These types of responses are almost hysterical in nature and reflect the symbolic nature of bodies as representative of the order, and thus rightness of a society's organization. This can be seen in the following quotes from an online newspaper and blog:

> "It's a very touchy thing, this deconstruction of our biological reality and the institutions that have existed across all kinds of societies over thousands and thousands of years to establish stability, respect and certainty. I think we're just playing with fire." (Margaret Sommerville qtd. in Elseworth)

> I don't want to know the deal [Beatie's pregnancy]. I don't want to hear. I'm gonna be sick. I'm gonna be sick. I am upset. That was not only stupid and useless, but quite frankly, disgusting. (Mika Brzezinski from *Morning Joe* talk show qtd. in Towle)

THINK OF THE CHILDREN

The last type of reaction that is generated in response to Beatie's pregnancy is that of concern for the 'welfare' of his child. As it has been noted, this kind of response is a typical reaction to the existence of transgender parents in general (McGuinees and Alghrani). This 'concern' over the wellbeing of transgender parents' children results from the social prejudice around transsexuality and transgenderism (Namaste; More; McGuiness and Alghrani). In part, the 'concern' with regard to children of transgender parents also reflects the larger social preoccupation with the nature of 'good' (appropriate) parents. In western society, the ideal family consists of a cisgendered man married to a cisgendered woman. Familial norms therefore buttress the essentialist frameworks of sex, gender and sexuality. Families that do not conform to this norm are thus judged to be inadequate or 'wrong' (Bernstein and Reiman 3). As a result of this hegemonic construction, motherhood and pregnancy are important sites of cultural and social meaning and control.

While all bodies are controlled and scrutinized in society, pregnant bodies are subject to especially close surveillance and regulation (Gross and Pattinson; Longhurst; Varcoe and Hartick; Doane). Multiple government health interventions and campaigns are targeted at pregnant bodies and parents. Pregnant bodies are also medicalized and monitored through the widespread acceptance of the routine use of medical technologies such as ultrasound, amniocentesis and genetic testing. Furthermore, upon the birth of their children, parents are subject to advice and surveillance with respect to 'appropriate' child rearing practices from a variety of 'experts' in the media, social institutions and the general public.

Current discourses construct motherhood as a dichotomy, either good or bad. Within the mythical ideal of the family, good mothers are those that are cisgendered, heterosexual and married (Bernstein and Reiman). Mothers who do not meet normative expectations of 'the good mother' are designated socially as 'deviant others' and are judged as unfit to parent (Wilson and Huntington 61). Wykes adds that, "Marriage and family [are] pivotal but conflictual sites of social/sexual control. Today these institutions are readily reified in the press, usually through the castigation of any 'other' manifestations of sexuality or reproduction and consequently of social 'problems'" (qtd. in Storrs 246). Within such a framework, Beatie's decision to become pregnant as a transgender man is read as deviant and wrong. Beatie is further judged as unfit to parent based on his decision to carry his own child rather than adopt or refuse to have children at all. This can be seen in the following quotes from an online editorial and from an online newspaper article:

> [W]hat about future consideration of the child when he or she is old enough to understand what has happened? As a parent, I can easily see that this could cause many psychological problems for this child in the future. The inability or refusal to consider this shows a lack of maturity and foresight. These qualities are essential to be a good parent. (Winslow)

> I feel that this is just too far and that they are trying to do an experiment with the child. If they wanted to have a child, they could take an infant from an orphanage. (Armen Hareyan qtd. in Paris)

Butler has suggested that the figure of the "the child" is a "dense site for the transfer and reproduction of culture" and the invoking of this figure reflects larger fears about gender, racial and sexual norms in contemporary society (*Gender Trouble* 110). Consequently, implicit in these reactions is the belief in the *naturalness* of heterosexuality and cisgender gender and that a family must reflect these norms by providing the child with the example of two (properly) heterosexual and cisgendered parents. The fear that is reflected in media accounts of Beatie's pregnancy, and in media coverage of LGBTQ parents in general, is thus the homophobic and transphobic fear that children raised in such families will be 'improperly' gendered or sexual as a result. This fear can be seen in the following quotes from an online magazine article and an online newspaper article:

> There were nurses who refused to refer to him as a he and a doctor who warned "that people would try to kill my baby because it is an abomination." His own brother, says Thomas, told him his baby would be a monster. (Tresniowski)

> [T]here is professional concern about the confusion the child may later experience. "There is going to be an extra degree of complication or confusion about 'where am I from?'" says Robert Withers, a psychoanalyst who has treated transgender patients. (Barkham)

CONCLUSION: BEATIE'S LEGACY?

Thomas Beatie's decision to become pregnant and to come out as a transgendered has elicited considerable sensationalist interest and transphobic responses from online and print media. It is interesting to note that Beatie became known as the 'first' pregnant man despite previous reports of other transgender men becoming pregnant (Califia; More). One possible reason for this designation and the subsequent interest in Beatie is perhaps that it reflects a conservative backlash against the recent successful challenges to marriage and family laws by LGBT people in the United States and elsewhere over the last ten years. Additionally, it is possible that Beatie's story was sensationalized as result of Beatie's insistence that he was the first pregnant man who was also legally recognized as male and as married. On the other hand, media's insistence that Beatie is the *first* may have simply occurred because Beatie has actively sought out publicity by coming out and agreeing to be interviewed on major television shows and by online and print media.

As I have shown, media responses to Beatie and his pregnancy fall into three types of discourses: gender essentialism, charges of obscenity, and 'concern' for the child. An analysis of these responses demonstrates that male pregnancy disturbs current hegemonic discourses of binary gender norms, heteronormativity and parenthood. Beatie's pregnant body poses a threat to the stability and coherence of the socially controlled body that relies on the illusion that there are two sexes and genders that are distinguishable by sexual difference. The pregnant male transgender body is thus seen as an 'incoherent' body (Noble). However, Beatie's decision to come out and narrate his own story of parenthood can be thought of as the production of a transsituated discourse of pregnancy and family formation that 'begin[s] to reord[er] the nature of things" (Cromwell 518).

Although this paper has focused on one example of transgender parenting and is a theoretical analysis, it nonetheless has implications for broader research, policy and activism. First, this analysis adds to the body of evidence that shows that transgender people experience discrimination and exclusion as result of systemic heteronormativity and cissexism. Second, while this paper has focused on negative reactions to Beatie's story, Beatie's story has simultaneously increased the visibility of transgender families in the mainstream. In the long term, this visiblity may have positive impact on social change and activism. Finally, this analysis can be used to continue to demand legal, social and institutional supports for transgender people and their families.

NOTES

[1] Cisgendered refers to an individual who identifies with the sex/gender identity that they were assigned at birth.

[2]Quotes are taken from clips and transcripts of interview available on the shows' websites.

WORKS CITED

Barkham, Patrick. "'Being a pregnant man? It's incredible.'" *The Guardian.* 28 Mar 2008. Web. 19 May 2009.

Beatie, Thomas. "Is Society Ready for This Pregnant Husband?" *The Advocate.* 28 March 2008. Print.

—. *A Labor of Love: The Story of One Man's Extraordinary Pregnancy.* Berkley: Seal Press, 2008. Print.

Bernstein, Mary, and Reiman, Renate. "Queer Families and the Politics of Visibility." *Queer Families, Queer Politics: Challenging Culture and the State.* Eds. New York: Columbia University Press, 2001. 1-17. Print.

Betcher, Talia Mae. "Evil Deceivers and Make Believers: On Transphobic Violence and the Politics of Illusion." *Hypatia* 22.3 (2007): 43-65. Print.

Butler, Judith. *Gender Trouble: Feminism and the Subversion of Identity.* New York: Routledge, 1990. Print.

—-. *Undoing Gender.* New York: Routledge, 2004. Print.

Califia, Patrick. "Two Dads with a Difference: Neither of Us was Born Male." *Village Voice.* 20 Jun 2000. Web. 01 May 2009.

Cramer, Elisa. "Pregnant Man, Pregnant Pause." *Palm Beach Post.* 25 April 2008. Web. 15 May 2009.

Cromwell, Jason. "Queering the Binaries: Transsituated Identities, Bodies and Sexualities." *The Transgender Studies Reader.* Eds. Susan Stryker and Stephen Whittle. New York: Routledge, 2006. 509-520. Print.

Davis, Erin Calhoun. "Situating 'Fluidity': (Trans) Gender Identification and the Regulation of Gender Diversity." *GLQ* 15.1 (2008): 97-130. Print.

Douglas, Mary. *Purity and Danger: An Analysis of the Concepts of Pollution and Taboo.* New York: Routledge, 1988. Print.

Elseworth, Catherine. "'Pregnant' Man Stuns Medical Profession." *Telegraph.* 28 March 2008. Web. 15 May 2009.

Fausto-Sterling, Anne. *Sexing the Body: Gender Politics and the Construction of Sexuality.* New York: Basic Books, 2000. Print.

Feinberg, Leslie. *TransLiberation: Beyond Pink and Blue.* Boston: Beacon Press, 2006. Print.

Goldman, Russell. "It's my Right to Have Kid, Pregnant Man tells Oprah." *ABC News.* 3 April 2008. Web. 1 May 2009.

Gross, Harriet & Pattison, Helen. *Sanctioning Pregnancy: A Psychological*

Perspective on the Paradoxes and Culture of Research. London & NY: Routledge, 2007. Print.

Halberstam, Judith. *In a Queer Time and Place: Transgender Bodies, Subcultural Lives.* New York: New York University Press, 2005. Print.

Hird, Myra. "The Corporeal Generosity of Maternity." *Body & Society* 13.1 (2007): 1-20. Print.

Jacoby, Jeff. "Pregnant, Yes- But Not a Man." *Boston Globe.* 13 April 2008. Web. 19 May 2009.

Jones, Jordy. "Gender Without Genitals: Hedwig's Sex Inches." *The Transgender Studies Reader.* Ed. Susan Stryker and Stephen Whittle. New York: Routledge, 2006. 449-468. Print.

Longhurst, Robyn. "Pregnant bodies, Public Scrutiny: 'Giving' Advice to Pregnant Women." *Embodied Geographies: Spaces, Bodies and Rites of Passage.* Ed. Elizabeth Kenworthy Teather. London & New York: Routledge, 1999. 77-90. Print.

Kessler, Susanne, and McKenna, Wendy. "Toward a Theory of Gender." *The Transgender Studies Reader.* Eds. Susan Stryker and Stephen Whittle. New York: Routledge, 2006. 165-182. Print.

Kipnis, Laura. *Bound and Gagged: Pornography and the Politics of Fantasy in America.* New York: Grove Press, 2008. Print.

King, Larry. "Pregnant 'Man' and Wife: We're a Normal Couple." *CNN News.* 18 Nov 2008. Web. 19 May 2009.

Leith, William. "Pregnant Men: Hard to Stomach?" *Telegraph.* 11 Nov 2008. Web. 15 May 2009.

McGuinees, Sheelagh, and Alghrani, Amel. "Gender and Parenthood: The Case for Realignment." *Medical Law Review* 16 (2008): 261-283. Print.

More, Sam Dylan. "The Pregnant Man—an Oxymoron?" *Journal of Gender Studies* 7.3 (1998): 319-328. Print.

Namaste, Viviane K. *Invisible Lives: The Erasure of Transsexual and Transgendered People.*Chicago and London: The University of Chicago Press, 2000. Print.

Noble, Bobby. *Sons of the Movement: FtMs Risking Incoherence on a Post-Queer Cultural Landscape.* Toronto: Women's Press, 2006. Print.

Paris, Natalie. "'Pregnant' Man Reveals Ultrasound to Oprah." *Telegraph.* 7 April 2008. Web. 15 May 2009.

Prosser, Jay. *Second Skins: The Body Narratives of Transsexuality.* New

York: Columbia University Press, 2006. Print.

Radford, Benjamin. "Pregnant Man: Real or Hoax." *LiveScience.* 28 March 2008. Web. 15 May 2009.

Rubin, Gayle. "Thinking Sex: Notes for a Radical Theory of the Politics of Sexuality." *Pleasure and Danger: Exploring Female Sexuality.* Boston: Routledge and Keegan Paul, 1984. Print.

Serano, Julia. *Whipping Girl: A Transsexual Woman on Sexism and the Scapegoating of Femininity.* Emeryville: Seal Press, 2007. Print.

Storrs, Elisabeth. "Mothers, Mothering and Christianity: Exploring the Connections between the Virgin Mary, Myra Hindley and Rosemary West." *Feminist Theology* 14.2 (2006): 237-254. Print.

Towle, Andy. "Morning Joe Hosts Disgusted by 'Pregnant Dude' Thomas Beatie." *Towelroad.* 4 April 2008. Web. 1 May 2009.

Tresniowski, Alex. "He's Having a Baby." *People Magazine,* 14 April 2008. Web. 15 May 2009.

Varcoe, Colleen and Hartick Doane, Gweneth. "Mothering and Women's Health." *Women's Health in Canada: Critical Perspectives on Theory and Policy.* Eds. Marina Morrow, Olena Hankivsky and Colleen Varcoe. Toronto: University of Toronto Press, 2007.297-323. Print.

Whittle, Stephen. "Foreword." *The Transgender Studies Reader.* Eds. Susan Stryker and Stephen Whittle. New York: Routledge, 2006. xi-xvi. Print.

Wilchins, Rikki. *Queer Theory, Gender Theory.* New York, Alyson Books, 2004. Print.

Wilson, Helen and Huntington, Annette. "Deviant (M)others: The Construction of Teenage Motherhood in Cotemporary Discourse." *Journal of Social Policy* 35 (2006): 59-76. Print.

Winfrey, Oprah. "Unprecedented Pregnancy. " *Oprah Winfrey Show.* 2008. Web. 1 May 2009.

Winslow, Jeffrey. "Pregnant Man Rebuts Transgender Arguments." *Nashua Telegraph.* 17 April 2008. Web. 15 May 2009.

5.

Stories of Grief and Hope

Queer Experiences of Reproductive Loss

CHRISTA CRAVEN AND ELIZABETH PEEL

Lesbian, gay, bisexual, transgender and queer (LGBTQ) pregnancy, adoption, and parenting have been at the forefront of the news in recent years. From the late-1990s there was speculation over the identity of Melissa Etheridge and Julie Cypher's sperm donor, the "gay surrogacy" boom including celebrities such as Neil Patrick Harris and Elton John, and the well-televised pregnancies of Thomas Beatie—dubbed "The Pregnant Man" in the media. However, a topic that frequently escapes mention is the losses LGBTQ people face in their efforts to become parents. This chapter centers on the personal narratives of LGBTQ people who have suffered reproductive loss: the loss of a child during pregnancy, birth, or adoption.

Both authors—Christa, an American anthropologist and Liz, a British psychologist—came to this topic through the personal experience of pregnancy loss. Christa and her partner lost a baby in 2009 at 18 weeks, and Liz and her partner experienced a "silent" miscarriage at 12 weeks in 2008.[1] Both Christa and Liz found few resources to help them cope with loss in queer families. When Christa searched for resources online, she found the survey research that Liz had begun (Peel "Pregnancy Loss"), and we ultimately agreed to work collaboratively on a cross-cultural and interdisciplinary study of LGBTQ reproductive loss.

This chapter draws from Christa's 40 qualitative interviews with LGBTQ parents in the USA and Canada and Liz's survey data from 60 non-heterosexual, mostly lesbian, women's experiences from the UK,

USA, Canada and Australia (Peel "Pregnancy Loss in Lesbian and Bisexual Women"). We argue that there are distinctive aspects of LGBTQ experiences of loss that deserve both scholarly attention and increased efforts to create resources for grieving LGBTQ parents. We explore in particular how, for LGBTQ people, challenges in achieving conception and adoption amplify stories of loss, and that both grief and hope suffuse stories of reproductive loss. We identify several factors, such as the severely under-researched experiences of non-gestational or "social" parents, financial concerns about loss surrounding the use of assisted reproduction, and fears of further marginalization as non-normative parents. These issues are particular, if not unique, to queer experiences of reproductive loss.

THE HEARTBREAKING EXPERIENCE OF LOSING A BABY IS UNIVERSAL… OR IS IT?

In this section, we offer a brief review of the literature that exists on queer experiences of loss. Despite the assertions of some queer bloggers who have been quick to ally LGBTQ reproductive experience with heterosexual experiences (e.g., "Fear of Miscarriage" in *A Lesbian's Pregnancy Blog*), queer scholars have long argued that the concerns that LGBTQ parents and prospective parents report are not always the same, nor experienced in the same ways as heterosexual parents. In her groundbreaking ethnographic studies of lesbian mothers and gay fathers, Ellen Lewin highlighted how prospective lesbian and gay parents can be excluded from adoption, fostering, and assisted reproductive options available to heterosexuals (*Gay Fatherhood* 31). As parents, LGBTQ people must navigate through stigma against homosexuality and gender transgression in their own and their children's daily lives (in childcare arrangements, school decisions and custody disputes, for instance) in ways that their heterosexual counterparts do not (*Lesbian Mothers* 87). Through our survey data and interview data, as well as the minimal academic literature on pregnancy loss (little is available on adoption loss), LGBTQ experiences of loss during pregnancy, birth and adoption all occur in the context of heteronormativity. The subtle ways that homophobia and what Liz has termed elsewhere "deafening heteronormativity" infuse our experiences are important to consider as we rethink the best ways to support LGBTQ parents who have experienced loss.

The first empirical study of lesbian experiences of pregnancy loss was published in 2007 by Danuta Wojnar, a nurse, in a midwifery journal. This small qualitative study drew on interviews with 10 white lesbian couples in the USA, all of whom had planned their pregnancies (she notes that about 50% of heterosexuals' pregnancies are unplanned). Wojnar found that, unlike some heterosexual mothers, lesbian mothers frequently bonded with their unborn child very early in pregnancy (482). She noted differences between the responses of what she terms birth (biological) mothers and social (non-biological) mothers to pregnancy loss. Whereas birth mothers felt they could grieve openly, social mothers kept their sadness more hidden with the intent of "being strong" for their partners. Wojnar and Swanson have also made a strong case for additional research on lesbian experiences of miscarriage, arguing that lesbians encounter unique reproductive challenges: "when lesbians face miscarriage [they do so] in a heterosexist society that questions their entitlement to have even sought motherhood in the first place" (8).

In the academic literature, studies of queer reproduction and parenting have made brief mention of miscarriages and failed adoptions[2], but literature considering these experiences in more depth is relatively minimal. In 2008, Michelle Walks called for research on infertility in queer families, noting in particular the flawed logic of previous studies which highlighted the "fairly unique advantage" for lesbian women that if one partner was unable to conceive, they could "swap" (Dunne 26). Walks emphasized the emotional challenges that such an arrangement posed for some queer couples, especially "people who do not embrace a stereotypical 'feminine' identity, such as butches, genderqueers, or some trans-identified individuals" (138). Jaquelyn Luce's 2010 book on narratives of conception among lesbian/bi/queer women in British Columbia, briefly addresses queer experiences of miscarriage and pregnancy loss. Luce wrote of queer women's experiences in seeking support in online and in-person assisted reproduction support groups; ultimately the homophobia queer women experienced "increased [their] sense of isolation and of not belonging" (27).

The publication of data from Liz's online survey in 2010 was the first major empirical study addressing queer women's experiences of pregnancy loss. Among other findings, Liz explained that 85% of mothers (both social and biological) felt that their loss—whether it occurred early or late in the pregnancy—had a "significant" or "very significant" impact on their lives. Further, the experience of loss for lesbian and bisexual women was amplified due to the emotional and financial investment respondents reported making in their impending motherhood, and the heterosexism some experienced from health professionals.

Although these specialized resources in midwifery and academic publications have broken important new ground, Lisa Cosgrove's feminist critique of the pregnancy loss literature rings largely as true today as when it was published in 2004:

> Assumptions about compulsory heterosexuality inform research agendas and conclusions. Despite awareness that technological advances have allowed many women to get pregnant who previously would not have been able to, the voices of single or lesbian mothers and nontraditional couples are nowhere to be found in the research literature (113-114).

This lack of research and resources is only magnified in the scarcity of research (or even mention) of the experiences of gay and bisexual men pursuing adoption or surrogacy, or the reproductive experiences of transgender and other queer parents.

Popular sources—including memoirs and blogs—have recently begun to address LGBTQ experiences of loss during pregnancy, birth, and adoption for broader audiences. For instance, Kristen Henderson and Sarah Kate Ellis' 2011 memoir, chronicles their simultaneous pregnancies, as well as their experience of two losses: Sarah's miscarriage at 11 weeks, and later her "disappearing twin." However, even these emerging resources remain relatively thin when compared to more publicly available memoirs of primarily heterosexual (usually also married, white, and middle-class) experiences that our LGBTQ participants have found, as well as copious self-help books and support websites devoted to heterosexual loss.

OTHERED GRIEF: "SOCIAL" MOTHERS AND ADOPTIVE PARENTS

A particularly under-researched area of LGBTQ loss, and LGBTQ parenting more broadly, are the experiences of what many researchers have come to call "social" mothers in contrast to "biological" or "gestational" mothers, and adoptive parents. Some scholars, such as Nancy Mezey describe lesbian motherhood solely in terms of a biological or legally adoptive relationship between a mother and child(ren), negating the experiences of "social" mothers who are not legally able to adopt their children (33). Even when "social" mothers narrate their own accounts, primacy is often placed upon the gestational mother's experience. In Henderson and Ellis' memoir mentioned above, for instance, although the authors shift back and forth between their own perspectives throughout the book (identified by their names), the discussion of both losses they experienced together were almost entirely written in Sarah, the birth mother's voice, though she notes on several occasions that "Kristen was in even worse shape" than she (82).

Additionally, little research addresses the experience of gay men or transpeople in this regard. Yet, as Lewin describes in her book on gay fatherhood, in the case of an adoption that does not go through for gay men, "such losses are experienced much as the death of an already existing child might be felt. The commitment is there, even in the absence of a physical connection" (85). Sullivan notes the particularly difficult experience of loss for an expectant non-biological parent who has not come out at work or to their family (188). Nevertheless, the experience of adoptive parents has received little attention in scholarly literature.

In Liz's survey, 22% (13 respondents) had experienced loss as the "social" mother, the partner of the woman who had carried the pregnancy (Peel 3). In Christa's interviews nine participants had experienced losses as "social" mothers, seven (four women; three men) had experienced loss during the process of adoption, six had experienced pregnancy losses both physically and as "social" mothers, two had experienced a physical pregnancy loss and adoptive loss, one had experienced loss as a "social" mother and through a failed adoption, and one had experienced losses in all three categories. Thus, although 65% (n=26) of her participants had experienced pregnancy loss physically, 65% (n=26) had (in some cases, also) experienced loss as a non-gestating parent.

When asked how they felt about their losses now, respondents to Liz's survey wrote "It's still [very] hard" (R2, lesbian, Canada and R37, lesbian, Canada)[3] and it "still hurts" (R28, lesbian, Australia). One particularly poignant sentiment was: "Filling this in has made me cry, but I don't often get upset about it these days. Our daughter … will always be thought of by us" (R53, lesbian, Scotland). For some, their sense of loss went structurally far deeper than the emotional loss of their child. After Nora, a lesbian graduate student, physically experienced a loss and later developed health complications that made another pregnancy dangerous for her health, she and her partner, Alex, a genderqueer, previously FTM trans-identified administrative assistant, decided that Alex would carry their next child. When Christa interviewed them, Alex was pregnant and Nora explained:

> In losing our daughter and in making the decision that it wouldn't be safe for me to carry again, and because we live in [a

> state that prohibits listing two same-sex parents on a birth certificate], I lost not only a biological and a physical connection and the possibility of breastfeeding my, our first child [...] I also lost the ability to have legal [rights to our future children], to have my name on this child's birth certificate [...] I'm not even going to be able to petition for that [where we live].

Nora's losses were amplified by the homophobic laws that will now govern her relationship—or lack of legal relationship—with her child born by her partner. As a fulltime graduate student, and with Alex's income as an administrative assistant, the couple was unable to consider moving to another state or country to give both of them legal status as their future child's parents.

LGBTQ parents pursuing adoption describe other ways of mediating their concerns about the ever-present possibility of loss. At the time of his interview with Christa, for instance, Mike, a gay man, had suffered the loss of twins several years previously in an open adoption. He and his then-partner Arnold, had traveled to Vermont for a civil union and begun the adoption process shortly afterward in their home state, which did not recognize their union. The adoption agency they worked with thought they were an ideal family to place bi-racial twins—Mike being white and Arnold being African-American. They moved forward with an open adoption, met the birthmother on multiple occasions, and attended all doctor's appointments. When the twins were born, the names that Mike and Arnold gave them went on their birth certificates. They spent ten days as a family, but on the tenth day, the last day that birthmothers in their state could legally reclaim their children, they received a call from the adoption agency asking for the babies to be returned. The adoption agency staff explained that the birthmother had contacted the biological father, whom she had been estranged from for months, to tell him that she had put the twins up for adoption to a gay couple. He did not approve of having a gay couple raise the twins and convinced her to reclaim them. After their loss, Mike experienced further trauma when their grief led to the end of his relationship with Arnold. Mike had recently begun the adoption process again as a single man. This time, however, he was pursuing the adoption of an older child.

> ...in the foster system, with parents whose parental rights had already been terminated [...] I don't want the chance of [a

> birth mother] reclaiming again. There's no way I could do that again [...] It was like they [the twins] had suddenly died. One minute they were here and the next hour they weren't here. It was horrible.

Additional research on the complex grieving experiences and coping strategies of non-biological parents is clearly something that is necessary to bring greater depth to studies of reproductive loss, as well as LGBTQ healthcare and mental health more broadly.

HIDDEN LOSSES: FINANCIAL CONCERNS FOR LGBTQ FAMILIES

Financial concerns are often an unspoken anxiety that queer parents, particularly those who have invested substantially in assisted reproductive technologies, surrogacy arrangements or adoption proceedings, have during the already emotional experience of the loss of a baby. Some participants noted that they felt like talking about the expenses associated with a baby they had lost seemed (to others) like it tainted the experience, but yet these were primary concerns for the parents themselves. As Liz's previous research has shown, "the resources (psychological, interpersonal and material) invested in achieving pregnancy shaped, and indeed amplified, the subsequent loss" for lesbian and bisexual women (Peel 6).

Liz's survey did not contain questions relating specifically to financial considerations, but Christa asked directly about this topic in her interviews. It is important to note that financial concerns vary widely across countries and jurisdictions based on whether access to assisted reproductive technologies is open to queer parents and/or which technologies are available free, paid for by insurance, or paid out-of-pocket.[4] Still, financial concerns in LGBTQ reproduction remain a significant issue that has received little attention in most academic and popular literature.

Many LGBTQ parents in Christa's study discussed—often with some ambivalence—the financial investment they had made in the child they lost, and many felt that the urgency to become pregnant or adopt again after a loss drove them to invest more (both financially and emotionally) in those efforts. For instance, Danielle, a lesbian who worked for her state government, and her partner took out a second mortgage on their home to fund additional artificial insemination attempts after their first loss. When her partner lost her job, they had stopped trying to conceive for several months.

But as Danielle neared her late 30s, they had recently begun to try again, and had suffered a second loss. At the time of interview, they were debating whether to invest in one in-vitro fertilization (IVF) treatment or a comparably-priced series of six intra-uterine inseminations (IUIs)—betting on which would have the better odds of achieving a viable pregnancy. As Danielle explained, "It's sad really. You don't look at the process [of trying again] as only emotional, you have to think about how you are going to afford it."

Another couple, Leah and Jessica struggled to make sense of both the financial burden they experienced during their loss, as well as when they sought to conceive again. Reflecting on their initial insemination attempts, Jessica, a bisexual administrative assistant who had conceived via IUI, explained:

> It is hard to look at all those months leading up to [our loss] and how much we spent, financially and emotionally, in getting pregnant the first time. And then you achieve pregnancy, and ... this isn't quite the word I want to use, but you're sort of like, 'why did I waste all that time and money?' It wasn't a waste, it is never a waste, but it feels a little bit like that.

Jessica's partner Leah, a lesbian author and editor who had suffered an earlier loss physically herself with an ex-boyfriend, as well the more recent loss with Jessica, continued:

> And I know that we were even a little overzealous after the miscarriage trying for a success, because a lot of that went on credit [cards]. And when there was no more credit, we tapped our retirement [savings]. It's not so much that we're feeling the pressure of time because [Jessica's] only 31 ... but I think just the desire to get it done successfully after the miscarriage was a big financial push.

Leah and Jessica ultimately had one child via IUI, and although they would like to have more children, they have postponed plans because of continued financial concerns. To conclude their story with Leah's dry humor: "They tell you children are priceless, but the children of queer families usually have an exact price tag."

Shameka and Vicki, a lesbian couple who worked in IT and as an office manager, respectively, also brought up financial concerns when they spoke with Christa. They described feeling "funny," because their emotional loss of their first child together at 13 weeks was so great, and they feared marring that with financial concerns, even in talking with each other. Vicki, who had carried their first child and planned to become pregnant again, explained:

> I feel a little apprehensive about talking about the financial factor [even] to Shameka, because we are considering IVF, which is a very expensive procedure. I think somewhere between 10 and 15 thousand dollars or something is what they were saying. It's a very expensive procedure, which is like an investment. It feels like in a funny place to mention that, to say that [the financial piece matters] without feeling really funny about it.

She continued by wondering aloud if her concerns about money, and what it might cost to become pregnant again, had affected her "subconsciously" and feared that the financial stress might even lead to another loss.

Although many of the participants in Christa's study who had experienced loss during adoptions did not share concerns about the financial burdens of forming their families, four lesbian women highlighted this concern. Karla and Edie's story offers a sobering counterpoint to common assumptions that all LGBTQ adoptive parents are wealthy and without financial concerns. Karla and Edie were in their 60s when interviewed. They had experienced several difficult pregnancy losses together in the late 1970s and early 80s and subsequently decided to put what they described as their "life savings" into the opportunity to complete an adoption in 1988. They explained that after the birthmother chose not to relinquish the child, they lost not only their son—for whom they had created a nursery in their home—but also their dreams of ever having a child. They were graduate students at the time and ultimately pursued relatively low-paying careers in public service. Although other factors, like personal illness, impacted their ensuing reproductive decisions, it was not until 2005 that they were finally able to adopt a 16-year-old girl into their family. Although their story has a "happy," and remarkable, ending, it is important to point out that Christa's sample is likely skewed towards those that do. Only five participants who have elected to participate in her study did not have children following their losses—all of whom were "ttc," popular Internet parlance for "trying to conceive," when they were interviewed.

Although the above examples show the gravity of financial concerns for some LGBTQ parents, most of Christa's participants have said that these concerns are not something they have talked openly about, thus they remain a hidden loss for many queer families.

FEARS OF FURTHER MARGINALIZATION: FROM DEAFENING HETERONORMATIVITY TO OUTRIGHT HOMOPHOBIA

Whether feared or actualized, most LGBTQ parents admit to being nervous about how others will react to their loss. Liz has discussed this in previous publications, noting that 26.7% of her respondents indicated that they had experienced "heterosexism, homophobia or prejudice from health professionals," and a further 8.6% were unsure (Peel 5). These experiences ranged in severity from assumptions of heterosexuality in clinic encounters to more extreme experiences of homophobia: "my partner was asked to leave during several exams, and was not allowed to answer questions regarding the autopsy or funeral arrangements after stillbirth" (R46, lesbian, USA; Peel 5). Others felt that healthcare professionals "treated me as if it [the loss] was my fault" because they were not (heterosexually) married (this same quote was given in Liz's survey [R52, gay woman, Scotland] and in Christa's interview with Tanea, a queer/bisexual woman). When Danielle, who was introduced above, had to undergo a "D and C" (that is, dilation and curettage, a procedure that removes tissue from the uterus, also known as ERPC [Evacuation of the Retained Products of Conception]) following her first loss, a nurse went so far as to ask her why, as a lesbian, she had bothered to get pregnant only to decide to abort, when she misunderstood the reason for Danielle's surgery.

Although many women in our studies who had encountered health professionals during their losses felt that they had largely positive experiences, many still noted that medical personnel had trouble understanding the experience of a grieving parent who was not physically experiencing the loss of a pregnancy: "Some health professionals seemed unable to understand my partner's distress at losing her child ... I don't think they understood what it meant for my partner, that she was a parent and she had lost her baby too" (R45, lesbian, UK; Peel 6). Leah, introduced above, also explained that friends and co-workers, both heterosexual and queer, expressed surprise that she didn't "get over" her loss faster as a non-biological mother, as they more consistently inquired about how her partner was doing after their loss.

While several participants in Christa's interviews benefited from general (primarily or entirely heterosexual) loss support groups, others chose not to attend for fear that they would ultimately have to justify their relationship, and were unwilling to do so during such a difficult time in their lives. Even for those who did not experience overt homophobia (Liz's survey reported an overall high satisfaction with healthcare [Peel 6] and Christa's interviews mirror those sentiments), many reported *fearing* negative responses, and several mentioned specifically that they would like health professionals to "realize how hard getting pregnant is for any lesbian and especially for someone who has dealt with infertility" (R30, dyke/lesbian, USA; Peel 6). In stories of failed adoptions, participants in Christa's study indicated a strong level of support among adoption professionals, yet several also noted that they felt "pushed" to accept "riskier" open adoptions with birthmothers who may not have felt ready to commit to adoption because adoption professionals saw them as "hard to place" parents because of their lesbian or gay identity. Instances of direct homophobia, as well as insensitive (and in many cases unacknowledged) biases displayed by friends, family, and healthcare or adoption professionals had significant impacts on LGBTQ experiences with reproductive losses.

CONCLUDING THOUGHTS

As our title, "Stories of Grief and Hope," suggests, the experiences of losing a child or children are by no means homogenous within LGBTQ families and communities. There is a great deal of variation regarding the legal status of LGBTQ relationships and parents throughout the world, and within countries like the USA, where legal rights vary by state (Peel and Harding 659). The experiences of LGBTQ families are also, inevitably, mediated by intersecting axes of privilege and marginalization based on ethnicity, social and economic capital, (dis)ability and so on. Yet we have highlighted some of the unique issues and concerns that LGBTQ people navigate around being social parents, financial difficulties associated with assisted reproduction and adoption, and confronting heteronormative assumptions about reproductive experience and, in some cases, blatantly homophobic responses to becoming parents.

Our goals in this chapter were twofold: to call for additional attention to reproductive loss in the academic literature on LGBTQ parenting and to suggest improvement in the support available for grieving LGBTQ parents. As previously mentioned, the existing LGBTQ parenting literature is notably quiet on this topic. Reflecting even upon her own work, Liz, in her co-authored book on LGBTQ Psychology (Clarke, Ellis, Peel and

Riggs 233-234) included pregnancy loss alongside grief and bereavement in the chapter on "Ageing and Old Age," rather than in the chapter on "Parenting and Family." No information was included regarding loss related to adoption, surrogacy or fostering. This example offers just one instance of a larger trend we see among LGBTQ researchers: the desire to tell positive stories about pathways to parenthood. These "happy ending" narratives also pepper the LGBTQ memoir market. And, of course, they are the easier stories to tell. Our concern, however, is that these positive portrayals belie the experiences of many LGBTQ people who experience loss, in addition to, and sometimes instead of actually becoming parents.

Finally, we suggest two main areas upon which efforts to improve healthcare and adoption resources for grieving LGBTQ parents should focus. First, it is crucial that health and adoption professionals not assume that all parents are heterosexual, and they must acknowledge and include non-biological (prospective) parents. Further, since there is growing evidence that non-heterosexual women's pregnancies (as well as all adoptions) are more likely to have involved lengthy planning and resources, professionals should be particularly attentive to how pre-conception experiences and adoption histories may contribute to and amplify experiences of loss. This could most simply be accomplished by asking questions about pre-conception reproductive and adoptive histories, and attending to patients' financial concerns. Although these kinds of structural changes would vary significantly in different cultural contexts, improving medical billing and insurance protocols around loss, or simply acknowledging the likely financial investment in the pregnancy, would improve not only the experience of grieving LGBTQ parents, but all grieving families. As the stories we recount above indicate, there is much to be done to create more sensitive resources and support that do not assume heterosexuality and conventional family structures. We need greater visibility of queer people's experiences of pregnancy and adoption loss—in academic, professional, and popular literature, such as blogs and memoirs—in order to generate better responses to the varied and often complex reproductive experiences of LGBTQ people.

NOTES

[1]See also Peel and Cain "Silent Miscarriage."

[2]See also: Lewin *Gay Fatherhood* 85, Mamo 52, Sullivan 188.

[3]Liz's survey respondents are identified by survey number, sexual identity, and country (e.g., R45, lesbian, UK). Christa's interviewees are identified by pseudonym.
[4]See also: Gunning and Szoke, and Frank.

WORKS CITED

Barry-Kessler, Liza. "Mission Impossible: Visibility and Inclusion of Pregnant Lesbians & Lesbian Mothers in Feminist Theory and Public Discourse." Paper presented at the Midwest Interdisciplinary Graduate Conference, 2011.

Clarke, Victoria, Ellis, Sonja J., Peel, Elizabeth & Damien W. Riggs. *Lesbian, Gay, Bisexual, Trans and Queer Psychology: An Introduction.* Cambridge: Cambridge University Press, 2010. Print.

Cosgrove, Lisa. "The Aftermath of Pregnancy Loss: A Feminist Critique of the Literature and Implications for Treatment. *Women & Therapy* 27: 107-122, 2004. Print.

Dunne, Gillian. "Opting in to Motherhood: Lesbians Blurring the Boundaries and Meaning of Parenthood and Kinship." *Gender and Kinship* 14.1(2000): 11-35. Print.

Frank, Zippi Brand. "Google Baby" (documentary film). Israel: Brandcom Productions, 2009.

Gunning, Jennifer and Helen Szoke. *The Regulation of Assisted Reproductive Technology.* Aldershot, UK: Ashgate, 2003. Print.

Henderson, Kristen and Sarah Ellis. *Times Two: Two Women in Love and the Happy Family They Made.* New York: Free Press, 2011. Print.

Hicks, Stephen and Janet McDermott. *Lesbian and Gay Fostering and Adoption: Extraordinary Yet Ordinary.* London: Jessica Kingsley Publishers, 1999. Print.

Josh, "Waiting for the Baby Who Might or Might Not Become Ours," *Regular Midwesterners: Two Perspectives on Gay Parenting and Life in the Midwest*, 14 February 2011. Web. 3 September 2011.

LesbianMom. "Fear of Miscarriage." *A Lesbian's Pregnancy Blog (Not Unlike a Hetero's Pregnancy Blog).* 23 Feb. 2010. Web. 5 Sept. 2011.

Lewin, Ellen. *Lesbian Mothers: Accounts of Gender in American Culture.* Ithaca, New York: Cornell University Press, 1993. Print.

Lewin, Ellen. *Gay Fatherhood: Narratives of Family and Citizenship in*

America. Chicago: University of Chicago Press, 2009. Print.

Luce, Jaquelyn. *Beyond Expectation: Lesbian/Bi/Queer Women and Assisted Reproduction*. Toronto: University of Toronto Press, 2010. Print.

Mamo, Laura. *Queering Reproduction: Achieving Pregnancy in the Age of Technoscience*. Durham: Duke University Press, 2007. Print.

Mezey, Nancy J. *New Choices, New Families: How Lesbians Decide about Motherhood*. Baltimore: The John Hopkins University Press, 2008. Print.

Peel, Elizabeth. "Pregnancy Loss in Lesbian and Bisexual Women: An Online Survey of Experiences." *Human Reproduction* 25.3 (2010): 721-727. Print.

Peel, Elizabeth & Ruth Cain. "Silent Miscarriage and Deafening Heteronormativity: A British Experiential and Critical Feminist Account." *Understanding Reproductive Loss: Perspectives on Life, Death and Fertility*. Sarah Earle, Carol Komaromy & Linda L. Layne (Eds.). Farnham: Ashgate, 2012. Pp. 79-92. Print.

Peel, Elizabeth & Harding, Rosie. "Regulating Sexuality: Contemporary Perspectives on Lesbian and Gay Relationship Recognition." *Sexualities*, 11.6 (2008): 659-666. Print.

Sullivan, Maureen. *The Family of Woman: Lesbian Mothers, Their Children, and the Undoing of Gender*. Berkeley: University of California Press, 2004. Print.

Walks, Michelle. "Breaking the Silence: Infertility, Motherhood, and Queer Culture," *Journal of the Association for Research on Mothering*. Special Issue: Mothering, Race, Ethnicity, Culture, and Class. 9:2 (fall/winter 2007 [March 2008]): 130-143. Print.

Wojnar, Danuta. "Miscarriage Experiences of Lesbian Couples," *Journal of Midwifery & Women's Health* 55.5 (2007): 479-485. Print.

Wojnar, Danuta and Kristen M. Swanson. "Why Shouldn't Lesbian Women Who Miscarry Receive Special Consideration? A Viewpoint," *Journal of GLBT Family Studies* 2.1 (2006): 1-12. Print.

II. Queering Practices, Practicing Queers

6.

Queer Mothering or Mothering Queerly

Motherwork in Transgender Families

BARBARA GURR

INTRODUCTION

The concept of "queer mothering" has come to be dominated by the politics and practices of parenting adults who identify themselves on a spectrum of gender and sexual identities (see for example Bernstein and Reimann; Epstein; Park). Therefore, "queer mothering," like "queer families," currently reflects a "grown-up" experience of queer gender or sexuality. What is not adequately considered in this frame are the politics and practices of parenting a queer child, particularly a young queer child. Further, the focus of queer family literature on lesbian, gay, and bisexual identity further marginalizes non- and counter-hegemonic gender identities as these may be understood separately from sexual identities (see Hines). Thus, the current hegemonic association of queer identity with sexuality works to preclude theoretical examination of mothering very young (assumed "presexual") children who blur, cross, and/or negate gender boundaries.

This essay complicates such a framing of queer parenting through an auto-ethnographic exploration of mothering a young transgender child. Anderson argues that autoethnography should serve an overtly analytical purpose, wherein the researcher is one member of the researched community, and provides one (reflexive) voice among many. These voices, according to Anderson, should generate sociological generalizations. Ellis and Bochner, on the other hand, propose that autoethnography should be evocative rather than generalizing, rooted in personal experience, and that its greatest merits lie in the potential of true stories to pull readers in and elicit personal connections. Relatedly, Denzin argues for an autoethnography that is pedagogical, grounded in personal narrative and producing a praxis of liberation in oppressive social conditions. I think autoethnography can and possibly should do all of these things. Perhaps more importantly for the purposes of this essay, there is simply no way for me as a sociologist to consider the meanings and productions of "queer families" without my own emotional presence: I am a queer mother. This queerness isn't based on my own sexual or gender identity; I'm a heterosexual, legally married, cisgender woman, seemingly pretty far from our current sociological understandings of queer mothers. My "queerness" derives from my daughter's transgender identity. The shifts her transition has prompted in my roles —as mother, as feminist, and as sociologist—have queered motherhood for me by producing what I hope is a multiplicity of practices that are liberatory. At the same time, these practices have been increasingly channeled through a hegemonic model of motherhood that is linked to gendered notions of availability, sacrifice, and heteronormativity, thereby queering my mothering work by "normalizing" it. In these ways, I'm a queer mother – or I'm mothering queerly, or my motherhood has *been* queered – not only because my daughter is transgender, but also because my own mothering work has shifted to a strange new landscape in the last two years, one marked by an ironic simultaneity of gender variance and the reproduction of a gender binary I had previously thought to reject.

In this essay, I examine my family's changing identity tasks in the year of our youngest child's gender transition as these tasks were understood and engaged by myself and my husband (a heterosexual, cisgendered man). I began by naming myself and claiming a queer space for my family as this queer space was produced by my daughter, who officially began her male-to-female gender transition just before she turned six.[1] Our family's recognition and affirmation of our daughter and our work to support her publicly and privately has been challenging and emotionally wrenching in many more ways than I will discuss here. However, because of my deep personal investment, it is not possible – and in fact, I believe it would be a disservice to the work of this essay as an ethnography – to mask the emotional experiences of transitioning to queerness. At the same time that this essay remains grounded in my personal experiences, I also seek to understand these experiences within a broader social context. In this essay, I consider how the work of helping my daughter transition publicly speaks to the context of what Patricia Hill Collins calls "motherwork," a "constellation of mothering activities...(which) reflects how political consciousness can emerge within everyday lived experience" (*Black Feminist Thought* 209). Motherwork can be further understood as the public/family work engaged by women of color to ensure the survival of their children in potentially hostile social environments. Collins argues that for women of color, "motherhood cannot be analyzed in isolation from its context...specific historical situations framed by interlocking structures of race, class, and gender" (*Shifting the Center* 56). In this way, social boundaries between what is presumed "private" and what is presumed "public" are proven false; the material consequences of oppressive structures outside of a "family" do, indeed, impact the maternal practices within that family, and vice versa.

I am white and aware that my race category affords both me and my (also white) daughter a privileged race location that is not similarly available to mothers and daughters of color (as we also share a class location not available to all families). During the year of our transition, however, I found many parallels between the ways in which I took on new forms of mothering and the work of mothers of children of color who seek safety for their own children in potentially hostile contexts. For me, these evolving motherhood practices served to produce a seemingly normative effect, which was, in actuality, a queer dis-location from my more radical hopes and beliefs.

I trace the development of motherwork in my newly queered role as the mother of a young transgender child to illustrate both the broad applicability of Collins' articulation of mothering across public and private spheres and the necessity of expanding our current conceptualizations of queer families. Throughout, I move between the personal and the political, the "private" and the "public," to illustrate the particular ways the socially constructed borders around my motherhood practices began to break down and dissolve into each other as we gradually incorporated queerness into our public family identity.

IT STARTS WITH PURPLE TOES...

My youngest child, Harry, was named after Harrison Ford, on whom I've had a mad crush since I was seven, although my husband still thinks he was named after his father. Steve and I had begun our parenthood two years earlier with the birth of our son Michael. We shared a commitment to raising both our sons in a proudly feminist, "gender neutral way," although we weren't quite sure what this could/should look like. We got innumerable eye-rolls from friends and family as we tried to figure it out, but for the most part our communities, the people we came to refer to as "the villagers," respected our goals. "Gender-neutral" was an unfamiliar concept for many, and our insistence on it seemed unnecessary to most, but our parenting choices were rarely challenged; no one questioned our commitment to our children's well-being or our ability to raise healthy children.

However, once our children began to "go public" (that is, enter daycare and playgroups) it became much harder to continue blurring the boundaries between social constructions of masculinity and femininity. This difficulty was clarified for me the first time I witnessed my oldest son being disciplined into masculinity by a peer. At three years old, Michael still enjoyed painting both my and his toenails, and that particular morning we had chosen a bright, glittering purple. We showed up at daycare and the door was opened by our provider's son Joey, also three. Michael, excited about his fun new toes, immediately pointed down to his sandaled feet and said excitedly, "Look! Look at my toes!," wiggling them for extra effect. Joey burst out laughing and informed Michael in no uncertain terms, "You can't wear toenail polish! That's for girls! Boys don't wear toenail polish!"

My crestfallen son looked at me for confirmation or denial. Biting back the rebuke I longed to give the gender police who had opened the door, I grinned brightly and assured them both, "Oh, no, toenail polish is for everyone! It's just for fun!" But my son wasn't buying it. Already, his peer (a boy who must surely understand boyhood better than his female mother) had more influence than I. He still occasionally paints my nails for me, but he never painted his own again.

Harry, on the other hand, was not so easily moved toward masculinity. During the four years he went to daycare, he moved seamlessly from toenail polish to playing with dolls, to playing kitchen, to dressing up (his favorite was a red velvet dress at daycare) while playing dolls in the kitchen. My husband and I shook our heads in wonder (after all, neither of us wore dresses or carried babies around or spent a whole lot of time in the kitchen – where did he even get it?), but we understood that he, too, was being socialized into gender. But in a very different way than his older brother. Steve and I assured our villagers (who were starting to do more than roll their eyes) that we were thrilled our child was able to explore his world without censure or criticism. The villagers, for the most part, kept whatever censure or criticisms they had to themselves. Even the teachers at daycare treated Harry's enactments of femininity as perfectly okay, developmentally appropriate, nothing to worry about.

Eventually, however, we started to worry. Oh, not about Harry's gender performances per se – we worried that other kids would tease him when he didn't perform the way they thought he should. We worried that the disciplining handed out by his peers would become far harsher than laughing at toenail polish (which had been bad enough). Many of the parents I know who are raising transgendered children share these worries, and in fact cite their fear for their child's wellbeing as their number one concern (see also Krieger). We, like many other parents, initially tried to steer our child toward what might be more traditionally gendered (masculine in our case) activities in the hope of providing some gender safety, but he had no interest. Soccer fell flat, and t-ball fell flatter. Karate was torture for all of us. Harry wanted a pink bike with a Disney princess, not a blue bike with thunderbolts. He wanted a doll for Christmas, not a train set, or even books. A backpack with flowers on it, not one with Pokemon or Transformers. He graciously accepted the little football we got him because it happened to have Dora the Explorer on it, but he never played with it.

Collins addresses the "delicate balance" between conformity and resistance that Black mothers must achieve in raising their daughters, asserting that "Black mothers emphasize protection either by trying to shield their daughters as long as possible from the penalties attached to their race, class, and gender or by teaching them how to protect themselves in such situations" (*The Meaning of Motherhood* 284). Steve and I found ourselves engaging in very similar work, trying to teach our son that he was "free to be," while at the same time teaching him that he would be safest if he…conformed somehow to a hegemonic model of boyhood. We understood the contradictions in this, but we were at a loss as to how to achieve both of these goals. Our concerns for Harry's safety pushed us into a project of masculinity we never expected as we sought to create a social safety for him, but we wondered if we were doing the right thing. Weren't we, after all, suddenly re/producing the gender binary we had sought to avoid? Wasn't Harry reproducing the same binary, by so thoroughly rejecting anything that could be perceived as belonging in the realm of boys, and so thoroughly enacting a hegemonic femininity?

We finally found a therapist, then another one, then a third, all of whom confirmed for us what we already knew in our hearts: Harry was a girl. I sobbed when I heard this the first time. I sobbed from the relief of having someone else – an expert, someone other than me – put a name to our experience, feeling like the pressure had been taken off me to label it, explain it, and manage it away. I sobbed because the well-meaning therapist immediately launched into "what we could expect," which included a litany of self-cutting, risky sexual and drug behaviors, or the seemingly best alternative of years of hormone therapy and surgical alteration as soon as legally possible. I sobbed because my precious baby's body seemed to be on an inevitable course to violation. It didn't occur to me then, weeping in our car after this appointment, that perhaps my child already experienced her body as a violation. I'm crying again now as I write this.

BECOMING A QUEER MOTHER

When Harry first began to transition, my outspoken identity as a feminist caused some conflict as friends and family tried to blame my feminism for Harry's gender "confusion." These conversations were some of my earliest experiences at bringing our newly transitioning family into the public sphere, as I struggled to find ways to educate people about gender, feminism, and transgender experience all in sound-bites they could digest quickly. Let's face it, most people were not going to sit through the regular gender lecture I deliver to students at the University where I teach. I felt acutely the need to do this well, as it seemed to me that my child's success at transition was going to depend on winning people over to our team, rather than alienating them. I had to swallow a lot of anger at those well-meaning people who thought we could "fix this problem" if I would just ease off a little on the feminism – "y'know?" As if my child's entire gender identity could be so thoroughly fashioned by my insidious feminist leanings (meanwhile, I have yet to succeed at getting either one of our children to use a napkin at dinner). Worse was the underlying implication that I, as a mother, was so tainted by my left-leaning politics that I would do something to my child as apparently horrendous as messing with his gender identity (see Hill and Menvielle for an historical overview on psychological studies which blame mothering practices for the development of gender identity disorder). When I was simply a Feminist Mom, my gender politics might be worthy of an occasional joke or two at my expense, but nothing more serious than that – after all, I was the primary caregiver and fairly good at it. No one *suffered*. In fact, our children thrived—well-fed, socially active, reasonably polite. But once my son became my daughter, particularly at such a young age, my public identity suddenly shifted from Feminist Mom to Bad Mom, one whose gender politics and mothering practices became suspect and potentially dangerous. It was easier for the villagers to believe

Harry was *not* transgender; he wasn't *queer*. Certainly not at five years old. Therefore, it must be me – mothering queerly.

We began our transition the Christmas Harry was in kindergarten. The year before, he had received books, trains, that Dora the Explorer football. I, the Santa Claus in our house, had bought him those things, part of my efforts to encourage a masculinity I had never thought I would particularly seek for my children. Shortly after that Christmas, I held him in my arms while he cried, asking me why Santa didn't like him, because after all, Santa brought all the wrong toys. It was perhaps my lowest moment as a mother. Maybe it was my lowest moment ever. The year we transitioned, Santa brought glittery clothes, dolls, even a musical jewelry box. Harry screamed with joy as each new package was unwrapped, trying on clothes, brushing the hair of his dolls and naming and then re-naming them, playing that music box over and over. My husband and I watched in awe, then amazement, then shame, profoundly shaken by our own complicity in denying this simple happiness to our child.

Over the winter break I called the school and told them my husband and I needed to meet with them, asking that the principal and assistant principal as well as the school nurse and Harry's teacher join us. I went to that first meeting with the phone number for the ACLU in my back pocket (literally), and I was fully prepared to pull it out and slap it on the table in my most threatening way. I was ready for a fight, aware that schools across the country are not handling transgender identity very well (see for example Grossman, Haney, et. al.).

But I think Harry's teacher and the school administrators already suspected the reason for our visit, because their response was flawless. Or maybe it just seemed flawless compared to the questions and burgeoning criticisms we'd been getting from friends and family, or compared to what I expected. We made a plan together, and decided that Harry would begin to transition at school following the winter break. They were on board, but I continued to check in regularly, speaking with the principal every other week and volunteering in Harry's classroom once a week to keep an eye on him and his classmates as he began wearing glittery shirts and jeans embroidered with flowers to school.

In fact, as we prepared to transition and then began, my husband and I both took on extra activities at the school and in town. I joined the school Parents Club, Steve began coaching basketball for our son's team. He was already a Sunday school teacher, but I began attending Church more regularly, giving up writing time to sit together in the second pew as a happy, well-adjusted family. Our previous project of masculinizing Harry, now abandoned, had been replaced by a project of impression management as we sought to publicly "normalize" our suddenly queer family.

Playdates took on a new urgency as we tried to cement our childrens' friendships, worrying about the changes that might come as we went increasingly public with our new identity and believing it would be harder to reject our child if her family was so clearly – well, normal, except for that gender thing. We became the most popular house to go to, always creating exciting activities – do you want to camp out in the backyard, or rent a movie? Do you want to make your own pizza and then make brownie sundaes? Anyone for laser tag? I was the parent who took on the lion's share of calling other parents and hosting their children. Is this because I was home more often than my husband, as my graduate school schedule allowed more flexibility? Or was it because I was the mom, trying so hard not to be a Bad Mom?

All of this was an added challenge for me as I tried to fit these new things into my life of family work and grad school requirements. I lost research time, writing time, and sleeping time as I took on more public roles in our town and spent more time socializing with other parents. My increased efforts were largely unremarkable in our bedroom community where it seems to be mostly mothers who take on this same lion's share. In some ways, becoming queer was reforming my motherhood practices into a more hegemonically feminine model as I sought to prove to a potentially, and at times actually, hostile community that we were just like them, really. Just another Church-goin', recipe-exchangin', school-volunteerin' family. Nothing much to see here, folks. The kids are alright.

By late February, Harry had changed her name to Hannah, and Hannah wanted to wear a skirt to school. But Steve and I were nervous about the skirt – I mean, girl jeans are one thing, but a skirt is an unmistakable statement (as if changing her name to Hannah had not been). I began my consumer foray into the world of girls for real, not as a sojourner, but as someone who was planning on making a home there. It's an uncomfortable place for feminist mothers. I, who had always only shopped for boys, was overwhelmed by the sparkliness, the sophistication, even blatant sexiness of young girls' clothing. I started to pay closer attention to what other little girls were wearing, turning to their mothers for guidance (always their mothers. Fathers – at least in our town—apparently still aren't doing much clothes shopping).

I delayed Hannah from wearing a skirt to school for several weeks, issuing a series of truly farfetched excuses – this one doesn't fit quite right, that one is too sparkly for school. The truth is, I was afraid of the reactions we would elicit. I was afraid of the reactions *she* would elicit. I was afraid of the other children and their parents hurting my child. I was afraid that the rage that was slowly building in me over the socially imposed need for all this gender management, management, management – make my child more masculine, make her more subtle in her femininity, build a solid public reputation, support my son Michael through his own transition as he came to understand his little brother as a little sister—would explode and un-do all we had tried to build if someone said just one small, hurtful word to my daughter. But finally I called the school to prepare them for our skirt debut. The principal responded by asking me to wait a while, telling me she thought it was too soon. I told her I had already put Hannah off as long as I could, and there was no real reason to keep telling her no. The principal responded by urging me to wait until summer, telling me, "this is when good parenting comes in." Oh. *This* is where good parenting comes in? Well, thank goodness, because I had been waiting and waiting for the opportunity to be a good parent! Once again, I swallowed my anger (I needed this principal on our *team*, after all), and offered to wait one more week so she could "prepare" the faculty and staff. Hannah wore her first skirt to school the day before spring vacation, carefully timed to give us, the school, and other parents a full week to sort through any consequences before we had to reconvene in the classroom. That week a well-meaning mother from Hannah's classroom stopped me in the grocery store to "check in," telling me she knew we had been dealing with some family issues. She asked if I was sure we were doing the right thing. I understood what she needed from me – laugh it off, kids will be kids, we'll be back to normal soon enough. I told her, "Yes, we're doing the right thing by supporting our child no matter who she is." It wasn't really what she wanted to hear from me.

WE'RE HERE, WE'RE QUEER, GET USED TO US

I cannot emphasize enough the need that all transgender people, but perhaps particularly trans-youth, have for support from their family. This has been made clear to us by our therapist, by our support group and the other parents in it, and by virtually every study I've read on queer youth (see for example Brill and Pepper; Grossman, D'augelli, and Frank; and Krieger). Most of all, it has been made abundantly clear to us by Hannah herself, who continues to thrive in school and in her social world, despite occasional challenges around friendships that have gone by the wayside, or conflict with me (Bad Feminist Mom) over what's appropriate school attire. This was made clear the Christmas we began our transition, when my child finally knew she was visible. However, the needs of parents who undergo their own shifts in identity as they seek to affirm and support their transgender children are less well-examined. When a young child is transgender and allowed to transition, the family experiences this transition, as well; the role of "mother" and the practice of mothering transgender children challenges social expectations of "children" as (properly) gendered, as the presumably private realm of family is fractured by the public needs of children who are queer and these needs are frequently opposed by resistant social ideologies. Scholars have noted how the practice of mothering may both require and justify public social activism in the name of "family" (see for example Collins; Earl; Naples; Shapiro and Tittle). The synthesis of "queer mothering" and motherwork provides a theoretical space for the consideration of this public family work as it links family identity tasks (presumed private) with social and political activism around gender (presumed public).

In the last two years, my husband has become an outspoken advocate for LGBT rights. I have worked with a state-wide organization to pass legislation protecting the legal rights of transgendered and gender variant people, and I continue to educate students and villagers about gender fluidity, even as I continue to learn. We have spoken at Church gatherings, demonstrations, and on national television about our experiences parenting a transgender child. These opportunities have become part of our "constellation of (parenting) activities…(which) reflects how political consciousness can emerge within everyday lived experience" (Collins *Black Feminist Thought* 209). Our everyday lived experience has queered our parenting and political consciousness simultaneously, and this queering has necessitated public work, at first in our efforts and hopes to ensure safety for our own child through producing and managing a public family identity, and increasingly in our efforts and hopes to ensure the safety of all trans-youth. This has been an unexpected development in our parenting, and the intensely personal commitment we feel in this work has shaped our perceptions of ourselves as parents, and our understanding of who and what our family is. Shortly after Harry became Hannah (although wasn't she always Hannah, just waiting for us to see her?), we decided to go to our first Pride parade as a family and march with our support group. As we milled around waiting for the parade to start, I spotted a vendor selling large rainbow flags.

"Let's get one," I suggested to my husband.
"A flag?" he replied, genuinely confused.
"Why? Those are for LGB...T. People." He looked at me with dawning comprehension. "Those are for LGBT people."
I smiled. "Yes, honey, those are for LGBT people. Like us." He just gazed at me a moment. On his face, I saw all the emotions of the last six months, the first six months of our transition: our denials, our fears, our anger, our anxiety. I waited. "Well," he said finally, fishing out his wallet. "We're here, we're queer, get used to us."

CONCLUSION

As I type this conclusion I'm looking out over our backyard, where Hannah is playing – something, it could be superheroes, that's a popular one lately – with her best friend Caren. Michael and his two best friends hover nearby, occasionally darting in to attempt some (super-villain?) escapade. Hannah and Caren scream, run away, twirl around and throw their hands up to ward off the boys. This queer mothering has not been an easy journey, and I know it's only just begun. I haven't figured it all out yet, and the truth is, I probably never will. This frustrates the scholar in me, and frustrates even more the mother in me. But I do know, watching my children run through the backyard swooping and diving, that I will be a Bad Feminist Mom, a queer mother, or a woman who mothers queerly for the rest of my days, happily and with enthusiasm, if the screeching, grass-stained contentment of my children is the reward.

Author's Note: *In the first two thirds of this essay, I most frequently refer to my daughter as my son, using his birth name and masculine pronouns; this is to reflect our parenting experiences and expectations when we thought he* was *our son. In the final third, I refer to my daughter by her chosen name and the proper pronouns. This shift is in no way intended to disregard my daughter's identity, but rather, to allow the reader to experience some of this transition as my husband and I did.*

NOTES

[1]In the first two thirds of this essay, I most frequently refer to my daughter as my son, using his birth name and masculine pronouns; this is to reflect our parenting experiences and expectations when we thought he was our son.

In the final third, I refer to my daughter by her chosen name and the proper pronouns. This shift is in no way intended to disregard my daughter's identity, but rather, to allow the reader to experience some of this transition as my husband and I did.

WORKS CITED

Anderson, Leon. "Analytic Autoethnography." *Journal of Contemporary Ethnography* 35.4 (2006): 373-395. Print.

Bernstein, Mary and Renate Reimann, eds. *Queer Families, Queer Politics: Challenging Culture and the State.* New York: Columbia University Press, 2001. Print.

Brill, Stephanie and Rachel Pepper. *The Transgender Child: A Handbook for Families and Professionals.* San Francisco: Cleis Press, 2008. Print.

Collins, Patricia Hill. *Black Feminist Thought: Knowledge, Consciousness, and the Politics of Empowerment.* New York: Routledge, 1991. Print.

——. "Shifting the Center: Race, Class, and Feminist Theorizing about Motherhood." *Mothering: Ideology, Experience, and Agency.* Eds. Evelyn Nakano Glenn, Grace Change and Linda Rennie Forcey. New York: Routledge, 1993. 45 – 66. Print.

——. "The Meaning of Motherhood in Black Culture and black Mother-Daughter Relationships." *Maternal Theory: Essential Readings.* Ed. Andrea O'Reilly. Toronto: Demeter Press. 2007. 274 – 89. Print.

Denzin, Norman. "Analytic Autoethnography, or Déjà vu All Over Again" *Journal of Contemporary Ethnography* 35.4 (2006): 419-28. Print.

Earl, Dave. "'A Group of Parents Came Together': Parent Advocacy Groups for Children with Intellectual Disabilities in Post-World War II Australia" *Health and History* 13.2 (2011): 84-103. Print.

Ellis, Caroline and Arthur Bochner. "Analyzing Analytic Autoethnography: an Autopsy" *Journal of Contemporary Ethnography* 35.4 (2006): 429-49. Print.

Epstein, Rachel. "Queer Parenting in the New Millennium: Resisting Normal" *Canadian Woman Studies.* 24.2/3 (2005): 7-14. Print.

——. "Butches With Babies: Reconfiguring Gender and Motherhood." *Journal of Lesbian Studies.* 6.2 (2002): 41-58. Print.

Fields, Jessica. "Normal Queers: Straight Parents Respond to their Children's 'Coming Out'" *Symbolic Interaction* 24.2 (2001): 165-87. Print.

Grossman, Arnold, Adam Haney, Perry Edwards, Edward Alessi, Maya Ardon, and Tamika Howell. "Lesbian, Gay, Bisexual and Transgender Youth Talk about Experiencing and Coping with School Violence: A Qualitative Study" *Journal of LGBT Youth* 6.1 (2009): 24-46. Print.

——, Anthony D'augelli, and John Frank. "Aspects of Psychological Resilience Among Transgender Youth" *Journal of LGBT Youth* 8.2 (2011): 103-15. Print.

Hill, Darryl and Edgardo Menvielle. "'You Have to Give Them a Place Where They Feel Protected and Safe and Loved': The Views of Parents who have Gender Variant Children and Adolescents" *Journal of LGBT Youth* 6.2-3 (2009): 243-71. Print.

Hines, Sally. *TransForming Gender: Transgender Practices of Identity, Intimacy and Care.* Bristol, UK: Policy Press, 2007. Print.

Kreiger, Irwin. *Helping Your Transgender Teen: A Guide for Parents.* New Haven: Genderwise Press, 2011. Print.

Naples, Nancy A. *Grassroots Warriors: Activist Mothering, Community Work, and the War on Poverty.* New York: Routledge, 1998. Print.

Park, Shelley M. *Mothering Queerly, Queering Motherhood: Resisting Monomaternalism in Adoptive, Lesbian, Blended, and Polygamous Families.* Albany: State University of New York, 2013. Print.

Shapiro, Johanna and Ken Tittle. "Maternal Adaptation to Child Disability in a Hispanic Population" *Family Relations* 39.2 (1990): 179-85. Print.

7.

Guy-Moms Unite!

Mothering Outside the Box

RAINE DOZIER

In 1991 I was arrested in Ithaca, New York during a spontaneous protest after the county council rejected a gay rights ordinance. The local paper labeled me a "militant homosexual" and reported on the opposition's fear that the ordinance would encourage "homosexual acts." I responded by organizing a public display of homosexual acts on the downtown pedestrian mall. I thought hard about what would best illustrate my most common behaviors as a homosexual, and settled on a large basket of clean laundry and my eight year old with her roller skates. I proceeded to spend the protest folding laundry and teaching my daughter to roller skate while surrounded by others who were also engaged in various and mundane homosexual behaviors.

Fast-forward twenty years. I now have a new daughter and another life as a single parent (my children are thirteen and thirty-one years old). A friend recently joked that she was going to nominate me for "Best YouTube Channel" in the TransGuys Community Awards. She said she thought my channel shows the real life of a trans person which, rather than detailing my transition[1] (common on YouTube), consists of my daughter's piano performances and a few vacation videos. These accounts illuminate what I think is one of the most important questions about queering motherhood: must we exhibit "queer" parenting behavior, or is our mere existence within the social institution of motherhood itself queer?

Queering is, "...by definition whatever is at odds with the normal, the legitimate, the dominant" (Halperin 62). Queering motherhood, then, describes any act of mothering that is transgressive or interrogates and deconstructs the normative. If we accept this definition, then single motherhood, mothering in extended families or trans-racial families, mothering as a primary earner, and many other types of mothering are queer. The danger of defining "queer" in this way, however, is that it removes the notion of queering motherhood from the realm of sexual orientation and gender identity. I believe that mothering[2] as a gay, lesbian, bisexual or transgender person occupies a particular social location relative to the heteronormative institution of motherhood and family.

As a masculine female, I assert that getting up, pulling on men's underwear and clothing, and making a school lunch is queer. Lucal suggests that gender atypical individuals who position themselves in gender-typical situations challenge the gender binary simply by existing. In her case, Lucal is referring to public bathrooms and whether, as a gender atypical person, the act of using the female bathroom challenges the gender order. In my case, I am referring to the institution of motherhood and whether simply participating in it as a masculine female disrupts the sex/gender binary. I believe it does not take a particularly radical act to queer motherhood; when I show up at the PTA[3] meeting with brownies, it illuminates dominant assumptions about motherhood, family, and gender simply due to my visible gender nonconformity.

QUEER PARENTS—DOING IT DIFFERENTLY

While female masculinity queers mothering in a particular way, to a certain extent, all LGBTQ parents queer motherhood. Queer parenting *can* be about engaging in decidedly different acts relative to other parents—and there is evidence that lesbian and gay parents do at times. For example, research suggests that children mothered by lesbians[4] have measurably different behaviors in some areas relative to those mothered by heterosexuals. They exhibit less gender-typical play, greater social and academic competence, fewer social and behavioral problems, and greater empathy for social diversity than children of heterosexual parents (Gartrell and Bos 32; Goldberg, Kashy, and Smith 511; Johnson 49; Stacey and Biblarz 168, 172, 175). As parents, lesbians feel more positively about their children choosing gender atypical toys than heterosexual parents, and children of lesbians report greater comfort in discussing their sexual development with their parents than their peers (Goldberg, Kashy, and Smith 511; Stacey and Biblarz 172, 175, 178; Tasker and Golombok 121). In addition, children of lesbians report extremely low rates of abuse and neglect relative to children of heterosexuals (Gartrell, Bos, and Goldberg 1204).

Given that children of lesbians are different in small, but meaningful ways such as "being nicer," more tolerant of gender nonconformity, and possibly more open to same-sex involvement (Stacey and Biblarz 170), we could say that, on average, queering parenthood involves a decidedly feminist slant. The few studies addressing gay fathers suggest they also differ from heterosexual parents, displaying more egalitarian parenting styles and placing less value on gender conformity in their children (Biblarz and Stacey 12; Goldberg, Kashy, and Smith 511). If the children of LGBTQ parents are different, perhaps it's due to the political orientation of their parents; the observed differences between children with lesbian and heterosexual parents may be ideological differences between the average lesbian and the average heterosexual parent. I asked an adult friend who was raised by lesbian mothers about their influence. After consideration, she replied, "It's hard to know what part is their being lesbians, what part is feminism, and what part is that they're hippies." Whether it's ideological difference or the influence of being parented primarily by women, when lesbian parents and their children differ from heterosexual families, it is in ways that favour lesbian-headed families (Biblarz and Stacey 11).

While LGBTQ parents might parent differently, they also differ in family structure. Queer families pose a visible challenge to the nuclear-normative family model due to biological necessity. Because same-sex couples need a third party to procreate and a transwoman or transman may not procreate in a gender-typical way,[5] making babies in queer families often involves more than two people and/or a radical disruption of gender norms. As a result, families with same-sex parents are constantly engaged in discussions about biology, legitimacy, and definitions of motherhood and family with a variety of individuals and systems (Chapman, Wardrop, Freeman, Zappia, Watkins and Kitzinger 1131; Lindsay, Perlesz, Brown, McNair, de Vaus and Pitts 1070; O'Neill, Hamer, and Dixon 44). For example, same-sex families are called upon to explain their family configuration to strangers at the playground, on forms at the doctor's office or preschool, to acquaintances who want to know how their family was formed, and to extended family members who contest the legitimacy of non-biological family connections (O'Neill, Hamer, and Dixon 45).

Biological limitations can also result in non-standard family arrangements (Dempsey 1151); an ongoing relationship with a donor father or a surrogate or birth mother can take many forms, queering family structure and dislocating the centrality of biology in family formation. For example, my middle schooler has a large and complex family including two legal mothers, two stepmothers, a donor dad, a half-sister, a stepbrother, and a brother-in-law. She is often called upon to explicate her family configuration at piano recitals and other public events where family turns out en masse. Families with queer configurations not only engage with the dominant culture in social situations, but also within institutions where they challenge the heteronormative family standard, emphasizing the potential diversity of families and family functioning (Chapman, Wardrop, Freeman, Zappia, Watkins and Kitzinger 1131; Lindsay, Perlesz, Brown, McNair, de Vaus and Pitts 1070).

The de-emphasis on biological reproduction in queer families uncouples parenting from biology, making it more likely for children to be raised in multiple households and with multiple "mothers" i.e., primary caretakers and nurturers. With multiple mothers, notions of motherhood as individual self-sacrifice, and notions of familial love as limited to the biogenetic family, are disrupted. The separation of biology and caretaking, common in many queer families, provides an opportunity to question the "business as usual" of families—the impermeable boundaries of the nuclear-normative family, a division of labor wherein the majority of caregiving and emotional labor falls to one person, and related power inequities that disadvantage mothers in typical family formations (Goldberg, Smith, and Perry-Jenkins 822).

QUEERING EVERYDAY ACTS

Same-sex parents don't need to engage in decidedly different practices in order to queer motherhood—they are always visible, thus queer, regardless of intention. Some queer parents have no interest in radical mothering or alternative family structure, instead aspiring to a more typical family form; yet their families can never be fully assimilated into heteronormative structures. Consider the middle class lesbian couple raising children in the suburbs of New Jersey—the white picket fence, the PTA and Little League—are they not queering motherhood? What about a gay male couple in the same situation? Certainly they are queering motherhood because there is no mother in the family at all—yet someone is surely mothering (as opposed to fathering) the children. Are these gay and lesbian versions of the nuclear family queer because the parents are?

Many queer parents do not want to challenge the institutions of gender and family, yet their existence results in profound challenge. The now numerous lesbian and gay parents who have had their children rejected from Catholic schools or prohibited from participating in Boy Scout activities in the United States have drawn public attention to previously unexamined heteronormative beliefs about family and childrearing. In one example, the archdiocese of Boston clarified educational policy after an 8 year old boy was rejected from a Catholic elementary school because of his lesbian mothers. The new admissions policy states parochial schools must not "discriminate against or exclude any categories of students" (Archdiocese of Boston). Thus everyday acts—whether deliberately or unintentionally political—queer family, disrupting the gender order and interrogating the institutions of family and motherhood.

Challenging heteronormative institutions does not always occur on a grand scale; small, everyday acts also serve to illuminate heteronormative operating principles within dominant social institutions such as the educational system. Every time I edit a school form that asks to identify "Mother" and "Father," it illuminates a gendered framework that is embedded in even the most mundane practices. These small, deliberate acts make visible the invisible—everyday practices that both create and maintain the gender order by promoting particular views of motherhood, gender, and family.

QUEERING QUEER PARENTHOOD

When considering what it means to queer motherhood, sexual orientation is often the focus. As "a positionality vis-à-vis the normative" (Halperin 62), sexual orientation can be used to interrogate unexamined processes in the family. Families with same-sex parents challenge virtually every aspect of family life including reproduction, the role of biology in kinship formation, parenting and relationship values, and the (gendered) division of labor (Biblarz and Stacey 10; Chapman, Wardrop, Freeman, Zappia, Watkins and Kitzinger 1131; Goldberg, Smith, and Perry-Jenkins 822; O'Neill; Lindsay, Perlesz, Brown, McNair, de Vaus and Pitts 1070; O'Neill, Hamer, and Dixon 44; Stacey and Biblarz 174).

Yet, while family is one of the most gendered social institutions, little research or formal discussion queers family through a lens of gender nonconformity. While there is now a sizeable body of research examining lesbian parents and their children, virtually none of it discusses gendered behavior and identities among mothers. In addition, what butch, stud, genderqueer, trans, or masculine-of-centre individuals bring to parenting and family structure is largely unexplored. Family is considered a major social institution by sociologists because it orders social life—the work of families is to raise and socialize children, pass on norms, and order gendered relationships. It seems likely that gender transgressive parent(s) might uniquely influence families and mothering. Because of the lack of research, I will use some of my own experiences to speculate about the effects of gender nonconformity on mothering and families.

As I was writing this chapter, I called my adult daughter to ask how having a masculine mother influenced her. This is a tricky question to answer. When she was a teen, we participated in a lesbian-gay panel at the juvenile detention center. An inmate asked her, "What's it like to have a lesbian mother?" She thoughtfully asked about the inmate's mother, then said, "Well, what would you say if I asked you, 'What's it like to have an African American mother?' or 'What's it like to have a tall mother?' Since it's all you know, it's hard to know what it's like, isn't it?"

She's thirty-one now and has the advantage of perspective. When I ask about being raised by a "guy mom," she immediately mentions being politically aware and more empathetic toward minorities. She gives the example of an extended conversation during anti-WTO protests about our racial privilege in interactions with the police, believing it resulted in a permanent shift in perspective. This first influence—greater social empathy—is not unexpected as it aligns with the research on lesbian mothers (Gartrell and Bos 9).

After further discussion, she agreed greater empathy might have more to do with lesbian status rather than female masculinity. She reconsiders my influence: "Having a mother with a non-standard gender makes you think a lot more about what it means to be a woman." She continued with a common theme in our discussions—the awareness that many gendered behaviors and social expectations are socially constructed. As an adult, she reports doing "those gendered things" less than her peers. "I'm more conscious and frankly more irritated when I feel like they are socially required, like in my career." She believes that having a gender transgressive mother most influenced her development by freeing her, to a certain degree, from gendered expectations. She explains, "In personality, I tend to be a feminine, conformist, rule-liking type. Had I been raised in a different environment, I would be far more extreme."

When we move "queering motherhood" beyond sexual orientation and consider transgender or gender variant lives, everyday mothering can challenge the gender binary, and more broadly, the institution of gender. I recall talking to a parent about his transition and how he explained it to his five year old. He told his son, "Some people are born girls, but they have the heart of a boy. If this happens, you can take medicine to make you more like a boy." With a more complex understanding of both the social construction of gendered expectations and the mutability of sex and gender, it seems likely that children would have a fundamentally different world view. I would like to think that this exposure also denaturalizes gender inequality, leading to a more critical analysis of gender inequality by children raised in gender nonconforming households.

Although our children may have a different world view, they still must negotiate the "real world" where they either become tireless champions or quiet critics of the status quo as they sit in class mentally tallying the teachers' and students' gendered assumptions. My daughter spends the summer in Provincetown among drag queens and a predominantly gay culture, then, during the school year, takes the bus to the local middle school where I appear to be the only LGBTQ parent. She primarily negotiates a world where her family structure or any of its queer derivations are invisible. Although she does not believe she has faced discrimination, she is aware we are outliers. When I picked her up from the first day of fourth grade, she introduced me to the other moms on the playground, "This is my mom. As you can see, she is not a typical mother." We live in a "progressive" college town, so they scrambled to cover, "She seems perfectly fine to me"—which is not really what my daughter said or meant.

Gender nonconforming parents typically come into contact with children beyond their own, providing an opportunity to expose numerous children to transgressive views of gender. For example, groups of tween girls at my house dressed up like pirates, racing through the neighborhood on an extended treasure hunt engineered by me and, on another day, assembled a racing chariot from a salvaged garden cart complete with spray-painted flames and luminous gold wheels. Especially at a time when many girls are focused on appearance, diets, and whether to wear eye liner, my gender atypical interests and skills offer a version of "female" that's profoundly different from their experience. What does it mean to make muffins to take to the motocross track? What does it mean simply to go to the motocross track with your mother? These everyday acts disrupt and problematize normative notions of femininity and masculinity, offering children a unique view of gender and gendered behavior.

I have questioned whether my gender transgression influences children in the long run, or whether they discount me as an outlier. My eldest daughter has always been relatively feminine in interests, behavior, and appearance. Since we are so differently gendered, I presumed I didn't fit into her category of "woman." I assumed that when I replaced the brakes on the car, it didn't translate into "women replace brakes on cars." However, my daughter claims otherwise, again pointing to her awareness of the social construction of gender. "When I went through puberty, I remember being really conscious that shaving your legs was a choice and that other girls didn't feel this way. I chose not to shave my legs. There are many things like that that have come up over the years—where I realized I had a choice to do or not to do something—it wasn't as automatic." She later explained that her behavior, in turn, influenced other girls. "As an adult, one of my friends from middle school told me that my unwillingness to go along with those [gendered] things in middle school influenced her too. She was less likely to go along with what was expected gender-wise."

In addition to questioning gendered behavioral expectations, my daughter is also a staunch queer ally. Even at a time when she had relatively little social power—her marriage to a wealthier man from a more conservative family—she insisted on my inclusion and visibility against their wishes. I believe that growing up with the inability to hide the queerness of our family due to my visible gender transgression required her to develop a different set of coping strategies including a strong sense of social justice and a commitment to advocacy. When our children grow into queer allies and publicly question "business as usual," it suggests that queering motherhood can result in broader societal change. How many lives are impacted when the mother of the bride at a big Indian wedding opens the wedding with a Buddhist meditation while wearing a vintage tux? If we think about the ripple effect, these relatively personal acts of queering motherhood might start the smallest of revolutions in how the world thinks about gender, sexual orientation, mothers, and family.

NO WAY OUT? THE INFLUENCE OF GENDERED SOCIAL POSITIONS

Gender nonconforming parents have unique opportunities to queer family, not only in parenting and interactions with children, but in how we engage with social institutions. However, even with intentionally and overtly queer identities, ideologies, and practices, we may be constrained by our socio-structural location—mothering makes us structurally vulnerable.

I identify as transgender in the most stereotypical of ways—I feel like a man and don't relate to being a woman at all. Yet even with this relatively black and white conception of gender identity, I do not identify as a father, but as a mother within the context of particular political, social, and legal systems. In my previous research with transmen, I conceptualized gender as a balance between perceived sex (appearance as male or female) and gendered behavior (Dozier, "Beards, Breasts, and Bodies" 314). However, I have come to understand that gender also includes our socio-structural positions. When a social position is highly correlated with being male or female, social policy, laws, and culture develop in response. The gendered social position of motherhood is inescapable in everyday life, impacting my personal life far more than my gender identity, appearance, or behavior. As I am fond of saying, "It doesn't matter whether I feel like a man doing laundry or a woman doing laundry, I'm still doing laundry."

"Mother" and "single mother" are specific, gendered social locations evoking particular expected behaviors in families, but also in interactions with social institutions. I have been a single mother for almost all of my adult life. The physical and economic constraints of single parenthood and the legal status of a primary parent with fewer assets is a uniquely gendered situation. Single parenthood is generally women's work and comes with the attendant hazards of poverty, legal troubles, and strained resources as the crises and costs of parenting fall disproportionately on one set of shoulders. For example, I have recently been engaged in a legal dispute over child support. These disputes are commonplace—the noncustodial parent feels they are an exception to the state-mandated support amount for one reason or another. Whether the noncustodial parent is a man or a woman, masculine or feminine, influences the predicament less than the social structural position of the parents. The gendered social locations "single mother" and "mother" affect individuals not because they are feminine or identify as women, but because there are gender differences in access to power and resources (Elizabeth, Gavey and Tolmie 475). I proudly claim the identities of "mother" and "single mother" and all they entail in resources, time use, legal history, oppression, resistance, and life chances while retaining my masculine and male gender identity. Surely, this is queering motherhood.

OPPRESSION AND QUEER PARENTING

Queering motherhood is often considered a theoretical exercise, but challenging heteronormative institutions and structures has material consequences. Structural inequalities, discrimination, and violence are unavoidable penalties for transgression. Some of our children continue to be picked on at school, we face a host of legal hurdles to parenting, and the lack of federally-recognized marriage or domestic partnership leads to painful realities for families. For example, Lisa Pond spent her dying hours alone after collapsing from an aneurysm in Florida while on vacation with her family. Even with legal documents including adoption papers and a healthcare proxy, her partner of 18 years, Janice Langbehn and their three children were not allowed to be with her for the majority of her final hours. As the social worker told Janice, "... this is an anti-gay city and an anti-gay state, and you are not going to get to see her or know her condition" (James 2009).

Unavoidable instances of homophobia and transphobia experienced by children can have lasting effects. When my daughter was six, a friend was shot and her girlfriend killed in an act of homophobic violence. This has profoundly affected my daughter's sense of safety. She has developed an acute awareness of her majority status (her husband is an ethnic minority in the United States) and her inability to protect the people she loves from violence and discrimination. Recently I picked her up, more than 20 years after the shooting, and she said, "I was just thinking about what you'd be wearing and wondering if you will ever stop dressing like a teenage boy... Do you know every time you are about to pick me up or I watch you drive off, I'm overcome by a wave of fear that I'll never see you again. That someone will kill you. Just by looking at you, everyone knows you're gay."

On a less dramatic note, everyday discrimination also takes its toll. For example, I have been unable to get a job as a sociologist, I believe, because I disclosed my transgender identity in an academic article (for an account see Dozier, "Odd Man Out"). My inability to pursue my profession has likely affected the life outcomes of my youngest child. Not only am I paid less, but I have to essentially maintain two careers—one in the discipline in which I teach and the other in the area in which I do research, leading to lower productivity. In addition to the negative impact on my immediate earnings, the trajectory of my lifetime earnings is attenuated, affecting my children's long-term outcomes. I recount these personal stories because I believe they are nothing special—the oppression faced by LGBTQ parents forever "queers" their families, affecting them both emotionally and materially. Individuals who are gender transgressive face even greater risks because of their continuous, visible challenge to gender and heteronormative family structures, a position construed as particularly hostile to "family values."

CONCLUSION

Queering motherhood can both illuminate heteronormative assumptions that structure mothering and family life and destabilize norms that maintain gender inequality in the family and other social institutions. Challenging the "business as usual" of families can be revisionist, such as when parents insist on the right to participate in society and social institutions by enrolling children in parochial schools or when they edit forms that don't reflect queer families. It can also be radical—upending the nuclear-normative family structure and redefining what it means to raise children and form families. Queering motherhood, however, does not just operate as we engage with social institutions; our personal lives also effect change when we come into contact with various people, institutions, and communities. In the case of gender transgressive parents, our version of "doing mothering" visibly defies the heteronormative rulebook and our everyday acts continuously trouble the waters of sex, gender, mothering, and family.

NOTES

[1]In this case, I use transition to refer to the process of changing physical characteristics via hormonal therapy or surgery. Although I identify as transgender, I have not transitioned.

[2]I use the term "mothering" to describe the daily processes of caring for and nurturing children.

[3]The Parent Teacher Association is a national parent association with parent-run groups in most public schools in the United States.

[4]I address the research literature regarding lesbians because of the paucity of work regarding gay fathers and families with a transgender parent(s). To my knowledge, no research investigates transgender parenting behaviors. Research regarding gay fathers is limited, but implies gay fathers exist between heterosexual families and lesbian families in parenting style, more closely resembling heterosexual mothers (see Biblarz and Stacey 12).

[5]I am aware that I am oversimplifying the term "trans" for the sake of brevity. The term can include a variety of identities in addition to those who identify as the sex other than which they were born.

WORKS CITED

Archdiocese of Boston. Archdiocese of Boston Announces School Admission Policy. 12 Jan. 2011. Web. 5 Nov. 2013.

Biblarz, Timothy J. and Judith Stacey. "How Does the Gender of Parents Matter?" *Journal of Marriage and Family* 72.1 (2010): 3-22. Print.

Bos, Henny M.W., Frank van Balen, and Dyphmna van den Boom. "Child Adjustment and Parenting in Planned Lesbian-Parent Families." *American Journal of Orthopsychiatry* 77.1 (2007): 38-48. Print.

Chapman, Rose, Joan Wardrop, Phoenix Freeman, Tess Zappia, Rochelle Watkins, and Linda Shields. "A Descriptive Study of the Experiences of Lesbian, Gay and Transgender Parents Accessing Health Services for their Children." *Journal of Clinical Nursing* 21.7-8 (2012): 1128-1135. Print.

Dempsey, Deborah. "Conceiving and Negotiating Reproductive Relationships: Lesbians and Gay Men Forming Families with Children." *Sociology* 44.6 (2010): 1145-1162. Print.

Dozier, Raine. "Odd Man Out: On Gender and the Job Market." Appendix I, *Report on the Status of Gay, Lesbian, Bisexual and Transgendered Persons in Sociology*. American Sociological Association. 28 May 2009. Web. 5 Nov. 2013.

Dozier, Raine. "Beards, Breasts, and Bodies: Doing Sex in a Gendered World." *Gender & Society* 19.3 (2005): 297-316. Print.

Elizabeth, Vivienne, Nicola Gavey, and Julia Tolmie. "The Gendered Dynamics of Power in Disputes Over the Postseparation Care of Children." *Violence Against Women* 18.4 (2012):459-481. Print.

Gartrell Nanette K., Henny M.W. Bos, Naomi G. Goldberg. "Adolescents of the U.S. National Longitudinal Lesbian Family Study: Sexual Orientation, Sexual Behavior, and Sexual Risk Exposure." *Archives of Sexual Behavior* 40.6 (2010): 199-1209. Print.

Gartrell, Nanette and Henny Bos. "US National Longitudinal Lesbian Family Study: Psychological Adjustment of 17-Year-Old Adolescents." *Pediatrics* 126.1 (2010): 28-36. Print.

Goldberg, Abbie E., Deborah A. Kashy, and JuliAnna Z. Smith. 2012. "Gender-Typed Play Behavior in Early Childhood: Adopted Children with Lesbian, Gay, and Heterosexual Parents." *Sex Roles* 67.9-10 (2012):503-515. Print.

Goldberg, Abbie E., JuliAnna Z. Smith, and Maureen Perry-Jenkins. "The Division of Labor in Lesbian, Gay, and Heterosexual New Adoptive Parents." *Journal of Marriage and Family* 74.4 (2012):812-828. Print.

Halperin, David. *Saint Foucault: Towards a Gay Hagiography.* New York: Oxford University Press, 1997. Print.

James, Susan Donaldson. "Lesbians Sue When Partners Die Alone." ABC News. 20 May 2009. Web. 5 Nov. 2013.

Johnson, Susanne M. "Lesbian Mothers and Their Children: The Third Wave." 2012. *Journal of Lesbian Studies* 16 (2012): 45-53. Print.

Lindsay, Jo, Amaryll Perlesz, Rhonda Brown, Ruth McNair, David de Vaus and Marian Pitts. 2006. "Stigma or Respect: Lesbian-Parented Families Negotiating School Settings." *Sociology* 40.6 (2006): 1059-1077. Print.

O'Neill, Kristal R., Helen P. Hamer, and Robyn Dixon. "A Lesbian Family in a Straight World: The Impact of the Transition to Parenthood on Couple Relationships in Planned Lesbian Families." *Women's Studies Journal* 26.2 (2012): 39-53. Print.

Stacey, J. and Biblarz, T.J. 2001. "(How) Does Sexual Orientation of Parents Matter?" *American Sociological Review.* 66.2 (2001): 159-183. Print.

Tasker, F. L., and Golombok, S. *Growing Up in a Lesbian Family: Effect on Child Development.* New York, NY: Guilford Press, 1997. Print.

8.

Shifting Families

Alternative Drafts of Motherhood

KARIN SARDADVAR AND KATHARINA MIKO

INTRODUCTION: QUEERING THE FAMILY

The term 'queer' does not refer only to sexualities, sexual practices and sexual desires, but also to readings and everyday practices of gender that go beyond clear-cut, binary definitions and ascriptions. While the meaning, potential, and problems of 'queer' have been debated (Pühl 2), the openness, ambiguity and unfinished definition of the term can be seen as inherent features (Jagose 124-128; Klapeer 13). Since the 1990s, a variety of ideas and perceptions regarding what 'queer' is supposed to mean and how it should be used have been put forward. Among them is the suggestion that queer studies also need to address the *institutional contexts* in which assumptions of heterosexuality, heteronormativity and concepts of gender dichotomy operate (Jagose 176). If we adopt this perspective, one social institution queer studies must address is 'the family.'

In this chapter, we are going to take such an approach seriously by reflecting upon the queering of motherhood in settings that may not seem queer at first glance or under tight readings of 'queer'. Our objective is to see where we end up if we look at particular empirical family constellations, which are not adequately addressed by mainstream family research concepts, through a queer lens. In so doing, we focus on a specific context: middle European countries where a Catholic tradition influences the legal restrictions concerning LGBT persons within family policy. Our results and examples are taken from empirical material collected in Austria, a country with conservative family politics in general and a very slow recognition of non-heterosexual relationship and family constellations in particular. As for the theoretical context, we start from a sociological perspective with a focus on European family sociology from the German-speaking countries but open it up towards a more interdisciplinary approach incorporating Anglo-American family studies, queer theories, and polyamory discourse.

FAMILIAR ASSUMPTIONS: DOMINANT SOCIOLOGICAL UNDERSTANDINGS OF FAMILY

In sociology, the family is generally conceptualized as institution (Nave-Herz "Familiensoziologie" 77). As such, it is linked to a number of specific functions, such as biological reproduction and the socialization of children (ibid. 79, 88). Inextricable from these 'functions' of the family is the historical differentiation of the roles of men and women and its diverse implications on the labor market and other aspects of society and inequality (Sieder "Sozialgeschichte" 131f.). In this chapter, however, we want to focus on 'the family' one step prior: we aim to deconstruct the dominant family concept and explicate how heteronormative parameters form its underlying assumptions (Miko "Sexing" 172f.).

Before doing so, it is important to clarify which theoretical frames we integrate our empirical analysis into. Concerning the debates within family research, we draw on the concept of *families of choice* (Weston) and the concept of *cultures of intimacy and care* (Roseneil and Budgeon). As such, we adopt aspects of the Anglo-American discourse, which is more diverse and fluid in terms of concepts than mainstream family sociology in the German-speaking countries. We critically assess how such concepts can be helpful for interpreting empirical data that was collected in a context of conservative family policies and a Catholic tradition. Indeed, this context of family conservatism is reflected in much of the family research and theory in Austria and Germany as well (for exceptions see, e.g., Lenz "Familie"; Sieder "Patchworks"; Schadler). Against this background, we consider it fruitful to apply a specific theoretical discourse (the Anglo-American literature on families of choice and intimacy and care) to a different empirical context (Austria as a middle European country with a conservative family policy).

Concerning the queer studies discourse, we draw on the polyamory debate in the USA and the European German-speaking countries (Easton and Hardy; Méritt, Bührmann and Schefzig; Munson and Stelboum) and

Gayle Rubin's "Thinking Sex." Rubin offered an important framework in providing the theory of the hierarchy of sexualities, in which members of society regard some sexualities as 'better' or 'more valued' than others and dismiss certain sexualities as 'bad' ones (Rubin "Sex denken" 44; Miko "Danke" 175). We argue that this approach helps to explain legal restrictions for certain family constellations based on presumptions about their sexualities. In addition, we refer to the polyamory discourse because it ties in with our concept of the *underlying assumptions* (Miko "Danke" 173) by questioning whether love, sexuality, sexual desire, etc. normatively and empirically always meet within a family frame. By *underlying assumptions* we mean the cornerstones of the mainstream family concept that are often kept implicit.

In the following, we identify five core assumptions that our empirical research calls into question, and which merit a 'queer' investigation (Miko "Sexing" 172f.):

I. Equation of family and household

Even if its adequacy has already been questioned by many scholars (Lenz "Familie" 491f.; cf. Burkart 506), the household is often used as one of the basic analytic instruments for family sociology (cf. Nave-Herz "Familiensoziologie," "Familie"). A family is still frequently defined as persons who live in a joint household. This underlying assumption has already been challenged in different aspects (cf. Peuckert 78), and living-apart-together (LAT), for instance, is an illustrative example for a type of intimate relationship which does not end at the entrance to a shared home.

II. Sexual intercourse as a basic condition for reproduction

It is a widely accepted assumption that a couple needs to have sexual intercourse in order to have a child together (cf. Lenz and Nestmann; Nave-Herz "Familiensoziologie," "Familie"). We argue that mainstream family sociology in the European German speaking countries often operates with a specific – and heteronormative – definition of the couple that then influences assumptions about reproductive processes and family formation (cf. Nave-Herz "Familiensoziologie" 79).

III. Sexual relationship as a basic condition for being a couple

Even if there is general consensus in couple and family sociology that it is possible to be a couple without reproducing together (Lenz "Soziologie" 11-13), it is broadly assumed that a couple must have some kind of sexual relationship (Lenz "Soziologie" 48). We will demonstrate in the discussion of the empirical data below that this assumption does not hold true for all couple constellations.

IV. The heterosexual couple as the heteronormative standard

Although there is a growing body of literature on same-sex relationships with and without children (cf., e.g., Miko "Sexing"; Miko "Danke"; Sawatzki; Streib-Brzic and Gerlach; Stacey; Weston), so-called 'rainbow families' are still marginalized in mainstream sociology (Stacey 130; cf. Nave-Herz "Familiensoziologie"). In this context, feminist family sociologists and queer theorists have argued that the LGBT people are being constructed as 'the other' with regard to the family (Weston 22). This phenomenon can be observed in scientific contexts as well as in popular discourses and everyday practices (Miko and Sardadvar "Visuelles Wissen" 215f.).

V. Monogamy as a core value of relationships

Monogamy as a core value between the partners is often implicitly anticipated in mainstream European German-speaking family sociology. This underlying assumption is related to the sexual relationship. The polyamory school of thought has challenged this aspect in recent years (cf. Easton and Hardy; Méritt, Bührmann and Schefzig; Munson and Stelboum). The key thought here is not only focused on questioning monogamy with regard to sexuality. In its broader sense, it refers to poly*amory* and thus to the fact that love can be lived (sexually as well as in other ways) not only with one person.

QUEERING MATERNITY: EMPIRICAL INSIGHTS BEYOND HETERO- AND HOMOSEXUALITY

Within the institution of the family, motherhood deserves particular attention. Several assumptions and consequences meet in the dominant constructions of motherhood (Sardadvar "Social Construction"; Badinter

"Mutterliebe"; Badinter "Conflict"; Schütze; Thomson et al.). First, constructions of motherhood rely on the system of gender binary that leads to a differentiation of parents into mothers and fathers. Non-gendered parents, i.e., parents who are neither fathers nor mothers, are thus not 'thinkable' (Dalton and Bielby 40). Second, the institution of motherhood (Rich; O'Reilly; DiQuinzio) is strongly linked to ideas of sexual reproduction and heterosexuality (for constructions of an opposition between family/parenthood and homosexuality see Weston; for discursive incompatibilities of motherhood and lesbian identity see Miko "Kind und Kegel" 131). Third, social constructions of motherhood are closely connected to constructions of biological particularities of women, such as the constructions of a maternal instinct, of a unique bond between mothers and their children, and of natural motherly love (Badinter "Mutterliebe"; Badinter "Conflict"; Schütze; Sardadvar "Social Construction"). These assumptions not only contribute to essentialist constructions of natural differences between sexes, but also have enormous social consequences with regard to the distribution of responsibilities for childcare, the gendered distribution of labor, and women's position in families and the labor market (Sardadvar "Geteilte Karenz" 88-93). A case in point is breastfeeding: Based on the ability to breastfeed, mothers are being constructed as the parent who is best suited to take care of a baby in the first months after its birth. Based on breastfeeding, then, parents develop a division of labor, and create routines with regard to the division of childcare and domestic work. Hence, the biology-oriented argument that only women are able to breastfeed expands to the social division of paid and unpaid labor and produces gendered parental roles (Sardadvar "Geteilte Karenz" 88-93; Hall Smith; Badinter "Conflict").

In order to illustrate the theoretical considerations presented above we offer four examples of families whose experiences highlight the gaps in mainstream sociology's assumptions about what makes a family. These cases are taken from two qualitative research projects conducted in Austria: first, a PhD project on the social construction of families drawing on the example of step-families with a special focus on homosexual step-families (Miko "Kind und Kegel"); second, a PhD project on social patterns of interpretation of older mothers (Sardadvar "Späte Mutterschaft"). Both projects worked with an interpretative research design and, inter alia, qualitative interviews with biological as well as social mothers and fathers.

EXAMPLE 1: SHIFTING RELATIONSHIPS, SHIFTING HOUSEHOLDS

Martha and Peter[1] (Miko "Kind und Kegel" 98) are married and have three children. Approximately two years before the interview, Martha fell in love with another woman whom she wanted to live with. Martha and Peter agreed to end their sexual relationship but they stayed in one household at first. The term separation was not appropriate in its typical usage. For instance, they considered sharing apartments with each other as well as their new partners in order to be a family for their children. Although at the end of the separation process they separated the households too, the example of Martha and Peter shows that in everyday practice, people may try to go beyond some traditional underlying assumptions of the family concept. In the interview Peter said:

> "We made considerations. For example, she told me: Try to find a girlfriend – each of us lives sexuality separately. [...] The relationship with me still meant security, continuity. The material aspect, the security, to like each other – we tried to conserve these aspects and go separate ways regarding sexuality."

The case of Martha and Peter shows that dominant sociological understandings of the family and the couple can be too narrow to grasp everyday practices, particularly in times of change. In particular, this example challenges the assumption that household arrangements automatically follow sexual and familial ties (*assumption I*). The separation process of Martha and Peter and their concern for motherhood and parenthood can be seen as 'queer' in that it challenges the classical concepts of family, motherhood, fatherhood and being a couple. In their words, they tried to find 'other solutions.' This case thus ties in to the discourses within the framework of queer studies that criticize the ideal of biological binary parenthood and plead for extending notions of kinship to the diversity of care models being actually practiced (Woltersdorf 922).

EXAMPLE 2: BEYOND THE 'GAY-STRAIGHT' DICHOTOMY

Renate and Wolfgang (Miko "Sexing" 288) are married. Renate is, according to her definition, heterosexual; Wolfgang defines himself as gay (and regularly has sexual contacts with men). They have adopted two children.

When asked whether they have a sexual relationship, they answer that it is a '*physical*' one. They live in a household together.

The case of Renate and Wolfgang raises questions with regard to different underlying assumptions towards families. Although they live a relationship that does not fit into heteronormative standards, it is a legal and – in legal terms – heterosexual relationship in Austria. In demographic statistics, Renate and Wolfgang would appear as a heterosexual couple with two adopted children. But their everyday practice goes beyond this simple labeling. They challenge several dominant assumptions. First, when asked about sexuality within their couple relationship, they cannot give a 'clear' answer. 'Clear' refers here to the sociologist's framework. Their bodies seem to communicate with each other, but they do not label this as 'sexual'. Second, according to their own definition they are a couple, even without a clearly sexual relationship with each other. It is interesting to note that couple sociology, which in the German-speaking context was established in opposition to mainstream family sociology (Lenz "Familie"), in fact also builds on specific assumptions about relationships (cf. Lenz and Nestmann; Lenz "Soziologie"). Although couple sociology criticizes the nuclear family model, it operates under other assumptions, including that sexuality is a foundation of the couple status (*assumption III*). Third, although Renate and Wolfgang define themselves as a 'couple,' the ideal of monogamy is not of value for them (*assumption V*). Fourth, they live as man and woman, as mother and father, as different sexes and genders – but are not a heterosexual couple (*assumption IV*). They are – as a couple – not homosexual either. Renate and Wolfgang leave us with questions and illustrate that sociological frameworks sometimes need to be 'queered' in order to grasp empirical reality.

EXAMPLE 3: SEEKING A BIOLOGICAL FATHER

Emma (Sardadvar "Späte Mutterschaft" 165-168) is 47 years old and the mother of a two-year-old daughter, Jenny. Emma raises Jenny on her own, although the biological father has regular contact to Jenny, visiting her about once a week. Emma planned to become a single mother when she decided to get pregnant. She said she had initially believed she would need to be in a relationship with a man in order to have a child:

> "And then, I think, yes, then I thought, I always had the illusion that a man, I mean that a child and a man go together, that a child needs a father, whom I absolutely need. And I

> would have argued with everyone who [raised children] you know, without a father. But then, when I turned about 40, I thought: If I'm going to wait for my final partner, I think I'm never going to get a child."

Emma then went to find a father for the child she wanted so much:

> "Yes, and that was when I swore to myself: Once in my life I want, I absolutely want to have a child. And somehow then I just went and selected a man. I have to admit this, yes, somehow I did [...]. Actually, I didn't care whether he was married or whatever, what was important was that he was a nice type of person. [That I] had a good feeling."

Emma constructed her desire to have a child rather independently from having a partner, in contrast with the dominant narrative that centers on a happy relationship as a reason for wanting a child together (Sardadvar "Späte Mutterschaft" 153-184). Emma broke away from several prevalent assumptions: with the idea of a stable relationship as a prerequisite for having a child (Lenz "Familie" 486), with moral norms regarding sexuality and conception (*assumptions II and V*) (Hertz; Bock), and with the ideal of monogamy which she challenged by not caring whether the father of her child was married or not (Sardadvar "Späte Mutterschaft" 166-168).

Emma's account challenges underlying assumptions about families by separating sexual desire, sexual practice and reproduction – albeit in a heterosexual way and context. We suggest that queer theory has something to offer to interpret this empirical case. Consider the widespread assumption that gay men will never be parents (Weston 22; Miko and Sardadvar "Visuelles Wissen" 215f.) due to the assumption of sexual activity and reproduction as belonging together (*assumption II*): in a different context, Emma, too, challenged this assumption. Meanwhile, Emma did rely on traditional ways of conceiving by having sex with a man. It is important to note that there were few other options for her due to the laws regarding assisted reproduction and adoption in Austria, where assisted reproductive technology is not open to single women (nor to lesbian women in a relationship) (Bundeskanzleramt "Bundesrecht").

EXAMPLE 4: ADOPTION AS A SINGLE MOTHER WITHIN A RELATIONSHIP

Charlotte (Sardadvar "Späte Mutterschaft" 162f.; Sardadvar "Empfängnisverhütung" 235-238) and her husband Fred had a baby at the time of the interview. Charlotte recounted that she had contemplated adopting a child as a single parent before her husband agreed to have a biological child with her. She said that she had been together with Fred, who already had a biological child from an earlier relationship, for a very long time when she decided she wanted to have a child. Before that, Fred and she had always agreed that they did not want to have children together:

> "And then, about when I turned 30, I noticed, every year in Spring I followed more and more baby buggies with my eye. And for me, the desire just became stronger and stronger and at some point it was clear: By any means I want to have a child. This wasn't as clear for my partner. Then it took two more years during which I was sure that I wanted a child and he actually preferred not to [. . .]. For me, it was also clear then that if he doesn't want to, I'll adopt. And he would be my partner, but somehow only the uncle [. . .]."

Charlotte's husband eventually changed his mind and they had a biological child together. Still, Charlotte's idea to adopt a child and raise it on her own, but *within* the existing relationship with her partner, is telling with regard to the kinds of family formations that are 'thinkable' and expressible. Charlotte's plan to adopt a child on her own challenges several underlying assumptions regarding families: the assumptions of biological and sexual reproduction (*assumption II*), the idea that, at least in an existing relationship, partner and father ought to be the same person, as well as more recent norms for couples to share responsibility for their children. Even if Charlotte's husband might have been just as (un)involved in parenting as many other fathers, it is remarkable that Charlotte explicitly constructed his role as that of an 'uncle', thus opening up space for a constellation in which the partner is explicitly not a father. Similar to Emma from example 3, Charlotte separated sexuality and reproduction (*assumption II*), but also family and household (*assumption I*), marriage and parenthood, and the heterosexual couple as the standard parent couple (*assumption IV*) – notwithstanding the fact that she was living in a heterosexual relationship.

This example illustrates the complexity of family constellations and definitions. In order to interpret this example, it is helpful to distinguish between self-definition, social construction and performative practice. Although the couple performatively plays the heterosexual norm, the queer aspect is visible in their definitions of couplehood (we are a couple, we have sex, but this has nothing to do with reproduction) and of fatherhood (although the couple relationship remains, he would be 'uncle').

Meanwhile, this case links with queer politics. Although living in a heterosexual relationship, Charlotte is in fact confronted with some of the legal restrictions with regard to having a child that a lesbian couple would have to face. Even if being married is not a legal precondition for adoption, in practice, adoptable children are preferably given to married couples in Austria (Bundeskanzleramt "Ablauf"). Non-married couples (neither in same-sex or two-sex relationships) cannot adopt a child together, and marriage is not open to same-sex couples (since 2010, there is, however, the option for a civil partnership, but this does not make adoption more available except as a 'step-parent'). At the same time, as a married woman Charlotte would be able to apply for an adoption alongside her husband in order to raise her chances for success, whatever their actual plans for his role or title.

CONCLUSIONS: QUEERING SOCIOLOGICAL FAMILY RESEARCH

Our empirical examples show that women, even if they live in seemingly traditional and heterosexual relationships, sometimes find alternative ways of becoming mothers, thinking about motherhood, or adjusting familial relations. We have presented cases that illustrate counter-narratives to the assumptions of conventional heterosexual conception, relationships and parenting. Empirical cases like these reveal how individuals actively shape the everyday practices of parenthood in diverse ways, thus creating family constellations that are rarely taken into account in mainstream family sociology – or, indeed, in queer studies.

In the past few decades, the term 'family' has been subject to substantial critique. Postmodern and feminist approaches have deconstructed allegedly constitutive aspects of 'the family', revealing underlying patriarchal structures and contesting the status of the bourgeois nuclear family as the norm (e.g. Doherty; Adler; see also Miko and Sardadvar "FAMinism" 49ff.). Social-historical research has contributed to this process by demonstrating the diversities of past family life and by pointing out how particular ideas and empirical representations of families emerged under particular social and historical circumstances (e.g. Sieder "Sozialgeschichte"; Badinter "Mutterliebe"). In his approach to couple sociology, Lenz (2003; 2009) has argued that personal relations have to be studied in their own right rather than as 'incomplete families', and thereby harshly questioned the very agenda of family research (see also Sieder "Patchworks").

What about queer theory then? Does queer theory have more to contribute to a critical and deconstructivist approach to family research than the combined forces of gender studies, feminism, postmodernism, social history, and couple sociology? And is queer theory adequate for a more general application to family research issues, i.e. including for instance couples living in heterosexual relationships, or single mothers? We argue that the answer is yes for several reasons.

I: We see the core contribution of queer theories to sociological thinking in their capacity to point out the prevalence, effects, and limits of gender and sexuality norms and categorizations:

> *Queer* criticism is directed against the perception that gender and sexuality as categories of human body appearances only describe the latter and classify them as 'normal' or 'deviant'. In a queer perspective, rather, gender and sexuality are perceived as effects of complex and in many ways interlinked linguistic-discursive practices that make the gender binary and heterosexuality seem 'natural.' (Klapeer 11, our translation)

In this article, we have pointed out that heterosexuality, monogamy, heterosexual intercourse and other assumptions implicitly function as cornerstones of dominant definitions of 'the family.' Queer theory challenges family sociology by calling these assumptions into question, particularly by challenging a binary gender system as the basis of being parent:

> Under postmodern conditions, processes of sexuality, conception, gestation, marriage, and parenthood, which once appeared to follow a natural, inevitable progression of gendered behaviors and relationships, have come unhinged, hurtling the basic definitions of our most taken-for-granted familial categories – like mother, father, parent, offspring, sibling, and, of course, family itself – into cultural confusion and contention (Stacey 120).

Queer theory allows us to combine analyses of gender and sexuality in a very rich way. This makes queer theory a promising approach particularly in those fields where interlinked norms of gender and sexuality play a vital part, such as the study of families.

II: Throughout its emergence and existence, queer theory has always been connected to politics (Klapeer 17-34). Social science sometimes looks at the political implications of its theories and findings with reluctance. At the same time, social science findings are often unavoidably political. This is also true for family research: on the one hand, family research agendas and terms can be shaped by politically-preferred family concepts. On the other hand, family policies often rely on family research (Lenz "Familie" 493; Miko "Kind und Kegel"). Finally, the social realities that family research tries to understand can be connected to political frameworks in very immediate ways. If we consider, for instance, research on same-sex parents, on surrogate motherhood or on joint custody, it is hardly possible *not* to take into account the legal and political conditions under which these social phenomena are organized, lived and experienced (cf., e.g., Burkstrand-Reid; Miko "Sexing"; Mense). It has to be noted, however, that queer theory and the term 'queer' itself have been contested with regard to their political usefulness (for an overview of the arguments see Jagose 129-159).

Broadening the scope of queer studies towards families and relationships which do not seem to have anything queer at first glance can be a boon for family research. This allows us to link the social and the political in cases where the importance of these connections may not be as evident. Hence, leaving space for investigating the 'queerness' of heterosexual constellations, too (cf. Doty 2f.), seems to be not only perfectly possible within the framework of queer theory, but also very promising for family research.

For example, to return to the empirical data, Charlotte might have benefited from the existence of an institutional framework that made it easier to adopt a child without a partner. Interpreted differently, she might have been privileged because she indeed had a husband who would possibly have *officially* adopted with her. Emma might possibly have found it easier to have a child, which she was prepared to raise on her own anyway, if assisted reproductive technologies had been open to single women in Austria. Renate and Wolfgang might have decided against a legal marriage if there had been a higher chance to adopt children without being married. From the standpoint of Wolfgang, perhaps he would have married a man if the adoption of children within a gay relationship had been legal in the country he

lives in. Martha knew that it would not be easy to take three children with her into a lesbian relationship because of general stigmatization, because of a lack of legal security and because of the restrictions of legal custody. If parenthood was not legally restricted to binary systems (father/mother) in Austria, maybe Martha and Peter could have organized their family life within a legal context with their new partners.
III: The undefined and unfinished character of the term 'queer' allows for experimentation. This quality of 'queer' has, on the one hand, been regarded as a weakness, as the openness and ambiguities of the term may also limit its significance and explanatory power. On the other hand, this feature is also a strength, as it makes the term adaptable to new developments, new ideas and new areas of research and theory. As such, a queer lens may help to investigate and interpret family constellations that can hardly be understood via traditional categories of mainstream family research, including new developments. Family research and gender and queer studies are often working separately. We argue that by adopting queer studies for analyzing mainstream family research questions, disciplinary boundaries can be challenged and new questions unearthed.

Queer approaches to family and kinship have dealt with topics such as differences, reinvention, and kinship remodeling in LGBT families (Ahmed 569; Halberstam 5; Weston 116). While not every 'unconventional' family challenges the gender binary, gender hierarchies, or hierarchies of sexuality (Miko and Sardadvar "FAMinism" 52), some apparently non-queer families may indeed be cases in point for differences, reinventions and remodelings of kinship and parenthood. Such family constellations would not necessarily be looked at by queer studies; at the same time, they would not be satisfyingly taken into account by mainstream family research either. Opening up family studies towards queer theories, even in cases outside the usual scope of 'queer', may help us understand alternative drafts of parenthood and family.

NOTES

[1]All names of the interviewees have been changed in order to ensure confidentiality.

WORKS CITED

Adler, Marina A. "Ideological Disputes and Feminist Discourse about an Inappropriate Concept: Let's Bid Farewell to 'The Family'." *Erwägen Wissen Ethik* 14.3 (2003): 485-498. Print.

Ahmed, Sara. "Orientations Toward a Queer Phenomenology." *GLQ: A Journal of Lesbian and Gay Studies* 12.4 (2006): 543-574. Web.

Badinter, Elisabeth. *Die Mutterliebe. Geschichte eines Gefühls vom 17. Jahrhundert bis heute.* München: R. Piper & Co Verlag, 1981. Print.

Badinter, Elisabeth. *The Conflict: How Modern Motherhood Undermines the Status of Women.* New York: Metropolitan Books, 2012. Print.

Bock, Jane D. "Doing the Right Thing? Single Mothers by Choice and the Struggle for Legitimacy." *Gender & Society* 14.1. (2000): 62-86. Print.

Bundeskanzleramt: *Ablauf der Adoption.* Stand: 01.08.2013. www.help.gv.at, 2013. Web.

Bundeskanzleramt: *Bundesrecht konsolidiert: Gesamte Rechtsvorschrift für Fortpflanzungsmedizingesetz.* Fassung vom 27.11.2013. www.ris.bka.gv.at, 2013. Web.

Burkart, Günter. "Sisyphos oder Der Kampf um die Familie." *Erwägen Wissen Ethik* 14.3 (2003): 506-509. Print.

Burkstrand-Reid, Beth A. "From Sex for Please to Sex for Parenthood: How the Law Manufactures Mothers." *Hastings Law Journal* (2013). Web.

Dalton, Susan E., and Denise D. Bielby. "'That's Our Kind of Constellation.' Lesbian Mothers Negotiate Institutionalized Understandings of Gender Within the Family." *Gender & Society* 14.1 (2000): 36-61. Print.

DiQuinzio, Patrice. *The Impossibility of Motherhood: Feminism, Individualism, and the Problems of Mothering.* New York: Routledge, 1999. Print.

Doherty, William J. "Postmodernism and Family Theory." *Handbook of Marriage and the Family.* Eds. Marvin B. Sussmann, Suzanne K. Steinmetz, and Gary W. Peterson. 2nd ed. New York: Plenum. 205-217. Print.

Doty, Alexander. *Making Things Perfectly Queer.* Interpreting Mass Culture. Minneapolis: University of Minnesota Press, 1993. Print.

Easton, Dossie, and Janet W. Hardy. *The Ethical Slut: A Practical Guide to Polyamory, Open Relationships & Other Adventures.* Berkeley, California: Celestial Arts, 2009. Print.

Halberstam, Judith. *In a Queer Time and Place: Transgender Bodies, Subcultural Lives.* New York University Press, 2005. Print.

Hall Smith, Paige. "Breastfeeding and Gender Inequality." *Journal of Women, Politics & Policy* 44.4 (2013). Special Issue: The Politics of Breastfeeding: 371-383. Web.

Hertz, Rosanna. *Single by Chance, Mothers by Choice: How Women Are Choosing Parenthood without Marriage and Creating the New American Family.* New York: Oxford University Press, 2006. Print.

Jagose, Annamarie. *Queer Theory. Eine Einführung.* 2nd ed. Berlin: Querverlag, 2005. Print.

Klapeer, Christine M. *queer. contexts. Entstehung und Rezeption von* Queer Theory *in den USA und Österreich.* Innsbruck: Studienverlag, 2007. Print.

Lenz, Karl. "Familie – Abschied von einem Begriff?" *Erwägen Wissen Ethik* 14.3 (2003): 485-498. Print.

Lenz, Karl. *Soziologie der Zweierbeziehung. Eine Einführung.* 4th ed. Wiesbaden: VS Verlag für Sozialwissenschaften, 2009. Print.

Lenz, Karl, and Frank Nestmann. *Handbuch Persönliche Beziehungen.* Weinheim: Juventa-Verlag, 2009. Print.

Mense, Lisa. "Neue Formen von Mutterschaft. Verwandtschaft im Kontext der neuen Reproduktionstechnologien." *Reflexive Körper? Zur Modernisierung von Sexualität und Reproduktion.* Eds. Ilse Lenz, Lisa Mense, and Charlotte Ullrich. Opladen: Leske und Budrich, 2004. Print.

Méritt, Laura, Traude Bührmann, and Nadja Boris Schefzig (eds.). *Mehr als eine Liebe. Polyamouröse Beziehungen.* Berlin: Orlanda, 2005. Print.

Miko, Katharina. *Mit Kind und Kegel – der Übergang von Kernfamilie zu Stieffamilie und wieder zurück. Konstruktion von Familie unter besonderer Berücksichtigung der homosexuellen Stieffamilie.* Diss., University of Vienna, 2007. Print.

Miko, Katharina. "'Danke, ich habe schon genug.' Die freie Wahl, die richtigen Eltern auszusuchen." *Freiheit und Geschlecht. Offene Beziehungen, Prekäre Verhältnisse.* Eds. Marlen Bidwell-Steiner, and Ursula Wagner. Wien: Studienverlag, 2008. 169-184. Print.

Miko, Katharina. "Sexing the family. Aushandlungsprozesse über geschlechtliche und sexuelle Identitäten in der Familie und ihre (rechtlichen) Konsequenzen." *Was heißt normal? Zum Verhältnis von Sexualität und Gesellschaft, SWS-Rundschau* 48.3, 2008. 285-306. Print.

Miko, Katharina, and Karin Sardadvar. FAMinism and FEMilies? "The comeback of the family as a feminist challenge." *New Feminism. Worlds of Feminism, Queer and Networking Conditions.* Eds. Marina Gržinić, and Rosa Reitsamer. Wien: Löcker. 49-56, 2008. Print.

Miko, Katharina, and Karin Sardadvar. "Das Unbehagen visuellen Wissens. Zur theoretischen Fundierung der Beziehung zwischen Geschlechterwissen und visuellem Wissen am Beispiel von 'Familienbildern'." *Körper Wissen Geschlecht. Geschlechterwissen und soziale Praxis II.* Ed. Angelika Wetterer. Königstein: Ulrike Helmer Verlag, 2010. 202-220. Print.

Munson, Marcia, and Judith Stelboum. *The Lesbian Polyamory Reader. Open Relationships, Non-Monogamy, and Casual Sex.* New York: Harrington Press, 1999. Print.

Nave-Herz, Rosemarie. *Ehe- und Familiensoziologie. Eine Einführung in Geschichte, theoretische Ansätze und empirische Befunde.* 2 nd ed. Weinheim: Juventa, 2006. Print.

Nave-Herz, Rosemarie. *Familie heute. Wandel der Familienstrukturen und Folgen für die Erziehung.* 3rd ed. Darmstadt: Primus Verlag, 2007. Print.

O'Reilly, Andrea. *From Motherhood to Mothering: The Legacy of Adrienne Rich's Of Woman Born.* Albany: State University of New York Press, 2004. Print.

Peuckert, Rüdiger. *Familienformen im sozialen Wandel.* 7th ed. Wiesbaden: VS Verlag für Sozialwissenschaften, 2008. Print.

Pühl, Katharina. "Queer Theory in Germany – Potentials, Questions, Critique." A paper presented on the workshop "Feminist Perspectives," Free University Berlin, 26th -27th May 2005. *Gender Politik Online* February 2006. Web.

Rich, Adrienne. *Of Woman Born: Motherhood as Experience and Institution.* New York: W.W. Norton, 1976. Print.

Roseneil, Sasha, and Shelly Budgeon. "Cultures of Intimacy and Care. Beyond 'The Family': Personal Life and Social Change in The Early 21st Century." *Current Sociology* 52.2 (2004): 127-134. Print.

Rubin, Gayle. "Thinking Sex: Notes for a Radical Theory of the Politics of Sexuality." *The Lesbian and Gay Studies.* Eds. Henry Abelove, David Halperin, and Michele Aina Barale. New York: Routledge, 1993. 3-44. Print.

Rubin, Gayle. "Sex denken." *Queer denken. Gegen die Ordnung der Sexualität.* Ed. Andreas Kraß. Frankfurt a.M.: Suhrkamp, 2003. 31-79. Print.

Sardadvar, Karin. *Geteilte Karenz und Geschlechterverhältnis. Erfahrungen aus Schweden, Aufschlüsse für Österreich.* Thesis, University of Vienna, 2004. Print.

Sardadvar, Karin. "Social Construction of Motherhood." *Encyclopedia of Motherhood.* Volume 3. Ed. Andrea O'Reilly. Los Angeles: Sage Publications, 2010. 1133-5. Print.

Sardadvar, Karin. *Späte Mutterschaft. Eine wissenssoziologische Deutungsmusteranalyse.* Diss., University of Vienna, 2010. Print.

Sardadvar, Karin. "'Wir lassen es jetzt drauf ankommen' – Deutungen von Empfängnisverhütung am Beispiel späten Kinderwunsches." *SWS-Rundschau* 50.2 (2010): 228-248. Print.

Sawatzki, Birgit. *Que(e)r zur Familie. Lebensentwürfe lesbischer Mütter.* Marburg: Tectum Verlag, 2004. Print.

Schadler, Cornelia. *Vater, Mutter, Kind werden. Eine posthumanistische Ethnographie der Schwangerschaft.* Bielefeld: Transkript, 2013. Print.

Schütze, Yvonne. *Die gute Mutter. Zur Geschichte des normativen Musters "Mutterliebe."* 2nd ed. Hannover: Kleine, 1991. Print.

Sieder, Reinhard. *Sozialgeschichte der Familie.* Frankfurt a. M.: Suhrkamp, 1987. Print.

Sieder, Reinhard. *Patchworks - das Familienleben getrennter Eltern und ihrer Kinder.* Mit einem Vorwort von Helm Stierlin. Stuttgart: Klett-Cola, 2008. Print.

Stacey, Judith. *Brave New Families. Stories of Domestic Upheaval in Late-Twentieth-Century America.* Berkeley: University of California Press, 1998. Print.

Streib-Brzic, Uli, and Stephanie Gerlach. *Und was sagen die Kinder dazu? Gespräche mit Töchtern und Söhnen lesbischer und schwuler Eltern.* Berlin: Querverlag, 2005. Print.

Thomson, Rachel, Mary Jane Kehily, Lucy Hadfield, and Sue Sharpe. *Making Modern Mothers.* Bristol: Policy Press, 2011. Print.

Weston, Kath. *Families We Choose. Lesbians, Gays, Kinship.* New York: Columbia University Press, 1991. Print.

Woltersdorf, Volker. "Queer Theory und Queer Politics." *Utopie kreativ. Diskussion sozialistischer Alternativen* 156 (2003). Ed. Rosa-Luxemburg-

Stiftung, Berlin. 914-923. Print.

9.

It Could Be So Different

Truth-Telling, Adoption, and Possibility

KELLY JESKE

I ache to tell the truth. There's so much to share that isn't pretty, isn't easy, isn't simple. My truths interrupt cultural narratives surrounding motherhood and lay bare my dynamic and shifting path as a mama. What is it about parenting that reaches under my skin, ignites my passion and my fury? Becoming a mother and loving another being so desperately and unequivocally has turned me inside out, affecting every aspect of my life. I've bumped up against the silences and stories surrounding motherhood, knocking my funny bone against conventionalities and stubbing my toes into the hard places of secrets kept by other mothers. When I tell my truths, I disrupt dominant discourse about parenting, knocking it askew just enough so that I can see my own mothering with new light shining through.

Before I became a parent, I swallowed cultural constructions of motherhood without a sideways glance. I imagined settling into my role as a mother without effort—finding myself happily filled up with mamahood. I was certain that being a mama would bring immeasurable joy and contentment into my life. Becoming a certain kind of mother—a perfect, competent, jubilant one—was something I never doubted, despite my habit of interrogating everything else. I accepted images of beaming, excessively hygienic mothers attending to their delightful, well kempt, accessorized children. In magazines, in movies, and at gatherings, I observed zipped-up mothers who exuded calm satisfaction. Even when I looked to queer role models, I found representations of mothers who were shredding expectations: strapping babies to their backs, climbing and reaching peaks with ease, energized and propelled by motherhood. Perhaps I only saw what I most wanted to, but my vision of motherhood was singular and transparent. Motherhood was a gleaming crystal goblet, shining with possibility and resplendent in its perfection.

Joy. Contentment. Delight. Certainty. Perfection. As I moved into my own parenting reality, I was knocked over by the intensity of my emotions, the brutality of sleep deprivation, and the despair of depression. My daughter's infancy collided with my deepest experience of crushing depression and immobilizing anxiety. While I marveled at the perfection of my daughter's tiny toes one minute, I moved through the murk of fear the next. I stood at the top of the stairs, terrified to move, convinced that I'd tumble and crush my baby—both literally and metaphorically. My daughter slept for no more than two hours at a time and she cried inconsolably for long stretches when she was awake. She'd sleep on my body, but would awaken anytime I tried to lay her down. When she cried, I obsessed about her separation from her birth mother—thinking about the grief they both must be feeling, the longing as their bodies screamed for each other. If my partner and daughter ever left our apartment without me, I shook with fear until they returned, steeling myself for the possibility that I might never see them again. Terror. Doubt. Exhaustion. Shame.

I queer constructs of motherhood by whispering my doubt, by scraping my nails along vestiges of strength, and by screaming out my truths. I queer motherhood by disarming images of perfection—tearing out magazine pages and setting them on fire, watching as flames lick at smiling and aproned clone mothers. I queer motherhood by owning my devastation as fully as I own my joy, by speaking my despair as readily as I speak my wonder, and by illuminating my otherness as brightly as I illuminate my desire to belong. So many times, during my first years as a mother, I felt a visceral sense of betrayal: why hadn't anyone told me how fucking hard it is to be a parent? Why didn't anyone share their wailing, raging, disintegrating moments? When mothers zip up, suit up, and put masks over our pain and uncertainty, we contribute to the silencing and erasure of other mothers. We flaunt our good days as if they are all there is, leaving folks who are struggling alone with the chill of doubt. It could be so different: mothers speaking our truths as we live them—sharing our strengths and our fears, our misses and our triumphs. Allowing ourselves imperfection and rawness and uncertainty.

When my daughter was a baby, as my depression and anxiety began to swallow me, I convinced myself that she'd be better off without me. Over and over again, my fear swelled that, as her mama, I'd irrevocably fuck her up. Driving down Southeast Powell Boulevard at rush hour, I repeatedly envisioned myself swerving into oncoming traffic. I could feel my hands clenching the wheel, my arms engaging muscles to cut sharply to the left, the jarring impact of metal and speed, the deafening squeal and blast of collision. I was wrung out, desolate, and terrified. I feared that I wasn't up to the task of motherhood—I mourned my daughter's loss of her first mother, I knew I couldn't be perfect enough to make it up to her (as if anything could), and I berated myself for the desperation I felt during my long days alone with her. I loathed myself for being so scared, for being so sad, and I was sure that my frailties would harm my daughter.

These are my truths. These are some of the devastating places I've inhabited as a mother. I did not parent the baby who would lie on a blanket and coo softly at her toys. I did not parent the baby who slept through the night. I did not parent the baby who could be content out of my arms. I mothered the toddler who slammed her head against the hardwood floor, again and again. I mothered the toddler who slapped herself in the face when she was frustrated. I mothered the toddler who shrieked and raged and threw things at me in the middle of the night. I mothered the preschooler who dissolved into angry tirades as we crossed the threshold of her preschool to head home. I mother a child who trusts me to hold her rage and fear and falling apart, who looks to me to share my strategies for keeping in one piece, who—oh, I hope—sees bountiful and unusual possibility by witnessing the raw complexity of my life. For her, I queer my own scripts about motherhood. I fuck with the imperatives by embracing my vulnerability. For her, I risk to tell the truth.

It was winter on the Oregon coast. The sky bloomed with the deep colors of a bruise settling across skin: the soft gray of a mouse's fur, charcoal streaking paper, seashell shimmers strewn throughout. Sharp, cold rain pelted staccato on my cheeks, with the wind acting as a rough towel—stiff and scouring as if it'd been laid out in the sun to dry in rigid peaks. I screamed my anguish into the wind, with Mama Ocean's roar mocking the smallness of my voice. I felt inconsequential and erased here, as if my pain were mere drollery up against the reality of the rest of the world. The ocean welled up, crested, and exploded again and again, washing broken bits onto the shore, pounding out a rhythm of unfurling. In the face of the ocean, I felt at once relieved and indicted. I felt the urgency of my distress like a kick in the stomach—it knocked the breath out of my diaphragm and sent me running for my dimly lit hotel room. Closing the door against the storming night, I eased open the bedside table and pulled out the white pages.

Guns? Ammunition? Where do people buy these things? For a brief—but terrifying—few moments, I knew that I needed to disappear. I needed to go away so that my pain couldn't reach my daughter. There, in that hotel room like so many others, I imagined my body reduced to the bits of myself: blood and bones just fragments scattered without reason. I imagined the mess I felt inside exploded onto the walls, the polyester bedspread, and the veneered wood furniture. I imagined the relief of exhaling once and for all.

When I think back to those days, I am angry beyond belief. Alone, surrounded by apparitions of perfect parenthood, I had fallen into a sinkhole of despair. I might have stepped over it entirely, or clambered from its depths with the appearance of a rope connecting me to other imperfectly embodied mothers. But in the earliest days of my mothering, there were no ropes, no other mothers, and no voices to interrupt my certainty of failure. It was only later that I happened into the embrace of other mamas who dared to speak their struggles and fears. In the basement of a solid graystoned Presbyterian church, under the warm gaze of a breastfeeding pastor, I found my mirrors in two other queer mamas who were parenting toddlers close in age to my daughter. On weekday mornings, we journeyed to this island of mothers and children—changing diapers, offering snacks, negotiating space and toys and mobility—where it was safe to murmur out fears to each other, leaning close to breathe in the cadence of each other's words. Pouring Goldfish crackers out of an enormous carton, melting into nubby plaid recliners, and witnessing our children reach towards connection, we dared to voice our unspeakable truths: terror, sadness, boredom, rage.

In the church play park, I tasted the delicious relief of revealing what I'd worked so hard to keep hidden. I smiled and cooed and laughed and played, but I also cried and whispered out the pain I'd been carrying around. I told about the stairs, I told about the crashing car, I told about the plan to buy a gun. I told about the days that felt endless and the ones where any movement at all came with exhausting effort. I told. And they reciprocated with their own stories of anguish. Peppered throughout our time together was a running commentary of wonder: our beautiful, capable, adaptable children simply amazed us. We'd never felt love like this before. We'd never imagined it possible to find so much joy in mundane days. Rushing through our conversations like water, leaving us breathless, was our love for our children. In this space, I became whole as a mama. I came back to myself as a whole person. With love in their eyes, my friends held me. And they held me up. My friends allowed me the support I needed to begin to reach towards my own best ways of caring for myself and for my daughter simultaneously. They reminded me that I needed to be whole and fed and resourced in order to parent the way I wanted to.

Here's the thing: I am not a perfect parent. I do not fit idyllic visions of what a mother should be, and I am not even *the* perfect parent for my daughter. I came to parenting flawed and—once a parent—met parts of myself that I'd never seen before. I dance and play and connect, but I also disengage and tantrum. Sometimes my frustration flutters into my chest, wraps around my neck, and pounds in my head until I have to sequester myself in the bathroom. I can hold space for my daughter's rage some of the time, but other times my fists clench and I can't stop myself from slamming the door or throwing the partner to the shoe she's just launched across the room. I am a queer, fat, chronically ill mama who battles depression and anxiety. I embrace radical, edgy, models of relationship and sexuality. I connect deeply with people and reject the suggestion that I should be fulfilled by material things. I don't believe anymore that there is such a thing as a perfect parent. My shoulders soften with the resonance that comes from hearing the strange chorus of imperfect parents all around me. I melt into the certainty that the voices screaming that I'm not enough, that other parents are inadequate, are coming from outside of myself. And they are power-hungry apparitions.

The saviour rhetoric of adoption suggests that children who are adopted will have a better life than if they stay with the families they're born to. Oftentimes, that "better" life is a capitalistic vision of financial plenty and the heteronormative nuclear family. In such a vision, poor folks and single parents are passed over as deficient. Adoptive parents are framed as benevolent saviours—especially if they're white folks adopting children of color. When people learn that my daughter was adopted, I often hear some version of: "Oh, how wonderful for her." Even when it's not explicitly voiced, I can hear the implication that I am doing something extraordinary in choosing to adopt a child. Even more so because she is brown-skinned. They say it like I've accomplished some feat that should be lauded and accompanied by a prize. They say it like there's no possibility that my daughter might have thrived with her birth family.

This is a ridiculously unwarranted assumption. People offer up their stunning bits of wisdom despite knowing nothing about my child's birth family. I can practically taste their Dickensian images of tattered rags and Reagan-era news clips shrieking about the epidemic of crack babies. The grief and trauma of adoption are smoothed and ironed out by these assumptions in order to make it more adoption palatable to adoptive parents, agencies, and to larger society. If first parents are constructed as inferior and unworthy, then everyone can just feel better about the whole enterprise. As long as first parents are demonized, the violence of parent-child separation is downplayed. Deeming first parents unworthy of parenting lifts adoptive parents into an exalted social position where privilege roots, spreads, and smothers out the possibility of anything else.

Who the hell can state with certainty that adoption is better for any child? Wrought with assumptions and privilege, the saviour complex erases the complexity of lived experience and whitewashes over the reality of oppressive social institutions. How does anyone know that my daughter is better off with me and with my ex-partner than she would have been with her first mom and birth family? The truth is that we don't know. In fact, we can guess that she might be better supported in her racial identity as a person of color if raised by her black first mother, instead of by two white women. Shared identity, history, and the physical connection of gestation and birth matter so much. My daughter grew in her mother's body, from her mother's body, with her voice, her rhythm, and her emotions as her own. When I see my daughter in her birth mom's arms, I imagine what life might have been like for the two of them to stay together. When it's time to end our visits, sobs are birthed as deep aches in my chest that crawl into my throat where I swallow them like dry bread. I wonder if they're choking, too.

I don't buy the rhetoric that says children need a particular type of parent or model of family to thrive. Voices from all over the political spectrum bellow out a standardized notion of family that attempts to prescribe models for success. I call bullshit. These voices aren't interested in the wellness of children; they're scrambling to maintain power and privilege in the hands of a few. Even progressive voices tend towards a politic of assimilation, pigeonholing, and uniformity. Discourse about children needing *both* parents and about the crisis of single motherhood creates a thinly veiled heteronormative ideal of parenthood that attempts to squelch all others. When culture strives for homogeneity, so much beauty is lost. When definitions of family are constricted, children suffer. Love seeps under doors slammed on single mamas and queer papas and grandparents raising children. Nurturing swells around the joints of cages intended to keep poor folks, people of color, chronically ill parents, and other outsiders separated from legitimized family. My daughter announces proudly that she has three mothers, she claims her dearest adult as an uncle even though he's not related by blood, and she beams with joy about her little brother who is the child of dear friends. We all have much to gain through expanding definitions of family, and by broadening kinship by choice.

I live next door to my ex-partner. In fact, my apartment shares a wall with hers. After fourteen years and a child together, we admitted that we were irrevocably estranged. Our daughter moves between our two homes without having to leave our shared duplex. When I was deliberating the possibility of divorce, I agonized over an image of my 6-year-old hefting a suitcase as she walked away from me. I saw her tears and bewilderment, meltdowns about belongings that couldn't move from place to place, and gut-wrenching goodbyes. These fears pierced me with such sharpness that I might have stayed in the relationship for twelve more years, if offered that option. My daughter's family terrain had already changed irrevocably once before, when my partner and I became her parents through adoption on the day after she was born. I couldn't bear the thought of this family dissolving into disconnected halves. I suggested that we find a duplex where we could rent both sides and still, sort of, inhabit one home.

When I imagined this solution to our divorce, I hoped we could soften the blow of our separation for our daughter. As a mother, I realized that I held the power to conduct myself in accordance with my wishes for my daughter. I could construct our divorce and future life in ways that supported her sense of security and family. I imagined that living in a duplex might allow her to continue on with her existing sense of family, despite our divorce. I pictured the way we'd throw a joint housewarming party, with our friends and loved ones filling our rooms. I imagined us sharing family dinners on the patio in the summer, and taking turns hosting soup suppers by the fire in the winter. I envisioned my daughter in her pajamas, bursting through my door to say goodnight before snuggling in with her Momo for the evening. A duplex, I thought, might pad the edges of our changing family, offering us possibilities for seamlessly shifting into our new reality.

Unexpectedly, this living arrangement created incredible emotional difficulty for me—second only to living in the same house, which my family did for the first eight months after my ex-partner and I decided to separate. I still grieve the dissolution of the family we had shared since our daughter was born and we were chosen to be her mothers. Sometimes with gulping sobs, sometimes with trembling anger, sometimes with numbed-out confusion, I process the loss of my family, my home, and my certainty. Some days, it feels like an unsettling dream that I can't shake upon waking, one that clings to my eyelashes and fogs my vision. It seems impossible then—impossible that this world can shift so treacherously that I can't stay upright, that my comfort can shatter into bits.

In this duplex, I can hear as my ex-partner walks across her floors, I can hear her toilet flush, and I can hear her laughing with guests. In the early days of our divorce, she seemed so damn joyful and sunny all the time—as if our parting was of little consequence. I woke myself from constrictive ruminations on the terrible way she'd moved on so quickly. Our daughter moves freely between our apartments when we're both at home, and through our open front doors some weeks ago, I overheard my ex-partner calling someone "baby" and expressing her love on the telephone. Hearing the phone call ignited a searing pain in my chest, a low boil in my belly. Sure, I wished my ex-partner well, but witnessing her joy punched me in the gut, made me double over on my intention to be strong and resilient. I longed for some distance to facilitate my own healing. I dreaded our interactions on the days when I was particularly hurting over our divorce—it would have been so much easier to move through my grief and anger without frequent crossings. In this situation, going with ease would require a selfishness that I'm not willing to enact. I prefer to shoulder the brunt of the difficulty so that my daughter might duck under some of the most brutal waves of our transition. If I take on the discomfort of proximity, then she gets to remain close to both of her parents. There have been days when I've wanted to run far away from my ex-partner, hide out where she couldn't see me, rebuild a life that she couldn't witness—but if I did, my daughter couldn't easily snuggle on the couch to read bedtime stories with me or jump into my living room to show me her newest creation. By taking on the intensity of negotiating healing in close contact with my ex, I have allowed myself to hold on to as much time with my daughter as possible. I also imagine that, in continuing to move as a family, our child is able to witness the buoyancy of possibility. We're modeling that family can shift without coming apart, that love can bend and twist without breaking, and that change can reap incredible growth.

The queers I call friends seem to do family a bit differently than other folks. Many of us maintain friendships with our exes, and we tend towards building chosen families of people who welcome and hold us in our complexities. Even as I grieve my divorce and smart at the meaning I assign to my ex-partner's actions, I still value her deeply. I spent fourteen formative years with her, from twenty-one to thirty-five. With her, I navigated the terrain of buying and selling a house, I learned to drive on the freeway, and I achieved my first master's degree. I suffered through health crises and surgeries in her arms. We held each other through the deaths of loved ones, dismantled and remade ourselves. We built a vibrant community together and delved into ourselves. When we finally moved toward parenthood, we had already spent years longing for a child and collaborating to create a home. She is my child's parent. Even without our connection as partners, she inhabits a sacred place in my life. My daughter deserves to see her Momo regarded with love and treated with respect. Nurtured and guided by her, my daughter intrinsically feels herself connected to her Momo, maybe even understands her Momo as a part of herself.

I cherish my place in the constellation of our family—just one of the many points that come together to create identities, harbors, and blueprints for our child. I am adamantly committed to queering the way we do family so that our daughter can grow certain of her place in the world within a loving and nurturing community of people who are devoted to her. Even through adoption, even through divorce, I strive to create space where my daughter can rest in the certainty of all of her parents' love for her. In tending the containers of family and community, we construct a reality where love is centred. In this centering, I am free to embody myself: my intensities, my paradoxes, the ways I struggle, and the ways I shine. I can step into my truths and invite my daughter to do so in her own ways. If I'm not hiding and reaching for artifice, my body hums with the relief of opening. If I am present and allow myself to truly show up for the vast diversity of my experience, I am better equipped to hold my child's complexity as well.

I didn't sign on to mamahood to be a half-time parent. I want to be with my kid every day—for the mundanity of tooth-brushing and weeknight dinners. I want to see her when she first wakes up every morning and before she falls asleep at night. I want her to experience me as consistently, unshakably present. But divorce changes all of that—even when I'm living next door. Now I parent my daughter three-and-a-half days each week. I watch her depart on family trips with my ex-partner's parents and extended family—the same trips I took for fourteen years. I miss full days of my daughter's life and I long for the moments that are lived away from me. Even a year into this, I still ache when I'm away from my kid, and I battle guilt for the times when she's reaching for me. I spent three years at home with my daughter, with days where we were in physical contact for twenty-four hours at a stretch. When we're apart, I feel a visceral strain—like we're attached by a cord that is overstretched, one that might snap at any moment.

But being apart also allows us to grow and expand, both together and individually. In my time away from my daughter, I tend to the parts of myself that require stillness and quiet, the parts that invite screaming and raging. I loosen my grip on holding everything together. The softness of my belly folds into itself as I round my shoulders over the expanse of my vulnerability. I feel the ache of my desire, slick wetness pooling between my legs, longing in my heart. I write. I fuck. I spend too much money. I scream. I eat popcorn. I gaze into the eyes of those I love. I laugh. I inhale campfire smoke. I binge on sugar. I read like I'm starving and words might save me. And when my daughter comes back to me, her bright eyes hook into my heart. Her silly stories ignite buoyant joy. We dance together to YouTube recordings of dance video games, sweaty and breathless. I chase her through our rooms, snapping my arms like an alligator's jaws, eliciting terrified and jubilant shrieks. We revel in each other's brightness—igniting light and reflecting it back. I am created through our connection and sustained in our parting. We fuel up together to do the work of becoming ourselves apart.

It has taken all of my daughter's six-and-three-quarter's years of growing for me to come into myself as a mama—and it's clear that I've only walked through the front door. As I've tried on my own power, my own voice, my own footsteps, I've tuned into other parents whose embodied lives glow like beacons. Centering on their warm lights, I urge myself to join their gatherings, trailing the lure of genuine connection. I am not my mistakes or my frailties, but I'm also not en route towards perfection. By shifting my gaze and reimagining motherhood as a place of contradiction, as a borderland of complexity, as a place where I can stand in truth, I make my way towards a new world with my daughter's hand securely in mine.

10.

Becoming Papa

From Daughter to Dad

T. GARNER

He's a storyteller, one of the best I know. He wraps me up in stories after dinner, smoking cigarettes together in his office. His cigarettes burn my throat, they're stronger than I'm used to, but I don't show it. I just listen as he winds tales around me.

His belief is so strong it rubs off on everyone and we all start to believe that he's just about to make a million, enough to buy that island he's always wanted. It doesn't matter that he's always just about to make a million. It doesn't matter that he never does. It doesn't even matter that he never will. What he's really selling are stories and the chance to play a starring role in them.

And when he gets up from the dinner table and puts his hand on my shoulder, he gives me that chance. He leads the way and I follow him in, gratefully leaving the others at the table. He's wearing suspenders stretched over his big belly, with a scotch in one hand and a cigarette in the other. He calls me scientist and expects me to understand his world. I do but I'm afraid of what happens when I don't. It's exhilarating being spun into a story, fearing the time when the words come crashing down. I live for those moments when I make him laugh out loud and he slaps me on the back.

> We spend a long time in there; neither of us wants the story to end. When we eventually come out, he doesn't let it. 'We just had a man-to-man chat' he announces as we walk into the kitchen. That makes me glow, that the 'we' includes me. He's joking but we both know he's not. After all, I'm the closest he's going to get to a son-in-law.
>
> I love all his stories but the one about me is my favourite.

As "papa" to three young children but most often read as "mama" in public, I live at the intersection of motherhood and fatherhood. As I try to derail the naturalised story of motherhood written onto my body from birth, and rewrite the transition to parenthood as a path from daughter to dad, my situation gives me a unique perspective. I constantly rub against normative assumptions, the friction making their social construction visible. My "queer" embodiment of fatherhood is marked by a failure to fully achieve the social status of fatherhood, which allows me to explore some challenging and productive questions about gender, sexuality, and parenthood. How is the category of "dad" naturalised? What does it mean to be a "father" once the biological "ground" of maleness is removed? How can one embody genderqueer parenthood? However, as well as engaging with the challenges of parenting beyond the binaries of sex and gender, I also want to affirm genderqueer parenthood as a source of knowledge and pleasure. Becoming "papa" is a story of joy and pain, gain and loss, and I would not change it for the world.

This chapter is an auto-ethnographic exploration of the attempt to occupy genderqueer parenthood as a female-assigned, trans-identified person. In contrast to the proliferation of academic and popular discourse on gay and lesbian families, there has been a relative absence of exploration of transgender parenting. Neglected within both sociologies of the family and mainstream gender research, the exclusion of transgender lives and experiences from these analytical frameworks means that they "rest on an uninformative and naturalized binary gender model that recognizes only male or female gender categories" (Hines 355). My reflections on trans parenting hope to address this lacuna and challenge the naturalized foundation of the sexual binary. In doing this work, I recognize that my experience as a trans parent can only be understood and expressed as such relatively recently. Drawing on Sandell's point that "... men and women have, for years, formed committed same-sex relationships, and had children, but what is relatively new is for men and women to self-identify as being part of a gay or lesbian family, and to have children with that identity" (qtd. in Hines 368), Hines asserts that, while the phenomenon of transgender parenting is not new, "self-identifying as a trans parent is a recent social development" (Hines 368).

The shift from act to identity, highlighted most notably by Michel Foucault (*History of Sexuality, Vol. 1*), is significant because it provides the conditions of possibility for the practice of trans parenting and the discursive moment of self-reflection. This piece is a collection of these moments; rather than a chronological narrative, it draws from past, present and future and mixes them together in the hopes of highlighting some of the most significant themes in my experience of becoming "papa." Forgive the lack of order; it is messy, just as life is.

> October 18, 2006: *sinking*
> I don't know if I'm a boy or a girl
> I don't know if home is here or there
> I don't know if there's any space in between 'he' and 'she,' and I don't know if I can squeeze in there
> I don't know if what I see in the mirror is real
> I don't know how to be true to my self, especially when my self is quite possibly some kind of 'discursive hallucination produced by a complex system of power relations'
> I don't know if I want to feel stubble on my face in the same way that you want to feel a size 4 against your skin
> I don't know if I want to be Brad Pitt like you want to be Angelina Jolie
> I don't know what other people see when they look at me
> I don't know what my children will think of me
> I don't know where all this doubt comes from
> I don't know if I can be this.

Looking back, I realize how far having children has brought me in providing me with more stability or, perhaps, in making this instability more liveable than before. I still don't know what other people see when they look at me, and that can be very disorienting in negotiating social contexts. But now I do know what my children think of me and much of my doubt about myself has dissipated. My children recognize me and love me as their "papa." We play and hug, wrestle and talk, read and draw, laugh and cry, and through all of these everyday practices of family care and intimacy, their recognition and love produces "papa" as a category of fatherhood that I can and do embody.

There is no misrecognition with my children because we operate within a conceptual and corporeal logic that we have created. We have lived this set of relationships and bodies since they were born. I have twin sons and a daughter (at least that's how they identify now), and they have a "mama" and a "papa." When my brother asks, 'Isn't it confusing for the kids?' he's the one that's confused, not them. Children are capable of complex ideas; in fact, they are more capable than most because their thoughts are not yet limited by traditional beliefs. For me, "papa" has become my primary gender marker, a better fit than woman or man, "mom" or "dad." Although my partner and I know that this framework of reference is in opposition to the dominant paradigm, my children don't. At least, not yet.

> March 10, 2010
> Right now, they just love me. Pure and simple. No questions asked. I'm here for them and they know that. I'm loving this age but, at the same time, it feels so fragile.
>
> Last night, we had dinner at one of the regular haunts we visit when we're feeling exhausted and overwhelmed (read: often): the local White Spot. The elderly woman behind me was quite taken with one of the twins (who wouldn't be?) and started chatting to him. He responded by reaching out with a straw and babbling at her, and then turned to poke me with the straw, at which she said, "Is that your daddy?"
>
> How terrible to feel both joy and sadness in response to such a simple question. Yes, I'm his dad but, if I turn around or say something, would you still think so?
>
> My partner and I exchanged a look weighed down with years of conversations about moments like this, but the kids were blissfully oblivious and continued to smear macaroni and cheese all over the table.
>
> They don't know the difference between boys and girls, and I wish it could stay that way.

Being rendered voiceless is a common experience for me. Not trusting my voice to maintain the reading of me, I have often chosen silence rather than disruption. The only way I could embody 'dad' in the moment was through the erasure of my voice. Staying silent is not a deceptive act—my voice does not reveal the reality of my embodiment. We come into being or, in other words, we become in the space between self and other, not as self and other, to the extent that there is no self and other, only space between. Drawing on Deleuze and Guattari's notion of becoming, Braidotti describes, "neither a sacralised inner sanctum, nor a pure socially shaped entity, the enfleshed Deleuzian subject is rather an 'in-between': it is a folding-in of external influences and a simultaneous unfolding outwards of affects" (159). In other words, the affective body of becoming "is as much outside itself as in itself – webbed in its relations – until ultimately such firm distinctions cease to matter" (Seigworth and Gregg 3). This is what Barad describes, in her iteration of "new materialism," as the "intra-active" character of materiality – the idea that 'things' do not precede their interactions but emerge through them (392). Thus becoming is inherently unstable. Uncomfortable though it often is, my experience is not unique. It simply makes visible this ontological instability.

Through the notion of becoming, I situate my personal experience within a political and theoretical framework that draws upon feminist theory, transgender studies, and queer theory, in particular, scholarship that highlights the contingency of current conceptions of the sexed (and raced, classed, and disabled) body, and focuses on the ways in which these beliefs are produced and naturalized (Butler *Bodies That Matter*, *Gender Trouble*; Davis *Enforcing Normalcy*; Foucault *History of Sexuality, Vol. 1*; Grosz *Volatile Bodies*; Haraway *Simians, Cyborgs, and Women*; Heyes *Self Transformations*; Laqueur *Making Sex*; Shildrick *Leaky Bodies*; Stryker "My Words"; Sullivan "Somatechnics"). The recognition that bodies are constituted through multiple forms of knowledges, spatial relations and practices, institutional and political regulations, and other culturally and historically located social "imaginaries" (Gatens *Imaginary Bodies* viii) provides a way of thinking beyond the natural versus constructed binary, a binary that is often used against transgender people. This perspective is described by Jennifer Terry and Jacqueline Urla in their introduction to *Deviant Bodies: Critical Perspectives on Difference in Science and Popular Culture*:

> Bodies do not exist in terms of an a priori essence, anterior to techniques and practices that are imposed upon them. They are neither transhistorical sets of needs and desires nor natural objects preexisting cultural (and, indeed, scientific)

> representation. They are effects, products, or symptoms of specific techniques and regulatory practices... Knowable only through culture and history, they are not in any simple way natural or ever free of relations of power. (3)

This idea has been taken up by some transgender and queer theorists within the framework of "somatechnics," which is a reconceptualization of the body, technology, and the relation between them. Outlined in the first book-length edited collection that engages with this concept, *Somatechnics: Queering the Technologisation of Bodies*, Nikki Sullivan and Samantha Murray define somatechnics as:

> an attempt to highlight the inextricability of soma and techne, of 'the body' (as a culturally intelligible construct) and the techniques (dispositifs and 'hard technologies') in and through which corporealities are formed and transformed. This term, derived from the Greek soma (body) and τεχνη (craftsmanship), supplants the logic of the 'and,' suggesting that technes are not something we add or apply to the body, nor are they tools the embodied self employs to its own ends. Rather, technes are the dynamic means in and through which corporealities are crafted, that is, continuously engendered in relation to others and to a world. (3)

Providing a challenge to the notion of static bodily being, somatechnics is grounded in the idea that, as Sullivan emphasizes elsewhere, all bodies are "entwined in (un)becoming," or, in other words, that "all bodies mark and are marked" ("Transmogrification" 561). The naturalization of the categories of "mom" and "dad" relies on a notion of biological continuity between sex, gender and parenthood, and erases the ways in which sexed bodies are engaged in a process of becoming "mom" or "dad." In contrast, my embodiment as genderqueer, as a body that has not experienced pregnancy but has gone through chest surgery, makes visible the operations involved in becoming "papa" and, by implication, in becoming "mom" or "dad."

In this work, I am joining Andrea Doucet in addressing the absence of the body in analyses of care and family, an absence that she notes is both understandable and surprising (298): understandable because of the history of biological essentialism that has been used to deny women equality and is particularly associated with parental care and domestic labour; but surprising because parents (and children) are clearly not disembodied subjects. In fact, Doucet finds in her exploration that the "weight of embodiment" permeates fathers' narratives of care giving (288). However, in her attempt to re-insert the body in her analysis, it is "not the body per se but the shifting material-discursive intra-actions of bodies across time and space" (299). My approach builds on Doucet's understanding of materiality as "a choreography of becoming" (300).

> What's in a name?
> I thought endlessly about what I would say when they asked. I replayed conversations, anticipating their question but never finding the perfect response. Because there isn't one.
> But then they never asked. I waited, I anticipated, I worried, but the question I imagined over and over again never came. They simply assumed.
> I thought my partner would occupy "mom" leaving me something else. But there was no something else. There was only "mom" or "dad." Sometimes I make it into "dad" but mostly, without my consent, I am "mommed."
> When and how to confront it is a dance. Mostly, I let it slide. Or I let my partner and the kids do the work of naming me and bringing me into existence. When my son says, "She's my papa," I know I am contained within that sentence. Within every word and between every word. There is space in there for me.

I started off as "dad" but it felt too hard to occupy. It was too far away from my name, my body, my history, and from the comfort of many. It remained unsaid or as a stumbling block.

So I settled on "papa." It fits. It allowed the conceptual and corporeal logic of the immediate family to extend, so that others are now engaged in the becoming of me as "papa." Not everyone, of course, but the important parts of a familial and community network.

In her exploration of trans parenting, Hines identifies the name change, part of the "linguistic shifts which accompany changes in gender identity," as a significant issue (366). I wasn't transitioning (in this sense anyway) nor were my kids (they were only just born), but the other people around me had to. Just as Dan, in Hines' case study, thought it "made things a hell of a lot easier" for his son to deal with the transition if he became "Danny" instead of "dad," it has been easier for me to be "papa" than "dad." That's a transition that others have been able to make in relation to me. It creates a space between that I can walk through.

I recognise the racial and cultural nature of this comfort. For many cultures and languages, "papa" is the equivalent of "dad" or "father." It's only in this white, English-speaking, middle-class, North American culture that there is a distance between "papa" and "dad" to the extent that "papa" is always 'not-quite' "dad." Only in this white culture could "papa" be said in reference to me, my name, my body, my history. Am I guilty of appropriation? Am I inserting and imposing gender-queerness on to a culturally-specific form of fatherhood? Am I maintaining the connection between racialization and feminization? I could have gone with some other name; supposedly, 'a rose by any other name would smell as sweet.'

But that's simply not the case. The guilt of those questions weighs heavily but the denomination of "papa" allows me to live. I need to borrow some of the cultural legitimacy of that fatherhood and live it within this white culture. It, at least, makes me 'not-quite,' (the story of my life) but not 'not-at-all.' Every utterance maintains proximity to the category of "dad" without placing me in it, and that's where I live to be.

I was surprised that some people are offended when I softly correct them after they "mom" me. I realize now that it's because I interrupt their expression of tolerance, their public affirmation of a queer family, their practice of "queer-friendliness" that has come to mark this North American city. They are well versed in acceptance, but then I disrupt the narrative. They literally don't know what to do with "papa," both my name and me. Tolerance, by definition, doesn't quite stretch far enough.

In some ways, appealing to the dominant transgender narrative, which is structured around a 'before and after,' a 'from and to,' would re-contain these moments, allowing them to slip into another understandable story, at least in this historical and cultural moment, under the rubric of "queer-friendly." However, the lack of a traditional transition story in my case denies this possibility.

The focus on transition as the central feature of the traditional transgender narrative is grounded in a static ontology of being – there may be movement but it must be absolute and uni-directional; transition is understood to be from one sexed category to another, (although it is never fully achieved because these categories are thought to be mutually exclusive). It denies all other intersectional axes of embodiment and brings only sex into view. My own experience repudiates what one might call "mono-optics" and incorporates, in particular, the nuances of age, gender and parenthood (or, more broadly, being with others) – without my children, I am (mis)recognized as a teenage boy, but with my children, I age into a "mom." In those rare moments when I am not aged, it's an interesting experience being a teenage father. This happened once when my partner and I were in an ultrasound appointment seeing the twins in black and white on the screen. I enjoyed receiving the mix of pride and maternal protection from the ultrasound technician, an older woman intent on passing on her advice. It's not often I feel such warmth from others.

In contrast to the dominant understanding of transition in relation to transsexuality, transition is constant in an ontological perspective based on becoming, never reducible to a single time span. Becoming is by definition transition. Thus, transition is not mine but all of ours. From daughter to dad does not just refer to me but my whole family.

> Tractor-Trailing
> My dad was driving me to school, which was unusual and I definitely wasn't pleased about it. I was going through a time when I hated my dad. He didn't really do anything wrong, it's just everything he did was wrong.
>
> So we're driving to school and we're stuck behind a long line of traffic trailing behind a tractor. This happened a lot where I lived so there were some unspoken rules about how to deal with this situation – the first car in the line waits for a break in the oncoming traffic, overtakes the tractor, and then all the cars behind move up one position. This can take a while because the road is narrow and there are lots of corners. But this is England. We're good at waiting patiently in line.
>
> Not my dad though. I could see his temper rising. He didn't shout—it was the silence that let me know he was raging. I sunk down into my seat while he attempted to overtake. He would veer to the right and then snap back into line as the traffic streamed past on the other side of the road. Eventually there was a gap. He sped up until he was practically touching the car in front. As the gap opened, he slammed the steering wheel to the right and gunned the accelerator. I closed my eyes. When I opened them, a car was coming directly at us. At the last moment, my dad veered back into line to the sound of car horns on all sides. My heart was racing. When I looked

> over at my dad, I could see a triumphant smile at the very corners of his mouth. He had overtaken one car.
>
> We repeated this game of chicken, one car at a time, until we eventually overtook the tractor and were on open road. I breathed again. We had broken all the rules, but at least now I might make it to school alive. We pulled up at a set of traffic lights and I heard the sound of a car door slamming. My dad looked in the rear view mirror and, without a word, reached over me and locked my door. Just as he locked his own, a man's face filled his window and shouted. I couldn't make out what he was saying but I got the idea. This was one of the drivers my dad had cut up. He screamed at us and tried to open the door. My dad just looked straight ahead, resolutely not making eye contact with him. The man hit the window with the heel of his hand and when that didn't work he moved to the front of the car, slamming his fist on the hood.
>
> The lights went green and my dad put the car in gear and tried to drive away. The man threw his body onto the hood, but he slid off and tried to hold onto the side mirror. We kept going and, as a final last attempt to make his point, he smashed his hand against the back of the car. We drove off with that thud. I looked over at my dad, he was still staring straight ahead. Neither of us said anything.

I have my dad's silent rage but, thankfully, it's tempered by my mom's abundant patience, so my kids rarely see it. I also have my dad's ability to stare straight ahead after breaking the rules. Like him, I keep going rather than taking up the fight. He rubs up against mainstream notions of masculinity and perhaps that has helped me do the same. Although we never talk about it, it's reassuring that he shares the concern of not embodying masculinity and fatherhood adequately. I think he nailed the absent father typical of his generation, but he recently revealed that he was jealous that my brother spent much of his teenagehood with another family where the other father was physically active and enjoyed playing and watching sports. My father enjoyed opera while other boys played cricket. My father talks about classical music while other men recount sports games. Throughout the stories my dad tells of his life, especially his childhood, his lack of interest in sports and the consequences of that is a recurring theme. In his explanation of this lack, he uses the excuse of over-competitiveness, an attempt to appeal to a masculine characteristic. Clearly, the strength of the association between physicality and masculinity has had an impact on my dad's life. For me, at least theoretically although not necessarily emotionally, I know that the ideal of masculinity that my dad is always measuring himself against is unattainable. My embodiment provides some reassuring distance from it and what I can learn from my dad is that any insecurity I feel is actually emblematic of maleness and fatherhood. As Stephen J. Ducat emphasizes, there is:

> a particular fear that has composed the very foundation of male selfhood from antiquity to the modern era...It is the fear of being feminized. For many men, masculinity is a hard-won, yet precarious and brittle psychological achievement that must be constantly proven and defended. While the external factors may appear to be that which is most threatening – gay men in military shower rooms, feminist women in civilian bedrooms, or audible female footsteps in the Taliban-era marketplace – the actual threat that many men experience is an unconscious, internal one: the sense that they are not "real" men. (1)

I simultaneously feel this insecurity and am protected from it because, while feminization is not comfortable for me, it is generally expected. For good and bad, I am not often situated in a position where my embodiment is measured against the ideal of "real" man.

I can't remember relating to my father in a particular, defined way as a daughter (or son). I certainly wasn't a 'daddy's girl.' There was a line drawn in the family and I was on my mother's side. More than a daughter, I became her confidante, her best friend. Now my mom misses me, not just because I live geographically far away, but more significantly because I am not the daughter I once was or she imagined me to be. In many ways, she's become closer to my partner who embodies the stay-at-home mom that my mom was. In this reflection on my parenthood, I have great respect for my parents. As any relatively new parent, only now do I realize what my parents gave me. I recognize that my dad gave me an inquiring nature that grounds my approach to life; and I know that my mom gave me love and time, through which to nurture that curiosity. I enter parenthood with those two figures, my "mom" and my "dad," never far from view, for good and bad. They still see me as their daughter, and I am and always will be, but I've also travelled far from there on a journey they don't recognize and often have difficulty following.

My older brother has now become a "dad" and I envy the ease with which he occupies the category. Where my becoming is always visible, his is erased; where my becoming is work – for me, my children, my partner, and others – his appears effortless. When he changes a diaper, he is congratulated; when he takes his son to swimming lessons, he is seen to be so involved; when he goes to work, he is the good breadwinner; quite simply, he is "dad." He embodies the "father-son" relationship. Sometimes, it seems as if my parenthood is invisible to my parents because they cannot recognize me as "dad" like my brother or "mom" like my partner. Despite the fact that we are a relatively homonormative family, with me occupying the role of breadwinner and my partner being a home-maker above all else, we are far from recognized as normative. Becoming "papa" is a journey into "no-man's land;" the terrain is unfamiliar and indescribable to many. Through this exploration of the "choreography of becoming" (Doucet 300), I have offered you a few dance moves to trace that landscape, this iteration of genderqueer fatherhood. The instability I live with makes visible the inherent instability of masculinity, fatherhood, and materiality itself, highlighting its "intra-active" nature.

What can I say? I truly do 'dance like a dad.' Becoming "papa" is a journey of pain and joy, although the joy far outweighs the pain these days, and I thank my children for that. I will never have what my brother has. But I do have this, and this is a space of possibility less confined than the traditional narratives of both motherhood and fatherhood. My attempt to walk a path in between is not determined and is not measured against those well-defined roles. Although the comfort of recognition would be appreciated sometimes, the openness of becoming "papa" has great potential. For one, it provides a relation with my children through which they live with, what is seen by many as, complexity and reduce it to simplicity. They take the awkward, unsatisfactory definition of "a little bit boy and a little bit girl" and just love me as "papa." They take the idea of sex and gender beyond binaries and apply it to their worlds, telling their friends that fairies aren't just for girls. My sons wear pink without even knowing they're not supposed to and my daughter is loud while other girls are told to be quiet. We don't divide the family along lines of sex with the 'boys' teaming up against the 'girls.' Some of this comes from an intentional practice of queer parenting but, to a great extent, it's informed by an unintentional embodiment.

Family is important to me and I love knowing and feeling my place among the generations that inform my heritage, both born and chosen. I feel connected through the past and the future, the threads of family reaching beyond me to my mother and father, my mother- and father-in law, the long lines behind them, and through me down to my own children. I hope, above all else, that I pass on that feeling of connection to them for we are quite literally nothing without it. My story of becoming papa could not be written without all these characters – from parents to children, and beyond – and I hope I continue to have a part to play in their stories as they continue to write them.

WORKS CITED

Barad, Karen. *Meeting the Universe Halfway: Quantum Physics and the Entanglement of Matter and Meaning.* Durham & London: Duke University Press, 2007. Print.

Braidotti, Rosi. "Teratologies." In *Deleuze and Feminist Theory*, edited by I. Buchanan and C. Colebrook. Edinburgh: Edinburgh University Press, 2000: 156-72. Print.

Butler, Judith. *Bodies that Matter: On the Discursive Limits of "Sex."* New York: Routledge, 1993. Print.

—. *Gender Trouble: Feminism and the Subversion of Identity.* New York: Routledge, 1999. Print.

Davis, Lennard J. *Enforcing Normalcy: Disability, Deafness, and the Body.* London; New York: Verso, 1995. Print.

Doucet, Andrea. A "Choreography of Becoming": Fathering, Embodied Care, and New Materialisms." *Canadian Review of Sociology* 50.3 (2013): 284-305. Print.

Ducat, Stephen J. *The Wimp Factor: Gender Gaps, Holy Wars, and the Politics of Anxious Masculinity.* Boston, MA: Beacon Press, 2004. Print.

Foucault, Michel. *The History of Sexuality, Volume I: An Introduction.* Tran. Robert Hurley. New York: Vintage Books, 1990. Print.

Gatens, Moira. *Imaginary Bodies: Ethics, Power and Corporeality.* London; New York: Routledge. 1995. Print.

Grosz, Elizabeth. *Volatile Bodies: Toward a Corporeal Feminism.* Bloomington: Indiana University Press, 1994. Print.

Haraway, Donna J. *Simians, Cyborgs, and Women: The Reinvention of*

Nature. London: Free Association Books, 1991. Print.

Heyes, Cressida J. *Self Transformations: Foucault, Ethics, and Normalized Bodies*. Oxford; New York: Oxford University Press, 2007. Print.

Hines, Sally. "Intimate Transitions: Transgender Practices of Partnering and Parenting." *Sociology* 40.2 (2006): 353-71. Print.

Laqueur, Thomas. *Making Sex: Body and Gender from the Greeks to Freud*. Cambridge, MA: Harvard University Press, 1990. Print.

Seigworth, Gregory J. and Melissa Gregg. "An Inventory of Shimmers." In *The Affect Theory Reader*, edited by Melissa Gregg and Gregory J. Seigworth. Durham & London: Duke University Press. 1-25. 2010. Print.

Shildrick, Margrit. *Leaky Bodies and Boundaries: Feminism, Postmodernism, and (Bio)Ethics*. London; New York: Routledge, 1997. Print.

Stryker, Susan. "My Words to Victor Frankenstein Above the Village of Chamounix: Performing Transgender Rage." *The Transgender Studies Reader*. Eds. Susan Stryker and Stephen Whittle. New York, London: Routledge, 2006. 244-256. Print.

Sullivan, Nikki. "Somatechnics, Or, the Social Inscription of Bodies and Selves." *Australian Feminist Studies* 20.48 (2005): 363-366. Print.

—. "Transmogrification: (Un)Becoming Other(s)." *The Transgender Studies Reader*. Eds. Susan Stryker and Stephen Whittle. New York: Routledge, 2006. 552-64. Print.

Sullivan, Nikki, and Samantha Murray, eds. *Somatechnics: Queering the Technologisation of Bodies*. Farnham, England ; Burlington, VT: Ashgate, 2009. Print.

Terry, Jennifer, and Jacqueline Urla, eds. *Deviant Bodies: Critical Perspectives on Difference in Science and Popular Culture*. Bloomington: Indiana University Press, 1995. Print.

III. Queer Futures? Yearnings, Alliances, and Struggles

11.

Borders, Bodies & Kindred Pleasures

Queering the Politics of Maternal Eroticism

JOANI MORTENSON WITH LUKE MORTENSON

The fight for Eros is the political fight. Herbert Marcuse

PRELUDE

This chapter is a mosaic of theory, practice, and process. I write from multiple self-claimed and fluid identities that currently manifest as partner, mother, post-academic, social worker, queer-identified woman, and creative non-fiction writer. I gather up and outline the threads of this chapter, a way through the labyrinth if you will, in order to provide context that I hope will incite contemplation, consideration, meditation. My intention is to tell and to show the processes surrounding my most treasured academic experience: co-presenting with my oldest son on maternal eroticism at a conference in 2010. I write from the voice of I—Joani—however, I share the conceptualization, memory and experience with Luke. While Luke was not interested in the writing of this chapter, I would like it to be known that his contributions were integral to the content, form and experience. I offer a poem that provides an aesthetic sketch of my relationship with Luke, informed by my graduate school textual crushes on Hélène Cixous, Audre Lorde and Sara Ruddick.

Baby: An Erotic Hunger for Goodness[I]

I sit down, with knife and fork; and eat my child
with some honey thick St. Hubertus Chardonnay,
Pop a rosy cheek, right in my mouth.
Chewing, I consume this child.

s
o
n

Wild little hunk of flesh.

His birth.
I do not scream. I do not sweat. I observe him rolling under my skin.
I whelp.
Vacuum extraction; enter: this pink and ocean-toned creature
A cusped Taurus, ruled by Venus, reluctant exile,
He does not cry

Who are you? Plumbed, plump and delicious.
The sweetness of his flesh
I want to gobble the chubby bubbles of his thighs

Second night, itching stitches
Numbed swell of milk
White Ink, you write on my chest
You are wheeled in, carted
Coal black, unblinking eyes, at me
Matrifocal,
I stare, back
I fall into your feral gaze,
blank yet full, curious
And I fall head over healing in love with you

We attach on every realm
Ferocious and vulnerable
Good enough mother

INCEPTION/INTRODUCTION

Life summons life. Pleasure seeks renewal. Hélène Cixous

The inception of this project began during my PhD studies. I performed research that extended my master's thesis in queer parenting to examine the birth and conception stories of queer-identified families who accessed midwifery services. During this research I was moved by the embodied way that mothers and midwives described birth with palpable emotion that (em)powered intense ferocity in their voices and inspired wild gesticulations. It occurred to me that their narratives about birth and birthing were passionate, joyous, deeply sensuous, and erotic. The participants told their stories not just with their voices, but also with their bodies. Both the mothers and the midwives ardently gestured with their hands and bodies to bridge the impossible gap between the meaning of their words and the surreality of the experience of birth. The mothers would open their hands and arms wide to elucidate the opening of their bodies into birth. The midwives would arc and dive their arms as though they were plumbing the depths of caves to mine the precious mettle of the mothers as they caught their babies. The participants would sway and stir their bodies as though they were divining the felt-sense of labour and delivery as a necessary ornamental offering to complete their oral narratives.

Their stories engaged and enchanted my imagination, and challenged my intellect, but they also stirred my body as I twitched, shifted and wept in response to their sharing. I identified through the lens of my own experience. Through this deep body-listening I began to reflect and make meaning of my relationship with my previously pregnant body and the early years with my children because I recalled it as such an intensely sensuous experience. I labelled this way of knowing through my body 'maternal eroticism.'

This chapter is presented in a bricolage; a collaged series of lyric poems that I wrote about my son interspersed with theory, musings on process, and my son's poetry, which is interspersed throughout. I unpack the poetics of queering maternal eroticism and the use of poetry as a potent antidote to the patriarchal heteronormative backlash against marrying the terms 'maternal' and 'erotic.'

METHODOLOGY

The presentation was for a graduate student conference held at the University of British Columbia Okanagan in 2010 in Kelowna, British Columbia. Luke and I wanted this presentation to replicate our embodied experience of intense connection, and yet we also wanted it to be open enough for others to enact their own interpretation. It was easy to talk with Luke about theory because he had two years of critical theory as part of his undergraduate studies in English. We share a love of poetry, although our styles are very different. Luke prefers a more avant-garde or cacophonic style of poem, where I tend to work in a lyric, free style. Luke spent many hours editing the 'too precious' out of my poems, and our conversations were evocative and stimulating. I realized a great deal more about how Luke thinks and feels as we negotiated this learning, and I fell into greater depths of love for his humanity and sophisticated maturity.

Luke was struck by the concept of 'quickening'; the mother's first felt-sense of the baby. Luke decided his contribution would include a loose poem that was the result of his pressing the two words 'quickening mother' through an on-line anagram machine. When we co-presented our paper, Luke read his poem as a quiet, pulsing drone layered under and over my delivery of theory and poetry.

We practiced our presentation beforehand, but our lived experience of presenting led us down a path that we didn't anticipate. Fortunately, we offered very little by way of explanation in our abstract, other than to say that we would be performing poetry. Before we started, we did ask people to release any expectations of a typical academic 'paper reading.' I felt into the moment with a sweet mixture of relaxation and excitement. Luke decided to improvise our production by 'wandering' around the room as he droned the words from his list, while I stood at the front of the room reading and changing the slides on our sparse, entirely visual power-point. Luke made the occasional word on his list POP, to mimic the sensation of the sudden and perceptible feeling of quickening in the mother's womb. The audience twinned their attention between my reading and Luke's, pulling towards Luke when he 'quickened,' which was a political interrogation and disruption of how quickening is always focussed on the mother's experience. Luke shifted that focus to himself as child, the active quickener. The organic way our presentation unfolded, led by our privileging our felt-sense rather than our intellect, caused us to entrain to each other intently by holding each other's gaze at times. The audience was silent as they watched us, and later many commented on the palpable and profound connection they saw in us.

The greatest challenge for me is to represent these rich, thick processes through an academic linear format when, like many human processes, the experience unfolded in a non-linear, iterative and spiral fashion. Because I am talking about pregnancy as the catalyst for my experiences of maternal eroticism, I will offer the content through the form of a triad of perceptions to represent the trimesters of pregnancy. I follow each of my poems with an excerpt from the poems of my son. I put them in a distinct font to highlight his work. Luke's poems appear as a simple list of words, though they are far from arbitrary. He pressed the words "Quickening Mother" through an on-line anagram machine and netted over 1000 words as a result that he compiled into intelligent, playful and sometimes acerbic lists.

Part One: First Perception/The Shock of Inception
Tuesday morning,
I fumble the phone in the crook of my neck
The medical clerk insists I must come in for the
results of my hysterectomy pre-op blood work

Nervously driving to the doctor's office,
listening to the quiet drone of "every breath you take,"
my anxiety slows to the steady pulse of Sting's hypnotic voice

I sit, across from the doctor,
self-conscious in elastic-waisted pants that feel premenstrual tight

He looks at me over his trendy round tortoiseshell glasses
Doubled vision,
his lunch hour Raybans still perched in the thick of his salted dark hair

He talks about my unviable womb in new hospitable terms

Joani, we can't do the surgery on Friday
P a u s e

You are pregnant
He grins at me as though he made it so

Collapsing into the wail and release of stored up grief
Having been hallowed out by 13 empty moons
I am at once full and suddenly succulent

Quicken Mothering Cheeking Quit Morn Cheeking Quit Norm Cheering Quit Mink Technique Rig Monk Cheek Morning Quit Hence Quirking Tom Hence Quirking Mot Quencher Miking To Quencher Kiting Om Quencher King Omit Quencher Toking Quint Creme Knight Quoin Creme Inking Quoth Quenching Mike Rot Quenching Mike Ort Quenching Mike Tor Quenching Trike Om Quenching Toke Rim Quenching More Kit Quenching Mote Irk Quenching Tome Irk Etching Quire Monk Etching Omen Quirk Quickening Hem Rot Quickening Hem Ort Quickening Hem Tor Quickening Them

Imagine a (m)other kind of journey. Imagine mothering as full, juicy living; as wild, luxuriant relationships; as an attitude, as an orientation towards a specific person; an intentional relational consciousness; and a consciousness that extends beyond that person, beyond the self, into the wider cultural and temporal contexts. Imagine mothering as messy texts, as embodied 'mistakes,' as servitude and terror, as surprise and as mundane. Imagine mothering as revolutionary, as transcendental, as meditation, as devotional, as praxis. Imagine releasing the tropes of mother as self-sacrificing, chaste, and able to demonstrate that her children are the centre of her life (Reich 47). Imagine mothering as erotic. Imagine mothering as a site of identity constitution, and paradoxically, as constitutional in the construction of dis/identification. Invoking the category of 'mother,' I engage in strategic essentialism (Spivak 3), as a political act; I intend to mark this category as erotic, and to explore how maternal eroticism may be taken up in service to social justice, personal empowerment and as a means of cultivating pleasure as both sacred and relational nourishment.

I have chosen to mother in my own way, outside the rhythms of my mother, or her mother, without the benefit of any symbolic architecture (Rich 275); living in rhythm with my sons (Rich 33), seeing and being in distinctive ways (Ruddick 100) super-'seeding' the entire matri-line and culture, contesting social prescriptions and subverting commercial and heterosexual master narratives. I intentionally chose to mother outside the bounds of how I was mothered; identifying priorities, attitudes, and virtues for myself and my sons, as Ruddick proclaimed, my "maternal thought *conceived* of achievement" (Ruddick 107). For me, this 'achievement' meant to break the cast of how I was raised and the limits I felt within our heteronormative culture. More than this, though, I also wanted to have a depth of relationship with my sons that struck me as uncommon, perhaps because my experience and social worlds were limited. I knew that I interpreted a sensuous relationship with my children as one of depth and substance because it spoke to me of an expansive way to interact. My mother's lack of demonstrative affection left me feeling cold, alienated and often times ashamed of what I felt, given that I am highly corporeal in knowing, learning and expressing. I craved to have all my senses sated and involved in my practice of mothering. In the absence of a model of practice, I turned towards cosmologies and spiritual systems beyond those of my upbringing.

I incline towards Goddess and earth-based lore, emboldened by Shakti, the divine feminine: "she who holds the Universe in her womb, she who is purest consciousness and bliss, the source of all creative energies" (Stone 216). I also want(ed) to be Sita: "she who exists only for love, she incarnates devotion." (Kempton 201). I want my sons to experience 'mother' in the way I'd read Fromm describe: "Mother *is* warmth, mother *is* food, mother *is* the euphoric state of satisfaction and security" (Fromm 36), and yet without essentializing or totalizing 'mother as nature' stereotype.

Since I employ both poetry and poetics, I operationalize two relevant terms: 'eroticism' and 'poetics.' The word 'erotic' comes from the Greek word 'eros', the personification of love and all its aspects, born of Chaos, and personifying creative power and harmony (Lorde 55). This fit perfectly, as my love for my children is chaotic, wild, oceanic and tidal. "Eroticism does not exist in a cultural vacuum, but is immersed in concepts of beauty, gender, and even political and economical arrangements" (Middleton 3). Audre Lorde claims "the erotic is a kind of ethical Geiger counter which we can use to determine which of our various life endeavours bring us closest to that fullness, that *jouissance*; as women, we need to examine the ways in which our world can be truly different" (Lorde 55). Poetics refers to both the theoretical orientation of a particular genre of writing, as well as the interrogation of language and social discourse. Poetry leans more towards the dialectical rather than didactic. Poetry interrogates, as the genre invites readers to make interpretations of the texts through invoking images and emotions. Fractured and fractal, any topic may be played widely, as the rules of poetry are different than those applied to academic and social discourse. While poetry is a craft with specific styles and conventions within its genre, the endeavour of poetry and poetics is hermeneutic, as 'meanings' are applied by the reader, independent of the intention of the author. Poems are intentionally ambiguous, and this word play invites examination beyond the 'face value' or taken-for-granted and socially constructed parameters of meaning. The semiotics of poetry—the structure and meaning—supports a rich exploration of maternal eroticism in ways that I cannot aptly nor fully state in theoretical terms. Poetry allows me to show "voluptuous moments" (Cixous 1651).

Both Hélène Cixous ("The Laugh of the Medusa") and Audre Lorde (53-59) have suggested that women write poetry as both a means of transcending the confines of patriarchal language and as a way of "writing with their bodies" (Cixous 1650); of exploring, investigating and embodying *jouissance* that is life affirming, that is our own, that is outside of the heterosexual economy "because poetry involves gaining strength through the unconscious and because the unconscious, that other limitless country, is the place where the repressed manage to survive" (Cixous 1646). The invitation that Cixous heralds is for women to destabilize and contest the analytical: "flying is a woman's gesture—flying in language and making it fly" (Cixous 1651). She implores women to not think of our bodies as transgressive; but rather as truly transcendent. "Censor the body and you censor breath and speech at the same time. Write yourself. Your body must be heard" (Cixous 1646) is the both the rallying cry and the invocation of Cixous' corporeal treaty for women.

While theory may drive the pulse of my ideologies, I feel confined by academic doctrine to describe my own experience of maternal eroticism. I write poetry as a means of subverting the cage of patriarchal and heteronormative discourse.

Second Perception/The First Movement

My mouth is full of stars

These are not cave wall flickers,
No.
Strange projections,

No.
This is commotion within a cave

This is my experiential maternal education
I know not this sensation
Foreign
This sensation knows me
Sovereign

This twitch that converses from my womb
the blurred purr and rumble
This bionic embryonic offering
from the cradle of my pelvis
Metonymic, it is you

Itching Queer Monk Hocking Mere Quint Hocking Queen Trim Hocking Queer Mint Choking Mere Quint Chroming Keen Quit Chroming Knee Quit Chroming Queen Kit Chroming Quiet Ken Chroming Quite Ken Chignon Meek Quirt Chignon Meet Quirk Chignon Mete Quirk Nicking Mere Quoth Nicking Queer Moth Nicking Hem Torque Ricking Queen Moth Tricking Queen Ohm Mincing Reek Quoth Mocking Here Quint Mocking Queer Hint Mocking Queer Thin Mocking Then Quire Mucking Thereon Uncorking Theme Queen Mirth Rocking Heme Quint Corking Heme Quint Gnomic Queer Think Coming Queer

In order to move the erotic from the silent margins that delimit the discourse on mothering and to contest the ideology of asexual motherhood, it is important to address the impact patriarchy and heteronormativity have had on motherhood as a theory and practice. My approach to this is to *queer* motherhood and maternal eroticism. I invoke the term 'queer' to describe those gestures or analytical models which dramatise incoherencies in the allegedly stable relations between chromosomal sex, gender and sexual desire (Jagose 3). Queer defies strict definition as it problematizes, interrogates, and challenges dominant regime(s) of sexuality and gender. Queer allows me to interrogate and push back against essentialism (Fuss 2); though clearly there are times I choose to strategically categorize, label and define as I seek to source, interrogate, and sometimes disrupt shared understandings. I also choose quantum shifts of meaning depending on context. "Queer" is slippery, and so am I. I identify with fluidity, and 'queer' lets me transform, reinvent, and 'be' all the torrents of who I am in the shifting river of my life. Queer, as I use it, values process over outcomes, and privileges 'doing' and 'becoming' rather than forcing essential categories.

I use queer as a noun *and* a verb. I queer as a way to disrupt and subvert 'norms,' to interrogate taken-for-granted, hegemonic operations of culture. I queer to encourage 'public surfacing' of sexualities under erasure and intend to make apparent the slippages in language, and the slipperiness of categories. Through queering, I am able to analyze discursive practices, to refute totalizing claims, and to privilege exceptionalities over any socially constructed 'norms.' Queer holds space for tensions and anti-binary ways of thinking and being as it seeks to re-narrate culture, to narrate culture differently, for example, through poetry. When I use the term queer, I am assuming that everything—every idea, concept, thought, feeling, action, identity—*is* political, and that language is patriarchal and problematic.

There is a patriarchal advantage for men's sexuality that women's sexual gratification should be restricted to heterosexuality, but the result is a denial of a life-force in mothering which constricts the actions of mothers in physical and psychological erotic expression with their children. Society is suspicious of the mother who enjoys the physical boundarylessness of a sensual/erotic relationship with her child. The construction of the good maternal body as being asexual is an expectation of both culture and the law. A 'good enough' (Abram 132, 220) mother, according to psychologist Donald Winnicott, is a woman who renounces perfectionism but who practices mothering within socio-cultural 'norms.' With regards to eroticism, a good enough mother knows that she is required to sterilize her affection towards her child, situating her pleasure under erasure and censorship in order to uphold the truth regime of compulsory heteronormativity. Good enough mothers are guided by gender role hegemony to believe that their erotic energies are to be directed towards their husbands and not towards other women, their children, or even themselves.

Third Perception: Performative Pregnancy

I cannot conceive,
Yet I do, and my body willingly accommodates
your every move

After endless foetus in foetu
Your cells surround a wild beating heart

Nested around the emblems of motherhood
Surrounded by stroller, high chair, diaper bags and washable wicking breast pads
Under a stupid party hat made of bows
I have been Showered,
replete with cloth nappies, green utilitarian onesies and yellow duck flannel burping bibs,
Your stirring moves to thrusts
You kick off the party plate of cake
tipped to the carpet, you never like angel food

Under the tents of my dresses
Your limbs bleat and whinge
This movement has sound
Resonance
Jelly fish in the aquarium of my belly
I hear you moving within me

Gin Quirk Om Reecho Gunk Mint Qi Cohere Gunk Mint Qi Trochee Gun Mink Qi Trochee Gnu Mink Qi Cheque Inking Mr To Cheque Kiting Mr No Cheque Kiting Mr On Cheque King Mi Torn Cheque King Mint Or Cheque King Rim Not Cheque King Rim Ton Cheque King Trim No Cheque King Trim On Cheque King Ti Morn Cheque King Ti Norm Cheque King It Morn Cheque King It Norm Cheque Grim Ink Not Cheque Grim Ink Ton Cheque Grim Kin Not Cheque Grim Kin Ton Cheque Grim Knit No Cheque Grim Knit On Cheque Grim In Knot Cheque Gin Mink Rot Cheque Gin Mink Ort Cheque Gin Mink Tor Cheque Gin Rink

Lorde suggests a feminist understanding of the erotic might reconfigure eroticism as a form of social and personal 'power' (Lorde 53-55). I believe that in order to conceptualize a maternal eroticism, the 'menu' of mothering—how to be a mother and how *to* mother—must be artfully widened to include a Cixousian *jouissance*; an exhilarating kind of joy that is born out of the loins of corporeal desire. But this kind of unconventional mothering runs antithetical to the discursive discourses of motherhood that script all women's lives (O'Reilly 15-16), given that the sexual/maternal dichotomy presupposes that these roles are mutually exclusive. The tabooed sensual/erotic behaviours and feelings that mothers may experience in relationship with their children are forced under erasure by pervasive cultural norms that suggest the best mother is an asexual mother who has been sanitized from all sensuality and sexuality, outside of her presumed physical relationship with her husband. The erotic mother is "forged in the crucibles of difference" (Lorde 112) and must claim her own space within the field of 'mother'. This creates an unnecessary burden, and also opportunity, for the mother who wishes to privilege the felt-sense of her body in relationship to herself and her children.

POST-NATAL TIME/SPACE CONCLUSIONS

Maternal eroticism might be described as transformational mother-child relationships that are marked by reciprocity, ritual, deep sensuality, fluidity and integrity. An eroticism of mothering invites interrogation of 'taken for granted' relationships between mothers and their children. "The alleged desexualisation and de-eroticization of the mother in both Eastern and Western culture notwithstanding, manifestations of erotically charged fantasies projected onto the maternal figure abound" (Taniguchi 123). The institution of motherhood in the West has been largely influenced by Freud, who depicted mothers as "the child's first seducer, though even this occurs as a by-product of their ministering to infantile needs for feeding and cleansing rather than an expression of intentional (if unconscious) seduction" (Chodorow 160). Where mothers have been socially constructed as self-sacrificing; maternal eroticism suggests that mothers and their children are freer to enjoy a wider range of physical, emotional, spiritual and social relationships that are based in the attainment of nourishing, pleasurable and enhanced consciousness within the geography of their shared and overlapping experience of mothering and being mothered. The erotics of maternal life are a significant source of power and vulnerability for women; often fraught with conflicting sensations and feelings, "produced at the intersection of a relational matrix, which might include desire, imagination, affect, emotion, power, discourse and signification" (Blackman 123). I believe one way to achieve a widening of the frame of reference for mothering to include eroticism is to create forums for mothers to openly, safely, creatively and productively discuss their own experiences of eroticism with their children.

I was surprised how easy, bonding, and healing it was to unpack my experiences with my grown sons, and yet struggle with vulnerability hangovers and the vexation of others when talking about the texture of my sensuous relationships with my children.

SOCIAL JUSTICE & MATERNAL EROTICISM

> Patriarchy is founded on the border between motherhood and sexuality. Freedom for women involves dissolving this separation. Iris Marion Young

I have collected, and identify personally with, stories of women that are fortified by 'the erotic'; a sensual life-force uncommon to the meta-narrative of the self-sacrificing, servitude of the everyday, heterosexual mother. My participants and I are inclusively queer-identified, though I imagine there are heterosexual mothers who would also appreciate a wider frame of socially accepted choice from within which to interact erotically with their children. I consider my graduate work a kind of Queer Cartography, where I map potential margins and blur borders of erotic and embodied mothering. Because my doctoral project focussed on conception and pregnancy, I have limited my discussion to these realms. It occurs to me that pregnancy is a 'safer' context within which to discuss eroticism because the nature of pregnancy and early motherhood call for close physical contact. I believe that our social worlds would benefit from future research that explored maternal eroticism throughout the lifespan of the mother-child relationship. I would also love to see research that included trans-identified parents.

I employ reflexivity in order to listen for the silences and stories that aren't told—not fully, not clearly, not yet; returning again and again, to the river of stories, accepting what can never fully, never unquestionably be *known* (Adams & Jones 111). For example, the interstices between my experience and that of my sons, like the spaces between fence boards, can never be filled in by me. Even within my own narratives, there are liminal spaces between what I remember and what I imagine; what I recall and what I feel sometimes elude my conscious awareness and/or language to express these sometimes ephemeral and slippery 'knowings.' I can never fully 'know' if I did my sons harm, or if I contributed to the depth of their compassionate and caring characters. I believe that there are always spaces for reworking and resisting the meta-narratives that forge mothering into a small and un-erotic box. With intention, spaces for agency and subject construction (Jackson 675) within the category and technology of mothering can be widened with creative language, with art, and with the creation of symbolic architecture.

Audre Lorde has re-inscribed the erotic as a deep well of replenishment that women could draw from as a source of productive power to re-engergize themselves beyond the tyranny of shallow beliefs. Thus, I consider this collaborative project with my son to be one of deep social justice. Together, through the presence of our bodies performing in tandem, we both 'show & tell' the material effects of embracing the erotic of everyday mothering as catalytic and corporeal. As a woman and mother, I invite all women to consider the ethics of self-care through self-knowledge by listening to their bodies for felt-sense, for the expansive path of the breath, for the pools of pleasure that feed from bodily connection to their children. I invite mothers to destabilize and disrupt notions of development. Mothers are shaped by their children iteratively, as they influence their children (Ruddick 306). I believe that this widening of awareness is act of social justice because it values the multiple and outlying communities of diverse mothering that can support an agentic path for mothers to take. Furthermore, in attending to such embodied experiences, mothers not only contribute to collective knowledge but also expand what mothering experiences can be.

The interrogation of the semiotics of maternal eroticism has led me to commit these acts of poetry in white ink as activism, as benediction, as service, as social justice. Lorde, like Cixous, invited women to understand the erotic as located within an embodied sensation, beyond the narrow fields of social perception. Rather, like the expansiveness of the sky, maternal eroticism is limitless when explored as sensation and expressed beyond the limiting language of patriarchy.

> Nothing, to be sure, had prepared me for the intensity of relationship already existing between me and a creature I had carried in my body and now held in my arms and fed from my breasts. (Rich 35)

My Uterus is a Compass

In the beginning, I adored[2].
You uncoiled within me
My ocular apple
Sprung from the cauldron of my pelvis

The pleasure of mothering
begins with the tender scent of your head
My nose, my lips, my closed eyes
find purpose gently pressed near your fontanelle
I inhale you
Devouring

I bury my face in your belly,
blowing raspberries,
while you squeal with delight
I am undone by your joy
When you cry, my milk seeks you

I both lose and find myself in the practice of mothering

What marks this relationship as fervent, ardent, erotic
Your unfurling, unfeigned limbs of Eros
You evoke frenzy within
My body heaves buoyant and weeping in our surreal embrace
My arms were made for this
Your body is mapped upon my body
I tuck your heart in my heart

The lyric covenant I strike with you
is my earnest resonance
That 'i' that is me is and is not
I am a hot mess
I am the root of a flame
I am the deep cavernous grooves of a cobalt salt lick
I am the unrevealed underbelly of the serpent
Guiding towards the Lilith fruit

My uterus is a compass
The arrowed dial spins wildly in your direction
My desire is the shape of your need
Potent, cosmic maternal gaze
Anchor and anvil

NOTES

[1]"Erotic hungering for goodness" (Ruddick 102). From Sara Ruddick's essay "Maternal Thinking." In her notes, she cites Simone Weil's essay "Gravity and Grace" (1951) as source, but suggests that the language and concepts extend back to Plato.

[2]First line in the essay "Coming to Writing" by Helen Cixous (1991)

WORKS CITED

Abram, Jan. *The Language of Winnicott: A Dictionary of Winnicott's Words and Uses.* 2nd ed. London: Karnac, 1996. Print.

Adams, Tony, E. And Stacy Holman Jones. "Telling Stories: Reflexivity, Queer Theory, and Autoethnography." *Cultural Studies/Critical Methodologies* 11/2 (2011). 108-116.

Blackman, Lisa. "The Re-Making of Sexual Kinds: Queer Subjects and the Limits of Representation." *Journal of Lesbian Studies* 13/2 (2009).

Chodorow, Nancy. "The Reproduction of Mothering: Psychoanalysis and the Sociology of Gender (Updated Version)." California: U of California Press, 1999. Print.

Cixous, Hélène. "Coming to Writing." *Coming to Writing and Other Essays*. Ed. Deborah Jenson. Massachusetts: Harvard University Press, 1991. 1-58. Print.

—, and Mireille Calle-Gruber. *Rootprints: Memory and Life Writing*. New York: Routledge, 1997. Print.

—. "The Laugh of the Medusa." *The Critical Tradition: Classic Texts and Contemporary Trends*. Ed. David H. Richter. New York: Bedford/St. Martin's, 2006. 1643-1655. Print.

Fromm, Eric. *The Art of Loving*. New York: Harper Perennial Modern Classics, 2006. Print.

Fuss. Diana. *Essentially Speaking: Feminism, Nature & Difference*. New York: Routledge, 1989. Print.

Jackson, Alecia Youngblood. "Performativity Identified." *Qualitative Inquiry* 10/5 (2004). 673- 690.

Jagose, Annamarie. *Queer Theory: An Introduction.* New York: New York University Press, 1996. Print.

Lorde, Audre. "Uses of the Erotic: Erotic as Power." *Sister Outsider: Essays & Speeches by Audre Lorde.* Freedom, CA: Crossing Press, 1984. 53-59. Print.

Kempton. Sally. *Awakening Shakti: The Transformative Power of the Goddesses of Yoga.* Colorado: Sounds True, 2013. Print.

Middleton, DeWight .R. *Exotics and Erotics: Human Cultural and Sexual Diversity.* Long Grove, IL: Waveland Press, Inc., 2002. Print.

O'Reilly, Andrea. *Rocking the Cradle: Thoughts on Motherhood, Feminism and the Possibility of Empowered Mothering.* Toronto: Demeter Press, 2006. Print.

Reich, Jennifer, A. "Maternal Sin and Salvation: Child Protection Services and the Policing of Mothers' Sexual Behaviour." Mothering, Sex & Sexuality. *Journal of the Association for Research on Mothering* 4/1 (2002): 46-57. Print.

Rich, Adrienne. *Of Woman Born: Motherhood as Experience and Institution.* New York: W.W. Norton & Company, 1986. Print.

Ruddick, Sara. "Maternal Thinking." *Maternal Theory: Essential Readings.* Ed. Andrea O'Reilly. Toronto: Demeter Press, 2007. 96-113. Print.

Spivak, Gayatri. *Outside in the Teaching Machine.* New York: Routledge, 2012. Print.

Stone, Merlin. *Ancient Mirrors of Womenhood: A Treasury of Goddess and Heroine Lore from Around the World.* Massachusetts: Beacon Press, 1990. Print.

Taniguchi. Kyoko. "The Eroticism of the Maternal: So What If Everything is About the Mother?" *Studies in Gender and Sexuality* 13/2 (2012). 123-138.

12.

Upsetting Expertise

Disability and Queer Resistance

MARGARET F. GIBSON

I was numb apart from a relentless headache as my five year-old daughter, Lindsay, and I sat on the bus, sweaty and tired. We got off at our stop, carefully crossed the street and walked home, holding hands and talking little. We entered the door of my home, where my father was looking after my three year-old, and left the kids to play in the living room. I kept going until I reached the kitchen. My father followed and asked how I was.

"I think that psychiatrist just accused me of trying to make money by getting my kid diagnosed. She said that since I was a social worker, I must know how much an autism diagnosis was worth."

I started to sob, long and hard. He assured me that nobody who knew me would believe such a thing, and then went to answer my children's questions about why I was so upset. I don't know what he told them.

Earlier that same day, I had gone with my daughter's class field trip to a "farm" with small carnival rides. When my daughter started to collapse into angry tears after another child claimed the exact car she wanted, the woman running the ride invited Lindsay to help with the buttons until the next turn. "It's

> no problem," she said when I thanked her. "I've got three kids, including one with ADHD." The three of us watched the cars spin around and around, my daughter suddenly calm and content. "You know," she said to me, "they all need different things. I just want the kids here to have a good time."[1]

So many published narratives about motherhood and disability revolve around a mother crying during or following an interaction with a professional, an 'expert' in the world of diagnosis or treatment. Indeed, some models of how mothers (and sometimes even fathers) *should* respond to disability start from a place of grief and sorrow, before (inevitably, the story goes) moving to a place of acceptance, both of the diagnosis and the professional's expertise. But that evening, I was not really crying with grief. No, what I felt was rage, and like my daughter when presented with the wrong spinning car, helpless fury emerged as tears.

I was furious not only that I had been personally insulted as a scam artist who would use my child for financial profit, but also because I had witnessed the psychiatrist's harsh assessment of my daughter. I was angry that so much time and energy had gone into this meeting. It had already taken eight months to get to this point—consulting with the pediatrician, the teacher, a friend's mother who was an occupational therapist, waiting for a referral that had been lost in the paperwork, getting another referral, waiting again for an appointment. Now we would be back at square one, phoning the pediatrician for another appointment, to get another referral, to wait for several more months.

Meanwhile, my daughter was clearly overwhelmed and miserable at her kindergarten, hiding under tables, hanging off the same corner of the play structure every recess, occasionally trying to leave the premises, with her teacher at a loss as to how to help. My partner and I were ambivalent about involving the medical system. We knew what could happen once children and parents were seen as "having problems," how the labels could fly fast and furious. But I had thought I could protect her, even control the process, since I had also worked for years in the same systems. And now I was crying and utterly drained, feeling I had failed to help my child. In that moment, I had no idea what to do with my rage.

In this chapter I explore my experiences of mothering a child with a disability, as a queer woman in an ableist society that holds mothers particularly responsible for the production and management of disability. I draw upon a combination of personal narrative and academic scholarship as I reflect on my roles as a parent and as a professional social worker. Throughout, I wonder about how notions of normalcy and expertise operate in particular encounters, and within larger discourses about what queer families should look like.

(QUEER?) MOTHERING, RAGE, AND RESISTANCE

Adrienne Rich wrote of mothers that "if we looked into their fantasies—their daydreams and imaginary experiences—we would see the embodiment of rage, of tragedy, of the overcharged energy of love, of inventive desperation, we would see the machinery of institutional violence wrenching at the experience of motherhood" (280). In Rich's telling, the patriarchal institution of motherhood makes such strong and conflictual emotions nearly inevitable in mothering experience. Rage is to be expected.

Here I consider rage as emotional *resistance* to unjust and overwhelming circumstances. Resistance: the term used by professionals to mean patients or clients who deny reality, by which is meant the professional's understanding of the situation. Resistance: the term used by feminist, anti-racist, and queer activists to mean life-giving battles—individual or collective, silent or voiced—against oppressive ideologies and practices. Sometimes, in my experience as a queer parent, these two meanings come together.

When I have talked with other mothers of children with 'special needs,' 'disabilities,' or any other identified (and stigmatized) difference, I have heard stories of similar rage and resistance.[2] I have heard stories of Rich's "inventive desperation" in the face of institutionalized motherhood and institutionalized ableism, as both oppressive forces combine to shape mothers' lives with their children. These stories, usually horror stories but often disguised as comedy, stay with me. So, too, do the moments of connection, of mutual understanding, such as my encounter with the carnival ride operator. In a matter of seconds, she sensed a kinship between my child and her own, and accepted her, and me, and "all kids," in a way that the psychiatrist did not. I have even encountered these stories and commonalities with a few (often queer) fathers.

So is there something particularly 'queer' about my rage and my resistance to the institutionalization of motherhood and disability? Other non-queer mothers certainly express rage, and straight mothers and I have talked at length about the inadequacies of services and supports for our kids and families, at gymnastics recitals or in schoolyards. I like to think that my partner and I are more comfortable advocating for our daughter and generally standing out after years of being openly queer, but I can't really verify this. Plenty of straight mothers raise a ruckus with schools and 'special needs' service systems.

I would say that, even if I can never put my finger on it exactly, the relevance of homophobia lurks as a menacing uncertainty in my encounters with 'special needs' professionals. Such ambiguity brings unending questions. Was the psychiatrist homophobic as she harshly dismissed my concerns about my child and proposed that I was out to make a profit? Did she assume that a lesbian mother will parent poorly (this doctor did mock my efforts to guide my daughter's behaviour)? But then, she certainly expressed regret that my partner, the 'birth mother,' was not there. So perhaps she was ruder to 'non-biological' mothers? Or to mothers who do not have fathers in evidence? Or to mothers dressed for field trips? Or to mothers who were social workers and presumed to know anything about children, including their own, rather than properly deferring to psychiatrists? But then she was also evidently hostile when she learned I was vegetarian (of *course* my child was a picky eater…), so it may be that she was judgmental toward mothers of all children who come into her office, and it was just a matter of finding an excuse. I will never know, but the questions whirl on.

Since this particular encounter, I have learned to attend appointments and meetings with my partner or another ally. Other parents have also affirmed that, yes, you need a witness if things go off the rails. Someone to take notes and help out if you are stunned by the latest turn of events.[3] In the moment, I even arranged a follow-up appointment with this psychiatrist that I later canceled.

Similarly, when other professionals have assumed, sometimes even once corrected, that our daughter is adopted rather than conceived and birthed by my partner, I never know if this is because they believe that queer women don't become pregnant, or because they judge my partner as somehow 'not the type' to give birth to a disabled child—this in an ableist social context that would make such distance from disability a warped compliment. Adopted children are expected to have 'special needs' in a way that children born to middle-class white people are not.

Our encounters with professionals have certainly not been universally awful. Indeed, this psychiatrist was the worst so far. Nor have my experiences of being found wanting as a mother been limited to such professional encounters. As Lisa Carver has written, "When you have a special needs child, it's your attitude on trial, your lifestyle, and the judge and jury is every 'helpful' stranger/ family member/ professional in the world" (ix). In the world at large, I have certainly felt others' judgment toward my child and me as her parent when she and I do not act as others think we should. The world is very harsh with children and mothers who stray out of line. Even when I receive unexpected accolades for mothering my child, I know it is too often because caring for a 'special needs' child is still seen as something outside the ordinary realm of everyday experience. People put mothers like us on a pedestal to keep us at a safe distance.

I will pause here lest this become a story of self-pity or individual outrage. Plenty of people familiar with disability, queer motherhood, and with the professional scrutiny that surrounds them both could immediately point to far more damaging stories, and to other causes for rage that people often cannot afford to reveal. Disability and suspicion go hand in hand; so too do mothering and assumptions of inadequacy. I am not being monitored by a child welfare agency or a psychiatric action team or a probation officer (if I had been, would I have quoted Rich's chapter on maternal violence?). I do not have to report regularly to a social service agency for my continued income. I do not have to repeatedly demonstrate my need for ongoing disability cheques or unemployment insurance or subsidized housing or money for childcare. I am not involved in a custody dispute in which any acknowledgement of my fallibility as a parent, or my dissatisfaction with professionals, can be used to take my children from me. I am listed on both my children's birth certificates. I am cisgender, and I have a femme gender presentation, both traits which fit with dominant societal images of mothers. I am white in a society that gives me extra kudos and support just for that. I am not in need of immigration papers, nor do I need translation services to interact with professionals. I am not 'too young,' 'too old,' 'too poor,' 'too sick,' 'too needy,' 'too disabled,' 'too high-risk,' or otherwise seen as unable to care for my children.

In many ways, my immediate rage at the psychiatrist showed the extent of my privilege. I was not already accustomed to professionals assuming that I was out to scam the system. Contrast my experience with what Audre Lorde has described as "the rage of Black survival within the daily trivializations of white racism" (76). Lorde has also recounted moments such as screaming at her own child rather than a racist bus driver, or getting a headache in a meeting, as manifestations of submerged and misdirected rage. She has convincingly argued that how we deal with the rage produced by injustice is a mothering imperative:

> If I could not learn to handle my anger, how could I expect the children to learn to handle theirs in some constructive way—not deny it or hide it or self-destruct upon it? As a Black Lesbian mother I came to realize I could not afford the energy drains of denial and still be open to my own growth. And if we do not grow with our children, they cannot learn. (Lorde 77)

How we use and direct our rage as mothers is no small matter. Our maternal anger may be inevitable and, at times, productive, but it can also destroy so much if we do not direct it constructively because the institutionalized violence I rage against is certainly not only the domain of mothers, queer or otherwise. My daughter was also present that day; she has her own experiences of such interactions with less preparation and fewer resources and privileges to protect her. She has her own rage, and sometimes it is directed at me. And she is an excellent self-advocate, making her preferences, her needs, known to all in the vicinity. One professional at a school team meeting, never having met my daughter, asked my daughter's teacher if adults were "speaking for" Lindsay rather than finding out what she wanted. This teacher observed, "I don't think Lindsay has ever let anyone speak for her." Lindsay is not a quiet, passive, "good little girl." Thank goodness.

Let me not pretend that my mother's anger is only of the selfless, outraged ally-and-protector variety. To do so is to hide my own complicity in ableism, in adultism, in social hierarchies that can take refuge in 'speaking for' others. Disability rights advocates have named and challenged the institutional violence of ableism, often pointing to how such violence has also operated *through* parents, from 'speaking for' their children all the way to murder (Bumiller 881-882; Shakespeare 187-189; Michalko 106-111). Being an adult, and a parent, who is socially categorized as able-bodied (a slippery adjective), I certainly have privileges that many disabled people and children do not. And yes, if I am honest, there are times when my anger with Lindsay, at her ways of being in the world, gets much of its steam from ableism, from my fear and anger at how she is (insists on being!) different from me and my assumptions of how children "should be." When she doesn't respond to repeated requests, when she refuses to do something "as simple" as brushing her teeth, when she starts on another round of an elaborate and ritualized game just as we need to catch the school bus...then the rage I feel gets vented at a child that I love. She will often call me on my actions, yelling, "Mummy! Stop it! You are behaving like a villain!" She is right. I am not proud of this.

QUEER PARENTS, DISABILITY, AND NORMALIZATION

> Lauren and I had many friends and acquaintances ahead of us on the path to queer mothering. We got information and referrals easily. We faced decisions almost immediately over what traits we believed to be both heritable and desirable as we decided between known and unknown sperm donors, and again as we flipped through the sperm bank catalogue. We emerged with a batting order of donor profiles. "I want a baby with green eyes, like yours," Lauren said, as we made the final decision. My daughter still has the beautiful blue eyes she was born with.

As cutting-edge and high-tech as our venture into queer parenting may have seemed as we scrolled through Internet searches of donor profiles and received regular voicemails announcing Lauren's blood hormone levels, none of the choices and responsibilities of contemporary reproduction and parenting spring out of a historical void. There is a danger in seeing queer parenthood as relentlessly modern, unprecedented, and divorced from historical legacies. Instead, new technologies offer new ways to rationalize the management of what traits should be reproduced, practices that hearken back to the early twentieth century eugenics.[4] Under "eugenic science" the categorization and measurement of both disability and sexuality became professionalized and systematized, using tools such as IQ tests and psychiatric diagnoses, and constructed both in explicitly racialized, class-based, and nationalist ways. Those deemed "unfit" (frequently labeled "feebleminded") could be deported, denied immigration papers, institutionalized, sterilized, given violent "treatments," or denied medical attention (although the precise "solution" varied by situation and time period). Many professions which continue to assert expertise over questions of reproduction and societal wellbeing also have strong historical links to eugenic practices and beliefs, including my own field of social work.[5]

Remembering such histories helps me avoid using words as hard dividers between people, including me and my daughter. As I think through my own choices and experiences in the journey to and through parenthood, it is important that I avoid any simple separation of queerness and disability. Many people belong to both disabled and queer communities and identities, parents and children included. Furthermore, in different historical and geographic contexts, to be queer is/was to be "disabled," since homosexuality or transgenderism have been (and still are) often categorized as a form of embodied deviance (Terry 191-219, Gibson "Intersecting Deviance" 5-14). Both disability and queerness continue to be fundamentally intertwined in complex ways with nation-building and race through strategies including "homonationalism" (Puar 4). In *Crip Theory*, Rob McRuer has argued that those seeking queer respectability simultaneously buy into "compulsory able-bodiedness," all in the search for normalcy (31-32).

At the same time, some of us, as queer parents and potential parents, have benefited from racist, ageist, classist, and otherwise eugenic notions of 'good parenting' or 'positive reproduction'. Some advocacy work and research in support of lesbian and gay parents has highlighted the 'fitness' of these parents based on class, education, age, and planning. For example, arguments for queer parenting rights have sometimes touted the benefits of having "two loving parents," thus distancing themselves from single parents, parenting grandparents, and other kinship arrangements. Reproduction discourses have, at times, contributed to the creation of 'respectable' queers.[6]

The institutional context that queer prospective parents encounter also highlights particular ideals of reproduction and parenting (Mamo 194- 202, Gibson "Adopting Difference" 413-421). In order to adopt a child, for example, parents need to demonstrate their suitability: meet income requirements, provide medical information, attend parenting classes, participate in interviews, and so forth. Transnational adoptions can be even more expensive and demanding. At a fertility clinic, people often have extensive medical workups, pay significant sums of money, and often participate in counselling or support groups. Donor profiles for sperm donors or egg donors and surrogates explicitly market what traits are deemed desirable, turning eugenic beliefs into profitable enterprises. Through adoption forms and interviews, parents list diagnoses, traits, ethnicities, and family histories they may or may not consider accepting in potential adoptees (see Burge and Jamison). While queer parents are restricted by homophobic beliefs and laws, the discourse of choice gives the illusion of control—at least, to those who have the means to pay for it. But of course, where bodies, people, and reproduction are concerned, control is always an illusion. You can try for green eyes, but you may very well get blue.

> Shortly before my daughter's birth, my partner and I went for lunch with a friend, a queer woman. Over burritos, we talked about the trend toward motherhood among women we knew.

> She told a story about friends of hers, a lesbian couple who were "getting older", who had tried for years to get pregnant. She described how they tried different sperm donors and medical procedures, until they finally had a baby. "But then," she said, "it turned out that their son is autistic. So sometimes your body really is telling you something." I remember feeling taken aback at her comment, but still I basked in the glow of Lauren's evident fertility. She, too, was "older", but she had gotten pregnant so quickly. We were lucky. We had done everything right.

Gail Heidi Landsman has argued that the techno-medical discourses surrounding pregnancy and birth in contemporary North America promote the idea that "perfect babies" can and should be achieved by the women who bear them. Consequently, when babies or children are deemed 'imperfect," the mother is taken to task. In contemporary North America, such 'imperfection' is usually categorized as disability, whether physical, intellectual, sensory, behavioural, developmental, or any combination of the above.

Mothers of disabled children are blamed for being the wrong thing (age, race, income), for consuming the wrong thing (food, drinks, drugs of all kinds), for doing anything that can explain their child's difference from an anticipated norm (Landsman 15-47). Prenatal testing has increased the illusion of choice, such that women are blamed for not testing, or for not aborting the fetus when an 'imperfect' result is reported to them. Mothers can be seen as caring too much, or about the wrong things, where disability is concerned. As Tanya Titchkosky explains, "Disability transmogrified as matter gone wrong helps to produce, and is produced by, women regarded as those who make things matter wrongly" (101)—disability is thus a site of blame, landing squarely upon women who 'choose' their children's existence and value over test results or medical interpretations. Women, in other words, are seen as primary producers of disability, especially through their unscientific emotions.[7]

Well past pregnancy and birth, mothers are judged for how they respond to their child's difference: "Unless I hate the things that make him different from others, I will always be a wayward mother," writes Kerry Cohen (40). Indeed, many women continue to blame themselves, and most at least wonder if there was something they could have (should have) done differently. Being questioned at the beginning of each professional encounter on the exact progress of the child's development certainly gives many opportunities for parental self-doubt. Mothers' conduct is open to constant scrutiny and judgment, and mothers are constantly revising and responding their narratives and actions within this context.[8] Even 'non-biological' mothers are questioned in their parenting decisions, or their decisions to parent their child at all, although perhaps less intensively because our mothering relation is not taken as seriously. I usually avoid mentioning the absence of a genetic connection between me and my daughter. Even though this may get me 'off the hook' in a particular encounter, to be so released is a distancing of myself from my child, and a further distancing of my child from the rest of the world.

As my friend's comment showed, just because we are queer does not mean we are immune to dominant ideas of who should reproduce, and who should be reproduced. Indeed, in the face of such fierce hostility, there is a danger that we will seek refuge in constructs such as "normalcy" and "respectability." Given the evident societal hostility to queer reproduction and parenting, queer motherhood starts with a knowledge that we, the mothers, will be called upon to defend our "choices." Why be queer? Why parent? Why get pregnant? Why not get pregnant? Why adopt? Why not adopt? We are asked, again and again, to assert a conviction that our children can, and will, be "okay," which usually means, "absolutely indistinguishable from kids of idealized heterosexual, middle-class, white, able-bodied, etc. etc. parents." The stakes are high. These defenses of our children and our parenting capacities have been made under the fear of losing custody of our children or of losing the possibility of having children in the first place. They have been made in the hope of gaining recognition as having any value as parents and potential parents (see Gibson "Queer Mothering and the Question of Normalcy," Thompson *Mommy Queerest*). In other words, the worth of queer parents has been set in terms of the well-being of their children, with the narrowest understandings of how children can be "well" (see Clarke "But What About the Children?").

What do we do, then, as queer mothers ready to defend our suitability (or even desirability) as parents, when our kids show us that they are not like all those mythical, 'perfect' children? What does it mean when getting things that our kids need means having them diagnosed, seen as one of the 'imperfect'? In Susan Wendell's term, responses to disability can be seen as a "flight from the rejected body" (85). In *not* rejecting the bodies of our children with disabilities, do queer mothers lose any chance of our own acceptance? How much difference, or 'abnormality,' can one family be allowed to assert? For queer parents of disabled children, these questions infiltrate our everyday lives, including our interactions with professionals and their domains of expertise.

When my daughter struggled in junior kindergarten, Lauren and I asked ourselves if we should seek professional services including a psychiatric assessment. Could we participate in a system that would define our child in terms of her lack, her inability, and her failure? This same diagnostic system, we knew, had once diagnosed same-gender sexual attraction (and continues to diagnose gender transgressions) as pathologies. But without the right piece of paper, a diagnosis, the educational system was not going to understand Lindsay, let alone bend for her.

AMBIGUOUS EXPERTISE: UPSETTING STORIES

> It took over two years for us to finally emerge with a diagnosis for Lindsay. The first school meeting we attended post-diagnosis, we met with another team, including another psychologist who had also never met our daughter. This psychologist proceeded to scan the assessment document for the first time in front of us, and explain it as if we had never read the assessment before or participated in its production.
>
> When asked, we acknowledged that we had not contacted autism-specific programs outside the school board because things were okay at home and we had been busy trying to line up school services. The psychologist smiled as she implied that we were also probably working through our own denial about Lindsay's diagnosis. "Sometimes we don't do things because we're busy. Sometimes it's a big gulp to do it."

In the journey between that first psychiatrist's office and that first post-diagnosis school meeting, the professionals involved repeatedly assumed that, as parents, we had a mistaken agenda: either we were trying to scam someone into giving our daughter an inappropriate diagnosis, or we were refusing to believe the diagnosis when it was given. All of this ignores the hours of work we and Lindsay had put into obtaining "the piece of paper" as Lauren and I took to calling it—the diagnosis that would open up more resources and options within the existing systems. The piece of paper was not an intangible arrival from nowhere, but a product of our needs, decisions, and efforts as we had coordinated with various professionals.

Children's program coordinator. Family specialist. Family therapist. Children's support group leader. My resume certainly suggests that, when it comes to children, parents, families, and service systems, I should have had a clue. Indeed, while often my job titles have focused on children, most of the actual work involved at least as much time talking to, advocating for, and monitoring parents. Where was this professional self in my subsequent rage at other professionals? As much as my daily commute traversed the terrain between professional and mother, the separation of the two roles turned out to be very real.

I had been working with parents for almost a decade before Lindsay was born. I was often in the professional role of evaluating parents, dispensing advice and judgment. Although I did pay a lot of lip service to how the parents were the real experts on their kids, there was no ignoring the power I held over their lives from the moment that their file folders fell onto my desk. I now also teach budding social workers. I am aware that they, too, will soon be dispensing advice to other parents with maximal enthusiasm and minimal preparation. Indeed, one of the early tasks often assigned to student interns and new hires is to run "parent information groups." Parents in the groups may have been on the waiting list to receive the agency's services longer than these workers have been in training for their chosen career. As professionals, we assume that the information parents need will be readily available to us, and yet somehow new to them.

In my journey through service systems, it has become clear that my expertise is entirely role-dependent. When I am a "social worker" I can say and do things that backfire when I am a "parent." Indeed, as a professional, my authority is both textual and relational. The person who fills in the document becomes, as Dorothy E. Smith would say, "the text's agent," empowered but also limited by the terms of the document and by his/her institutional relationship to it (108). I have the authority to determine what is (and is not) relevant, guided by the form, my degrees, the accepted discourse of my practice, and my job contract. When I am in the parent role, I have learned that I need to hang back, to pick my battles, to work within the language I am given.

I know that my daughter has benefited from our family's social location, and also from my professional 'expertise.' Even though it took longer than I would have believed, we had private insurance to cover the necessary assessments, which would have taken much longer to obtain through the public system. I know how to write letters that use the terms that educational systems respond to. I have found allies within these systems. I am a parent that schools pay attention to. And my daughter, as a result, has had more resources allocated to her at her public school. Not more than she needs or deserves, mind you (indeed, often we have to fight to hang onto what she has), but I have heard stories of children with similar diagnoses receiving less.

None of this is to say that most professionals are incompetent or mean-spirited. As a parent I have chafed at phrases that I could imagine myself having said, were the tables turned. Most often, the grating phrases are meant to placate upset parents. As I teach future social workers, I am aware that most are young and still identify far more with the children than with the parents they encounter. Many are drawn to those placating phrases to soothe themselves and reassert their own authority. I try to encourage them to allow for upset and uncertainty, both for themselves and for other people they encounter.

It should be noted that my perspective, as both professional and mother, offers only one story. My daughter has her own story to tell. I have no doubt that will share more of her thoughts in years to come, as we continue to navigate social expectations and the language of difference. For now, some differences are simply more salient to her than others. Having two mothers is something that she speaks about easily (for a while she would announce "I have two mothers" to her school bus driver, two times every day). She also knows that certain things are "different" for her at school than for other people, and that she has things she can do "on her own time" that other children are asked to do in a more clearly-defined way. She has a beloved aide who is with her much of the day. She explains her own difference from other children as resulting from the fact that she is "part-cat." This works remarkably well

I do not want to tell my story as hers even though this is the role that many professionals both demand and resent in parents of disabled children. As mothers, we are interviewed to provide 'the story' for professional assessment, even as our motives and trustworthiness as narrators come under scrutiny. My daughter does not need me to tell her story. She is a prolific writer and artist in her own right, as shown by a work in progress entitled "Bald Kitty and the Babysitter." Can "Bald Kitty" be a hero of defiant difference? We will have to stay tuned.

I want to clear space in the official narratives that crowd us both, to make room for my daughter's stories as well as my own. To extend Adrienne Rich, there is transformative potential in attending to our experiences, not just of mothering, but of retelling. In my account of imperfect mothering, in my daughter's telling of the adventures of Bald Kitty (I suspect that babysitter is in for a wild ride), we each resist the rigid narratives imposed by the institution of motherhood, the institution of normalcy, and the institution of expertise.

NOTES

[1]This research has been supported by both a Joseph-Armand Bombardier Canada Gradute Scholarship through the Social Sciences and Humanities Research Council and an Ontario Graduate Scholarship
[2]Throughout this chapter I use scare quotes around 'special needs' since I do not endorse the idea that some people's needs are special. Rather, the means and resources required to meet these rather ordinary needs (e.g. safety, connection, adventure, community) have not been institutionally or socially anticipated or provided for.
[3]The "other parents" I refer to in this chapter include both people I have encountered in the community and participants in my research on LGBTQ parents of children with disabilities. All detailed narratives come from my personal experience rather than from participants.
[4]See books by McLaren's *Our Own Master Race* and Ordover's *American Eugenics* on the scope and history of eugenics in North America. Also see Mamo (238-239) on queer women's interactions with the eugenic assumptions and technologies of reproductive biomedicine.
[5]See Gibson "Intersecting Deviance" on the legacy of eugenics in social work.
[6]See Ward *Respectably Queer* and Gibson "Adopting Difference" on the development of respectability discourses across difference contexts. See also Epstein "Queer Parenting in the New Millennium" and Gibson "Queer Mothering and the Question of Normalcy" on the pressures of normalization on queer parents.
[7]See also Gibson "Stressing Reproduction" on cultural constructions of mothers as responsible for disbility as both carriers and carers.
[8]See Goodley on the narrative strategies of mothers in the face of ableism.

WORKS CITED

Bumiller, Karen. "The Geneticization of Autism: From New Reproductive Technologies to the Conception of Genetic Normalcy." *Signs*, 34. 4

(2009): 875-899.

Burge, Philip and Margaret Jamieson. "Gaining Balance: Toward a Grounded Theory of the Decision-Making Processes of Applicants for Adoption of Children With and Without Disabilities." *The Qualitative Report* 14.4 (2009): 566-603. Web. 15 Oct. 2010.

Butler, Judith. *Undoing Gender.* New York & London: Routledge, 2004. Print.

Carver, Lisa. "Introduction." *My Baby Rides the Short Bus: The Unabashedly Human Experience of Raising Kids with Disabilities.* Eds.Yantra Bertelli, Jennifer Silverman and Sarah Talbot.. Oakland, CA: PM Press, 2009. ix-xi. Print.

Cohen, Kerry. "Evaluating Ezra." *My Baby Rides the Short Bus: The Unabashedly Human Experience of Raising Kids with Disabilities.* Eds. Yantra Bertelli, Jennifer Silverman and Sarah Talbot. Oakland, CA: PM Press, 2009. 32-40. Print

Clarke, Victoria. "What About the Children? Arguments Against Lesbian and Gay Parenting." *Women's Studies International Forum* 24.5 (2001): 555-570.

Epstein, Rachel. "Queer Parenting in the New Millennium: Resisting Normal." *Canadian Woman Studies* 24.2/3 (2005):7-14. Print.

Gibson, Margaret F. "Adopting Difference: Thinking Through Adoption by Gay Men in Ontario, Canada." *Signs* 39. 2 (2014): 407-432. Print.

—. "Intersecting Deviance: Social Work, Difference, and the Legacy of Eugenics." *British Journal of Social Work* (2013). Web. 30 Sept. 2013.

—. "Queer Mothering and the Question of Normalcy." *Mothering Across Difference.* Ed. Andrea O'Reilly. Toronto: Demeter, 2013. 347-366. Print.

—. "Stressing Reproduction." *Disability Studies Quarterly*, 2012. Web. Online only.

Goodley, Dan. "Becoming Rhizomatic Parents: Deleuze, Guattari and Disabled Babies." *Disability & Society* 22.2 (2007): 145-160.

Landsman, Gail Heidi. *Reconstructing Motherhood and Disability in the Age of 'Perfect' Babies.* New York & London: Routledge, 2009. Print.

Lorde, Audre. "Turning the Beat Around: Lesbian Parenting 1986." *I Am Your Sister: Collected and Unpublished Writings of Audre Lorde.* Ed. Rudolph P. Byrd, Johnnetta Betsch Cole, and Beverly Guy-Sheftall. New York: Oxford University Press, 2009. 73-80. Print.

Mamo, Laura. *Queering Reproduction: Achieving Pregnancy in the Age of Technoscience.* Durham, NC: Duke University Press, 2007. Print.

McLaren, Angus. *Our Own MasterRace: Eugenics in Canada,* 1885-1945. Toronto: McClelland and Stewart, 1990. Print.

McRuer, Robert. *Crip Theory: Cultural Signs of Queerness and Disability.* New York: New York University Press, 2006. Print.

Michalko, Rod. "Coming Face-to-Face with Suffering." *Rethinking Normalcy: A Disability Studies Reader.* Eds. Tanya Titchkosky and Rod Michalko. Toronto: Canadian Scholars' Press, 2009. 91-114. Print.

Ordover, Nancy. *American Eugenics: Race, Queer Anatomy, and the Science of Nationalism.* Minneapolis: University of Minnesota Press, 2003. Print.

Puar, Jasbir B. *Terrorist Assemblages: Homonationalism in Queer Times.* Durham, NC: Duke University Press, 2007. Print.

Rich, Adrienne. *Of Woman Born: Motherhood as Experience and Institution.* New York: W. W. Norton, 1986 [1976]. Print.

Shakespeare, Tom. *Disability Rights and Wrongs.* New York: Routledge, 2006. Print.

Smith, Dorothy E. *Institutional Ethnography: A Sociology for People.* Lanham, MD: AltaMira Press, 2006. Print.

Stacey, Judith and Timothy J. Biblarz. "(How) Does the Sexual Orientation of Parents Matter?" *American Sociological Review* 66. 2 (2001): 159-183. Web. 1 Nov. 2009.

Terry, Jennifer. *An American Obsession: Science, Medicine, and Homosexuality in Modern Society.* Chicago, IL: University of Chicago Press, 1999. Print.

Thompson, Julie M. *Mommy Queerest: Contemporary Rhetorics of Lesbian Maternal Identity.* Amherst and Boston: University of Massachusetts, 2002.

Titchkosky, Tanya. *Reading and Writing Disability Differently: The Textured Life of Embodiment.* Toronto, ON: University of Toronto Press, 2007. Print.

Ward, Jane. *Respectably Queer: Diversity Culture in LGBT Activist Organizations.* Nashville, TN: Vanderbilt University Press, 2008. Print.

Wendell, Susan. *The Rejected Body: Feminist Philosophical Reflections on Disability.* New York: Routledge, 1996. Print.

13.

Transgender Women, Parenting, and Experiences of Ageing

DAMIEN W. RIGGS AND SUJAY KENTLYN

Despite positive changes in public attitudes towards transgender people amongst some sectors of society, for many transgender women the process of transitioning brings with it considerable loss. Transgender women may face the loss of friendships, the loss of employment, the loss of housing, and as is the case in this chapter, the loss of family. These losses can be exacerbated for transgender women who transition later in life, who may be married to a woman, and who may have had children. Cook-Daniels (2006) suggests that there are definite cohort effects for transgender women, such that older transgender women are likely to have delayed transitioning because of fears related to the social stigma and risk of violence associated with identifying as transgender. Older transgender women may also have felt compelled to conform to the norms expected of their natally-assigned sex, as a participant in Hines' research suggests:

> In the 1960s and 1970s the scenario was very different from how it is now. You left school and did your duty. You didn't query anything. You got your career and marriage and had children. You didn't have time to think about what you were, and that was the environment that I was in. (Christine in Hines 128)

For some women, like Christine, transitioning later in life can be negotiated 'successfully,' such that close family remains supportive. A recent summary of published research on transgender people and ageing conducted by Finkenauer, Sherratt, Marlow and Brodey suggests, however, that women like Christine may be in the minority. Finkenauer and colleagues suggest that "for many trans and gender-nonconforming older adults, family and social support relationships are either fraught with difficulty or nonexistent" (318). In countries such as Australia and in many states of the United States, the issue of transitioning later in life may be further complicated by laws which prohibit marriage between two people of the same gender, such that for those transgender women who were married prior to transitioning, the only way to be issued a new birth certificate acknowledging their female gender is to divorce their wives. Whilst in some instances this may be appropriate given the likelihood that some relationships will break down when a partner transitions, for some transgender women, such as Christine (above), this may be inherently disruptive to long-standing and ongoing committed relationships. Further, such divorce typically also involves considerable financial cost. The average cost of a straightforward divorce in Australia has been estimated at $3,600 per couple, while a contested one was just under $10,000 (Browne).

The ongoing legacy of financial and familial strains can become particularly crucial as transgender women age. Throughout the United States and Australia, government-supported aged-care facilities are finding it increasingly difficult to cope with the demands of an ageing population. Even when places in such facilities are available, the cost may be beyond the reach of many transgender people, given both the costs of transitioning and the potential impact of transitioning upon employment options. Even if there are places available that are affordable, there is no guarantee that these will offer trans-affirming spaces for transgender people. Barrett's 'My People' report, for example, documents the experience of 'Nancy,' a non-operative transgender woman in supported accommodation. Nancy reported experiencing verbal and physical abuse from other residents, so much so that she rarely left her room and had her bags packed because she was desperate to leave, but had nowhere else to go. Cook-Daniels similarly opens her chapter on the topic of transgender ageing with a particularly harrowing story from a transgender man who experienced extreme discrimination and violence in a care facility, but felt unable to challenge it for fear of his life and access to ongoing support. Stories such as these are all too common, and sit alongside examples of what has elsewhere been termed 'mundane transphobia'

(Riggs), referring to the everyday ways in which the broader society fails to accept or comprehend the lives of transgender people.

In addition to the limited availability of care facilities and the limited or non-existent inclusivity on offer within care facilities for transgender people, there is growing recognition (e.g., Fox) of the fact that older people prefer to, and have better outcomes if, they 'age in place' (i.e., here Fox refers to people being supported to continue living in their own home, though in Australia 'ageing in place' may also refer to staying in one facility if living at home is not possible, rather than moving between multiple facilities). For transgender people, and given the context of ongoing discrimination in the broader society (and compounded by past experiences of discrimination), it is likely that being able to remain living in their home will be of key importance to faring well as they age. Yet as Witten suggests,

> Given that many trans-persons are marginally connected or are disconnected from their birth families, we can hypothesize that trans-elders will experience growing difficulty with respect to aging in place with family support. (44)

In this context of transphobia, lost or strained familial ties, restricted financial resources, and limited supported housing options, who will care for transgender women (and men) as they age? If, for many people, families have ceased contact, and if aged care facilities are unavailable, unaffordable, or unapproachable, what options do ageing transgender people have to be supported to stay at home?

The remainder of this chapter examines these questions through a case study taken from the US documentary *Gen Silent*. As part of the documentary we learn of the story of KrysAnne, a transgender woman who, post transition, was diagnosed with lung cancer. She was understandably wary of health care professionals, but had little support from her family. By exploring KrysAnne's story, this chapter highlights the lived experience of the issues we have already raised about transgender women and ageing, and contributes to the growing body of literature that recognizes the need to examine experiences of ageing among transgender women who are parents.

In the broader context of this collection, KrysAnne's story queers notions of motherhood not because she herself identified as queer, but rather due to the fact that her relationship to normative notions of motherhood and family challenges commonplace assumptions about what it means to parent as a woman. The chapter explores the experiences that some transgender women may have with the category 'mother' that are in many ways incommensurate with the experiences of mothers who were assigned female at birth.

KRYSANNE'S STORY

Broadly speaking, KrysAnne's story may be considered indicative of the experiences of many older transgender women, in that transitioning brought with it both many joys (i.e., finally being able to live the life she had longed for as a woman) and many losses (i.e., children and other family members who ceased contact with her). The degree of loss experienced by KrysAnne is highlighted in the documentary through both her words and the images that accompany them, as outlined below:

> *KrysAnne*: Most people that transition expect losses, sometimes a great many losses, but I didn't expect [to lose] everyone. I haven't heard from them since. For two years I desperately tried to connect with my family. And some of [the letters] weren't even opened. [The letters were returned saying] 'this person is dead' [images of letters with name struck out saying 'no such person!' and 'deceased']. It was horrible. It was vile.

For the viewer the images of the letters highlight the depth of loss and rejection experienced by some transgender women. The discounting of KrysAnne's experience as a woman, whilst not undermining her own sense of herself as a woman or her decision to transition, is clearly presented within the documentary as bringing not only loss, but also loneliness. Whilst, through her own admission, pre-transition KrysAnne often sought to be a difficult character to those around her so that she would be left alone, she still devoted a considerable portion of her adult life to her family and children. This loss is perhaps, for some women like KrysAnne, even beyond what they might have predicted.

Cook-Daniels's work summarises why an older cohort of transgender women may have transitioned later in life. Many transgender women, when living as their natally-assigned gender, will have made many sacrifices for their family, but they get to a point, often when children have left home, where they decide it is time to pursue their own desires. But for KrysAnne and many women like her, 'her time' becomes one marked by loneliness and rejection, rather than the perhaps dreamed of halcyon years in which being true to oneself would be embraced and endorsed by others.

When KrysAnne received a diagnosis of lung cancer, then, and was given only 18 months to live, she was faced with the need for in-home care, or to move into a care facility. In regards to the latter, she says of previous health care professionals that 'They didn't want to touch my body. I believe that as I sit here with you today." Such experiences are also reported by lesbian women living in Australia (Birch). An experience of emergency transport to a hospital included in the documentary highlights that this belief was well-founded, when KrysAnne's case worker shares the transphobic attitudes and opinions of ambulance staff. For KrysAnne, then, in-home care is the best option. Yet as the following extract from the documentary demonstrates, for KrysAnne this may not be an option:

> *Jenifer* (KrysAnne's case worker): To hire someone to stay with you 24/7 is a lot of money. Most people have some people to take care of those things.
> *KrysAnne*: I have desperately tried to develop a support network. Most of my seeds fell on barren ground, but that's ok...
> *Interviewer*: What are you thinking about?
> *KrysAnne*: The truth? What am I going to do when I can't do that myself? When I can't walk to the oxygen tank and turn it on.

The documentary poignantly shows KrysAnne washing her (new model, expensive looking) car, overlaid with text indicating that the sale of the car would only cover one month of care in a facility. What KrysAnne needs, instead, are people in her life to care about her, as her caseworker Jenifer indicates. However help is not forthcoming from family, despite KrysAnne's best efforts. As such, not only has her family's reaction to her transition left her at a loss for social contact and caring relationships, but it has also left her at risk in terms of her physical health and wellbeing.

Whilst at one point in the documentary KrysAnne states that she doesn't want treatment as it involves being potentially subjected to the transphobic attitudes of healthcare staff, she is left with little choice following being rushed to hospital. Word of this emergency, however, reaches KrysAnne's family, as the documentary relates:

> *KrysAnne*: The word is out about me being pretty sick. So now my family starts to come back into my life. But are they

> coming here because they accept *me* as KrysAnne, or because I'm just a person dying?
> *Adam* (KrysAnne's son): I obviously want to contribute as best as I can.
> *KrysAnne*: What is it that you want to do to help?
> *Adam*: Anything that you need.
> *KrysAnne*: Well, I need acceptance.
> (Adam says I love you and walks out the hospital room and says 'bye Dad')
> *KrysAnne*: I don't know what their motivations are, and I don't have time to figure them out. For me to go home, I can't take care of the house. I need people to help me take care of myself. Maybe with my son. [Text then says that Adam subsequently visited much less than KrysAnne hoped whilst she was in hospital].

For KrysAnne, the return of family to her life is bittersweet. On the one hand seeing her son is positive, while on the other, as she states, she doesn't know the terms on which he visits her – whether it is a sign of acceptance of her as a woman or a sign of the end of her life. Arguably this cynicism is legitimated within the documentary when her son Adam is unable to refer to KrysAnne as anything other than 'Dad,' and when subsequently his promise of support is not fulfilled to any substantial degree. These experiences demonstrate that for transgender women the loss resulting from transition is not a once-off event. Rather, it can be repeated again and again as family members put their own concerns ahead of those of their loved one.

Whilst a recurring theme for KrysAnne is her need for acceptance, it is important that we also acknowledge KrysAnne's own complicity with a lack of acceptance for others. For example, she shows little insight into how her own behaviours might have made supporting her difficult for her family. Describing her life pre-transition, and as alluded to above, she says:

> I lived 50 years of my life as a male. He was a sad, miserable person: angry at himself and the world…and just received no joy or happiness. If I was the best athlete, if I aspired to being 'king of the hill,' maybe I could just drive this out of myself. I mean I looked as ugly as I possibly could. Smoked cigars…I did that for a long, long time. And no one ever knew this about me…I was in a serious, serious depression. Tried to take my life twice.

> Then I just said, "I know what I need to do," and I did it! Cured the depression!

She describes the anguish she experienced during this period, but she never reflects on how her behaviour impacted on her family. A family photo shows four children, and the vision of a small statuette labelled 'NO. 1 GRANDPA' would suggest at least one has partnered and had children, but Adam is the only one of KrysAnne's children who is featured in this documentary. He says:

> I found out at 17. So it was pretty difficult at 17, just finishing high school and everything... There was a major depression. Random spots on the floor she'd pass out...and it was just hard to come home from practice or anything like that just to see that. Then she got off the floor with the transformation and I was happy for that, but I just wasn't ready to really accept it I guess.

Adam's use of the feminine pronoun 'she,' even when referring to KrysAnne pre-transition, demonstrates that he is clearly doing his best to accept her. Adam is expressing such support in a family context, which appears extremely hostile, as evidenced by the comments on the returned letters, and the doubts Adam expresses that many family members would visit KrysAnne in hospital because they're "set in their ways." KrysAnne, along with many older trans women, is hurt when her children refer to her as 'Dad,' perceiving this as a lack of acceptance of her gender. But the word 'Dad' is more than just a gender signifier: it carries huge emotional significance around a particular kind of relationship with a parent. Adam has never experienced KrysAnne as a 'mother' with all the emotional and behavioural properties invested in that term.

KrysAnne is understandably disappointed by Adam's apparent lack of engagement at her time of need, which she clearly attributes to transphobia; "I paid a dear price for this transition." She acknowledges that her family may be "stuck in mourning," but seems to show no awareness of how her depression and suicide attempts may have affected them. Similarly, she does not seem to acknowledge how difficult it can be for families to reach a point of acceptance. It took her 50 years to reach a point in her life where she was prepared to accept her gender identity and do something about it. Families who live in societies, like Australia and the US, where normative gender ideologies are mostly unquestioned and socially enforced, may need a lot of education, social support, and time to deal with a family member's transition.

Older transgender women who are parents may also not be aware that older women in general are often neglected and even abused by family members. Many transgender women experience considerable negative affect post-transition from the unanticipated loss of male privilege and the experience of general social misogyny, which they may attribute to transphobia in general, and/or trans-misogyny in particular. Koyama says, "... we often confuse the oppression we have experienced for being gender-deviant with the absence of male privilege" (253). Further, some transgender women may not be aware of the particularly abject status of older cisgender women, and the prejudice, discrimination, neglect and abuse they routinely experience, especially those living with illness and/or disability.

In the scenes that followed the interaction between KrysAnne and her son Adam, we are told about the efforts of KrysAnne's caseworker Jenifer to establish a community of people who could support KrysAnne to return home. These people, drawn from the local lesbian, gay, bisexual and transgender community, offered their time to support KrysAnne. This is important to KrysAnne, given as Jenifer suggests below, other options would have been extremely negative:

> *Jenifer*: The goal with this radiation was that it would buy her some time at home. And I think it's been devastating to her to think that she may have to go to a nursing home at age 59 because she didn't have enough people in her life who could help her out.

Despite this support, and as we see in the final parts of the documentary that feature KrysAnne's story, support from caring strangers is not the same as acceptance and care from her family. KrysAnne, talking in the form of a video diary, shares the absolute loneliness of her illness, left with a body that no longer functions in ways that allow her to live a full life, and with no one in her life with whom she has established connections. As such, while the documentary highlights the ways in which community members may rally around people (which, as Jenifer suggests, echoes the community supports provided to people living with HIV in the early 1980s), for KrysAnne this support appears to fall short of providing her with the quality of life she desires. The difference, it could be suggested, is between care from strangers (and as KrysAnne notes, having people in her house all the time is as challenging as it is supportive), and care from those with whom one has built long-standing relationships.

This conclusion is not intended to idealise birth families as an *a priori* place of sanctuary, nor is its aim to dismiss the genuine and meaningful caring relationships that can be built between people who are part of a 'chosen family' (Weston). Rather, the point here is that in a society such as the United States where KrysAnne lived, being cared for by a stranger is not necessarily a desirable goal for many people. Independence is a privileged commodity that is enshrined in laws and public policy in western neo-liberal societies (Fox). Having to adapt to being 'cared for,' it could be argued, is more easily reconciled when the person doing the caring is a family member with whom the individual requiring care has a reciprocal and mutual relationship. That KrysAnne was precluded from such care as a result of transphobic attitudes, compounded by other societal attitudes towards older women and societal inadequacies regarding elder care, placed her in a precarious position in terms of having to choose between the care of (potentially transphobic) strangers or no care at all. Whilst KrysAnne received some care from community members, the final images of her contained in the documentary show her home alone. Being alone, as it is represented in the documentary, is thus the ultimate cost of transphobia, resulting in KrysAnne spending her final days at home alone and in distress.

DISCUSSION

It is possible that much of this chapter isn't an obvious candidate to appear in a book on mothering. Not because of KrysAnne's transgender identity, but because so much of it is about factors other than mothering. Yet, at the same time, what sits at the heart of this chapter is the loss of family experienced by transgender women, and perhaps more precisely, the loss of the expectation that in raising children, one will be able to call on one's children for the support one may need in times of crisis or as one ages. For many transgender women, and in the case of KrysAnne specifically, the standard narrative of family (in which it is presumed that parents care for children who in turn may contribute to caring for them) is destabilized by the fact of transphobia and the rejection that many transgender women experience when transitioning later in life. While for much of her life KrysAnne may not have been seen as a mother by her children, and while her children have another mother, KrysAnne's experiences are part of a broader social issue that relates directly to mothering: the recognition we accord to people as they age, and the familial and non-familial supports we make available to them.

There are several implications of this chapter for how we understand transgender women's experiences as mothers. In their study of children whose parents transitioned after they were born, White and Ettner debunk the belief that has guided many transgender women's decisions to come out later in life: namely that young children cannot comprehend gender transitioning, and that it is a challenge to the children's own (normative) development of gender identity. White and Ettner found that all children other than those aged 14-16 were able to understand, and to varying degrees accept, their parent's transition. Even for teenagers, this was still possible, with adequate support from their other parent and from professionals. Contrary to received wisdom, which has encouraged people to delay transitioning until children are adults, and to shield children from information about their parent's transition, White and Ettner found that the worst outcomes (such as those experienced by KrysAnne) arose when children were not told anything. Coming out as transgender to children in as open and early fashion as possible may thus be an important tool for transgender women to ensure ongoing support from their children into the future.

A second implication of this chapter is that health and aged care professionals must strive harder to adhere to their mandate to 'do no harm.' Clearly we cannot know what KrysAnne's prognosis might have been had she had different (or earlier) treatment for her lung cancer. Nevertheless, we know that she delayed and avoided medical treatment out of the fear of how she would be treated as a person. Such fear is warranted in regards to some professionals. In a recent study of Australian transgender men, Riggs and Due found that many transgender people avoid interacting with health care professionals on the basis of well grounded concerns over how they will be treated. It is suggested here that to 'do no harm' means more than simply avoiding malpractice. It also requires actively trying to contribute to the betterment of an individual's life by offering them inclusive and affirming treatment.

Finally, the present chapter has implications for any discussion of the concept of 'successful ageing' in regards to whether or not it is possible for transgender women to age in ways where they are in control of what happens to them—as would be expected of any neo-liberal citizen within a framework of 'successful ageing.' Obviously, no individual can be entirely in control of their health or ageing, and when it comes to transgender women specifically, we do not yet know enough about the effects of long-term hormone dosing to be able to predict the impact of hormone therapy upon transgender women's lives. What we can say, however, is that in current parlance, 'successful ageing' refers to individuals who, throughout the ageing process, remain active and positive and able to contribute to the world around them. With regard to transgender women, and as discussed in this chapter, there are significant social and personal factors that impact upon transgender women's capacity to live a life that adheres to the norm of 'successful ageing.' This is not to say that many transgender women do not age extremely well, despite the negative social and personal contexts they live in. Rather, it is to say, well-founded critiques of the neo-liberalism of the concept of 'successful ageing' aside (e.g., Fox), transgender women continue to face significant barriers to active participation in the world around them.

In conclusion, and to return to KrysAnne's story, the documentary depicts KrysAnne's military funeral, and the honour bestowed upon her there as a Vietnam veteran. Thankfully, and unlike what has occurred for some other transgender women (Cook-Daniels), KrysAnne was recognized as a woman on her gravestone, due to her own efforts in ensuring that her funeral was respectful of her identity as a woman. That such issues are of concern in the end of life decisions of some transgender women is a sign of how far we have yet to go towards the full inclusion of transgender people. As a woman and as a parent, even if as one who was not easily accepted into the category of 'mother,' KrysAnne's story has much to tell us about the costs of transphobia, and about the need for ongoing societal and scholarly attention to the experiences of transgender people in a framework of ageing and family.

WORKS CITED

Barrett, Catherine. *My People: A Project Exploring the Experiences of Gay, Lesbian, Bisexual, Transgender and Intersex Seniors in Aged-Care Services.* Victoria: Matrix Guild Victoria, 2008. Print.

Birch, Helen. "Dementia, Lesbians and Gay Men." *Alzheimer's Australia* Paper 15. Victoria: Alzheimer's Australia, 2009. Print.

Browne, Rachel. "High Cost of Divorce." *The Age* 22 April 2013. Print.

Cook-Daniels, Loree. "Trans Ageing." *Lesbian, Gay, Bisexual and Transgender Ageing: Research and Clinical Perspectives.* Eds. Douglas Kimmel, Tara Rose, and Steven David. New York: Columbia University

Press, 2006. 20-35. Print.

Finkenauer, Sabine, Jackson Sherratt, Jean Marlow, and Andrea Brodey. "When Injustice Gets Old: A Systemic Review of Trans Aging." *Journal of Gay and Lesbian Social Services* 24.4 (2001): 311-330. Print.

Fox, Nick. "Cultures of Ageing in Thailand and Australia." *Sociology* 39.3 (2005): 481-498. Print.

Gen Silent. Dir. Stu Maddox. Interrobang Productions, 2011. Film.

Hines, Sally. *TransformingGgender: Transgender Practices of Identity, Intimacy and Care.* Bristol: Policy Press, 2007. Print.

Koyama, Emi. "The Transfeminist Manifesto." *Catching A Wave: Reclaiming Feminism for the Twenty-First Century.* Eds. Rory Dicker and Alison Piepmeier. Dartmouth: Northeastern University Press, 2003. 244-261. Print.

Riggs, Damien W. "What Makes a Man? Thomas Beattie, Embodiment, and 'Mundane Transphobia'." *Feminism and Psychology March* (2014). Online.

Riggs, Damien W, and Clemence Due. *Gender Identity Australia Report.* Adelaide: Flinders University, 2013. Print.

Weston, Kath. *Families We Choose: Lesbians, Gays, Kinship.* New York: Columbia University Press, 1991. Print.

White, Tonya, and Randi Ettner. "Disclosure, Risks and Protective Factors for Children whose Parents are Undergoing Gender Transition." *Journal of Gay and Lesbian Psychotherapy* 8.1-2 (2004): 129-145. Print.

Witten, Tarynn M. "Graceful Exits: Intersection of Aging, Transgender Identities, and the Family/Community." *Journal of GBLT Family Studies* 5. 1-2 (2009): 35-61. Print.

14.

Queering Feminist Antimilitarism

Rethinking Motherhood Mobilizations in American Anti-War Actions

MARY JO KLINKER

Outspoken American anti-war activist Cindy Sheehan, the mother of a U.S. soldier killed in Iraq during combat, pled for "an end to the immoral bloodshed in Iraq" in preparation for the 2006 Code Pink Mother's Day celebration. Sheehan declared that "Matriotism is the opposite of patriotism—not to destroy it, but to... balance out the militarism of patriotism..." (Sheehan "Matriotism").

This essay asks, what does it mean when motherhood is invoked for antimilitarist political purposes in the current American context? Sheehan's words provide just one example in an impressive history of transnational feminist antimilitarism utilizing maternal identity as a mobilizing tactic against war. At the same time, maternal images and motherhood are a contested terrain within contemporary U.S. media, political, and consumer culture. Proceeding from a consideration of the long history of peace activism and scholarship and how it has used motherhood as an organizing principle against war, I argue here that such a strategy has been complicated by the current context in which motherhood is also deployed by socially conservative and anti-abortion movements. Using queer temporality as a methodological framework, I examine motherhood-based peace activism in relation to popular maternal imagery and point to imperial repronormative[1] capitalism and fetal "personhood" as points of contention for future feminist antimilitarist actions.

(DE)NATURALIZING METHODOLOGIES OF TIME AND SPACE

Integral to this project is an examination of time and space, not as neutral depoliticized concepts, but as socially constructed, nationalized terrains of thought where power is naturalized and largely unquestioned. David Harvey theorizes that societies naturalize time according to the logics of capitalism, through concepts "like 'industrial' time and 'family' time, time of 'progress,' 'austerity' versus 'instant' gratification, 'postponement' versus 'immediacy'" (Halberstam 7). In a critical examination of Harvey's theories of late capitalism, Judith (Jack) Halberstam asserts that this analysis fails to recognize cisgendered and heterosexualized normativity (8). Halberstam uses Harvey's work to construct a notion of "queer time" that diverges from "the time of reproduction" (Halberstam 5). Examining the scheduling of reproductive-time as connected to a 'biological clock' for women, essentialist (hetero)sexist assumptions are mapped onto women's bodies as solely tied to reproduction. Reproductive-time assumes that all families are tied to heteronormative time and the reproduction of nuclear families. Queer time refutes the conception of a natural progression of life goals (i.e. marriage, family, children, etc.) and instead exists as a temporality of resistance to the rigid and fixed binaries of the public/private spatial divide.

'Queer' moves beyond the project of connecting sexual identity to bodies; rather, it "refers to non-normative logics and organizations of community, sexual identity, embodiment, and activity in space and time" (Halberstam 6). Hence, queer time and space are ways to account for temporal frames outside of those designed around the reproduction of individuals and, indeed, the nation state. In this chapter, I expand upon Halberstam's examination of "queer temporality," which offers a new framework to denaturalize repronormative futurity by queering the trajectory of adulthood, and is central to understanding how sexuality, family, and women's identities as mothers are tied to the social production of imperialist capitalism. Thus, queer temporalities become critical in the investigation of political economy, militarism, and the parallel constructions of time and space.

In a controversial queer analysis of time, Lee Edelman suggests that queer people should refute the nation's attempt to reconfigure queer identities as consumptive for capitalist futurity (19-21). Much of his analysis is tied to Lauren Berlant's concept of infantile citizenship, which renders the nation an entity existing solely for the future of children and the protection of their innocence (27). The appropriation of paternalism constructs citizens as the children of the state, whereby national change becomes impossible because repressive parents control the nation (21-22). Edelman argues against "reproductive futurism," which he defines as "an ideological limit on political discourse as such, preserving in the process the absolute privilege of heteronormativity by rendering unthinkable, by casting outside the political domain, the possibility of a queer resistance to this organizing principle of communal relations" (Edelman 2).

My analysis of queer temporality, repronormativity, and nationalist futurism are situated in the context of American feminist antimilitarism. I am interested in contextual examples of the contemporary marketization and spectacle of motherhood in celebrity and political culture, which undermines the platform feminist antimilitarists employ to mobilize motherhood strategically. Exploring the relationship between these forms of politicized motherhoods, I argue that queer temporalities pose new ways of confronting war in a time of perpetual militarism.

MAPPING THE MATERNAL IN ANTIMILITARISM

What can scholars make of this use of motherhood as an antimilitarist strategy? Micaela Di Leonardo's 1985 essay "Morals, Mothers, and Militarism: Antimilitarism and Feminist Theory" described the dubious relationship that motherhood discourse has to anti-war activism, asserting that utilizing modernist character constructions of women as "nurturing," and therefore peaceful, is a continuation of biological determinism that simultaneously renders militarism and processes of the nation-state obscure. She reminds us that the Moral Mother— which she defines as "nurturant, compassionate ... instinctive spokeswoman for all that is vulnerable"— privileges heterosexual reproduction, thereby reinforcing heteronormativity (Di Leonardo 602).

The quintessential theoretical work on maternal/mother identity in relation to feminist peace action has been Sara Ruddick's 1989 work, *Maternal Thinking.* Mothering, Ruddick argues, is a gendered labor, yet anyone who cares for the "preservation, growth, and social acceptability" of children has the capacity to be maternal (17). Ruddick is careful to make a distinction between maternal thinking and motherhood as an ideological apparatus that exploits women's labor and biologically essentializes women as nurturing beings. Ruddick's theory of "maternal thinking" insists that feminist scholars must recognize the material importance of maternal labor. Thus, Ruddick's work insists that instead of assigning attributes to an innate female identity, maternal discourses need to recognize gendered social constructions.

In *Maternal Thinking*, Ruddick lays out the ways in which maternal epistemology, which is self-consciously constructivist, is diametrically opposed to socialized militarism and to violence that threatens peace (152). Turning towards the political utility of maternal thinking, Ruddick argues that while those who mother have scant access to many resources necessary to fight governments or militaries, they do have nonviolent tools, the very tools often used to teach and care for children. Nonviolent mothering can offer an "invigorating image of peace as an active connectedness" (183). Ruddick's definition of "women's politics of resistance," includes the use of cultural imagery/symbolism of femininity, women unified in solidarity and resisting practices or policies of their government (225). Ruddick, however, is careful not to romanticize women's resistance as solely nonviolent.

Here I offer a brief, and in no way complete, history of the integral role "maternal thinking" has played in women's anti-war organizing. One of the most important historical uses is Julia Ward Howe's "Mother's Day Proclamation" of 1870—the "true" origins of Mother's Day—in which she urged U.S. mothers to bind across difference to oppose the civil war, because she argued it allowed "our sons to be trained to injure theirs" (Howe 83). Similarly, U.S. Quaker women used this sentiment in early arguments for women's suffrage and the abolition of slavery. Another important utilization of the maternal identity includes the 1961-1980 U.S. "Women Strike for Peace" Movement in Washington D.C., which used motherhood as a feminist standpoint, and in which predominantly white, middle-class women argued that they had forgone careers to produce and raise the next generation, a language problematically tied to nation building (Swerdlow 1-6).

During the 1980's nuclear era, the participation of women in the antiwar movement often utilized motherhood rhetoric. The "Mothers and Others Action" originating in Santa Cruz, CA, actively opposed the Reagan-imposed imagery of the "militarized white mother" by critiquing essentialist ideological assumptions that mothering is inherently a feminine identity and opening the definition to include "mothering" in a variety of identities (Sturgeon 73). While this action built from the importance of mother movements, it actively addressed Di Leonardo's concerns of the "Moral Mother."

The use of mothering images and models have also existed in multiple national contexts, as in the struggle of Mothers and Grandmothers of the Plaza de Mayo who opposed the military dictatorship in Argentina from

1976-1983. Raging Grannies, originating in Victoria, Canada in 1987 and now existing in the U.S., Europe, and Canada, began as an anti-nuclear movement that radicalizes popular songs and "rage for peace, social and political justice, and environmental preservation... and to create a better world for our children and grandchildren" (Rohrer 226). In the late 1990s, women affiliated with Four Mothers protest, a group of Israeli women and mothers who had raised sons that were involved in the Israeli infantry, stood in Lebanon to protest Israel's war in southern Lebanon. It has also appeared in Turkey in 1995, where Turkish mothers opposed the militarized government and disappearances of activists held under police custody.

A more contemporary use of activist motherhood has been Code Pink's 2006 Mother's Day celebration about the necessity of mothers in the anti-war movement. Code Pink began in the United States in 2002 in opposition to the Bush administrations plans to invade Iraq. They play off of cultural representations of femininity in relation to the red/orange security threat statuses in the United States. As they state:

> Women have been the guardians of life — not because we are better or purer or more innately nurturing than men, but because the men have busied themselves making war. Because of our responsibility to the next generation, because of our own love for our families and communities, it is time we women devote ourselves— wholeheartedly — to the business of making peace. (Code Pink)

Clearly their work resembles Ruddick's analysis of maternal thinking and is a contemporary example of motherhood as a mobilizing principle for anti-war activism.

Mothers Acting Up (MAU)[2], an affiliated organization with Code Pink, began in Boulder, CO in 2002 to mobilize the efforts of women as a means to "show motherhood as a large, impressive force to be reckoned with" (Osnes 81). Beth Osnes, a MAU activist, articulates that "mothers are a natural lobbying group for children" and that it is mothers' political obligation to be a "voice to the voiceless" (82). The groups organized events for Mother's Day to address the need for children in the U.S. and abroad, drawing specific attention to material issues like education and health care, a subject of great importance to feminist antimilitarism.

I deeply respect the contributions of these activists and the continued importance of these actions against war and violence. My concern is that these actions are undermined by an already existing insistence on women's care-giving roles within other political agendas, which persistently utilizes motherhood tropes to mold an acceptable version of domesticity in modern feminine subjectivities. Hence, these actions are undermined by their reliance on overdetermined images of women's care-giving roles. In addition, much of this maternal symbolism rebinds us to gendered dichotomies and a (hetero)sexist division of labor. Such discursive formations normalize and render natural the compulsory relationship of women to the (re)production of nation.

In the next section, I discuss the ways other political deployments of motherhood and maternal imagery dominate public attention and utilize racialized repronormative futurity, thereby subverting the critiques of nationalist militarism that peace activists seek to promote.

MAMA GRIZZLIES AND REPRONORMATIVITY: MAKING A FUTURE FOR THE CHILDREN

A complication for any analysis of antimilitarist uses of maternal symbolism is the long history of militarist, nationalist, capitalist, and imperialist discourses also deploying maternal imagery. For example, in Laura Briggs' important work *Reproducing Empire* she describes how U.S. reproductive medical companies appropriated feminist rhetoric, utilizing an "imperial feminism" in order to institute exploitative medical testing and population control policies (74-107).

More generally, imperialist bourgeois nationalism reconstructs women as "mothers of the nation" to assert that the nation is, in fact, women's domestic sphere, and in need of their protection and loyal labor. Thus the construct of the "Moral Mother" offers women a double-edged sword when the nationalist political identities being offered to women are:

> ...particular reincarnations of particular visions of the past. These visions, usually called 'traditions,' are no such thing: They embody the hopes for future power and domination... Yet these 'traditions' generally have one thing in common: the subservient status of women and often the restriction of women's lives to a rosy vision of domesticity and motherhood. (Papanek 70)

Furthermore, motherhood politics can not only supplement the argument for protecting the "nation" but also be used in anti-immigrant, class-based, white supremacist arguments. Reproductive motherhood, as articulated in the theories of Briggs and Papanek, utilizes the capitalist space of the private/public divide to construct white, middle class bodies as properly reproducing bodies, while constructing women of color and working class women's bodies as politically public spaces and "threats" to the nation. This threat is one that must be taken seriously in queer theoretical accounts that demand a reordering of temporality. As Andrea Smith argues: "If the goal of queerness is to challenge the reproduction of the social order, then the Native child may already be queered... the Native Child is not the guarantor of the reproductive future of white supremacy; it is the nit that undoes it" (48). Too often queer theoretical analyses are premised upon settler colonialism and the future of whiteness, an assumption that must be challenged in order to fully engage anti-imperialist critique (Smith 45-49).

Contemporary peace activists sometimes engage directly with imperialist concerns and discourses. For example, Mothers Acting Up addresses the neocolonial context of globalization as they acknowledge how "American politics has far-reaching effects on the quality of children's lives. Whether babies in South Africa get the antiviral AIDS drug they need is based on a political decision to allocate aid to that country... I must speak up and advocate on behalf of these children" (Osnes 82). While MAU's actions recognize an imperial process that impacts the lives of children globally, it too is situated in the neoliberal and racial framework that affords U.S. women a public maternal platform as voices for children from all over the world.

Within national borders, the use of children as an emotional appeal serves the ideological function of constructing "good families" and model consumer citizens. Set in opposition to a politics of peace and anti-war motherhood is a resurgence of the conservative women's movement brand of motherhood politics. Former Alaskan governor and GOP 2008 vice presidential candidate Sarah Palin has become a central figure for the neoconservative right and a tokenized image of nationalist femininity. During the 2008 campaign, a raced/classed/sexed repronormativity became a spectacle as her daughter, Bristol, became an iconic figure of patriotism through teen-pregnancy. As a pregnant, white, affluent teen, she became identified with "family values" and was afforded the privilege of a private identity rather than being presented to the public as a social ill, as teen pregnancy is so often depicted when it involves racialized, low-income young women.

Using her fame from the 2008 election, Palin has continued to speak on behalf of conservative women using maternal rhetoric. The November

2010 election was termed the "Year of Women" due to the number of female candidates running. Palin used this to rally women around a romanticized essentialist notion of "Mamma Grizzlies." Speaking to the newly formulated Tea Party, a fundamentalist branch of the Republican Party, Palin informed women that such rhetoric is successful:

> It seems like it's kind of a mom awakening in the last year and a half, where women are rising up and saying, 'no, we've had enough already.' Because moms kind of just know when something's wrong... Here in Alaska I always think of the mama grizzly bears that rise up on their hind legs when somebody's coming to attack their cubs, to do something adverse toward their cubs. ("Sarah PAC advertisement")

"Mamma Grizzlies," is a political celebrity motherhood that calls upon maternal femininity as a political resistance to national change. Her political stances are vehemently anti-social welfare, anti-healthcare reform, queerphobic, and against reproductive education and options for women. Palin's political version of celebrity motherhood actively engages with the nationalist stance of women embodying and publicly protecting the nation, as their family, or what Berlant has theorized as the "intimate public sphere" (Berlant 4-6).

How, then, does women's reproductive temporality operate in this vision of women mothering the nation? Reproductive futurism, or the ideology of defending the nation for the children, plays an important role in the continued logic of imperial nationalism that constructs an "us" and a "them" in order to protect and expand the nation for the futures of children. This defense of heterosexual reproduction obscures the drive of the nation "as the biological fact of heterosexual procreation bestows the imprimatur of meaning-production on heterogenital relations... the Child, [carries] the cultural burden of signifying futurity" (Edelman 13).

In July 2011, Michelle Bachmann, a Palin-identified "Mamma Grizzly," and other Republican leaders signed onto The Marriage Vow. The Marriage Vow, advocated by Iowa-based conservative group The Family Leader, called upon racist nostalgia to argue that African American families were more healthy during slavery than contemporary times, utilized homophobic bigotry to argue for monogamous heterosexual marriage as both the "natural" and social order, and called for nativist white-centric reproduction, stating the need for "robust childbearing and reproduction [for the benefit of] U.S. demographic, economic, strategic and actuarial health and security" (The Family Leader 2). This pledge politicizes conservative ideologies about the classed, raced, and sexed underpinnings of family in nation building.

The dynamic is further complicated when feminist antimilitarists draw on similar sentiments. Politicizing national patriotism in favor of maternal activism, Cindy Sheehan, the anti-war mother activist quoted at the beginning of this essay, states: "War will end forever when we matriots stand up and say: 'No, I am not giving my child to the fake patriotism of the war machine which chews up my flesh and blood to spit out obscene profits.'... Matriotism above all is a commitment to truth and to celebrate the dignity of all life" (Sheehan "Matriotism"). What Sheehan's analysis of "matriotism" points to is a shared nationalist framework between anti-war maternalism and "Mamma Grizzlies," which doesn't subvert patriotic belligerence, but employs a differing vision for the future of the nation.

Queer temporalities offer a new structure that denaturalize this shared framework, which depends on repronormative time and "connects the family to the historical past of the nation, and glances ahead to connect the family to the future of both familial and national stability" (Halberstam 5). Simplistic formations of heterosexual reproduction and consumption for national stability have also been more recently challenged through the introduction of "normative" lesbian and gay family. Jasbir Puar's *Terrorist Assemblages* argues that the current U.S. imperialist endeavors in Iraq and Afghanistan have been shaped by the illusion of an expanding sexual citizenship. Puar challenges us to critically deconstruct the way U.S. nationalist politics of "sexual exceptionalism"—by which the American nation-state positions itself as unique in its "tolerance" of certain forms of homosexuality—have constructed a "homonationalism" that is complicit with heterosexual configurations of the nation (3-11). Puar asserts that neoliberal sexual politics of homonormativity depoliticize queerness by advocating consumption and monogamous domesticity as keys to accessing both private sphere protections and public sphere rights, thereby upholding and supporting the framework of the public sphere as a heteronormative nationalist space. Her analysis points to the necessity that we move beyond a critique of radicalized anti-war motherhood as solely heterosexist. The ideological function of appropriating non-heterosexual families benefits imperial nation-building. Such questions need to be addressed in advancing a queer critique of repronormativity and futurity as they may be (re)produced through some non-heteronormative families.

As Lauren Berlant argues, this repronormative discourse is the biopolitic that controls our concept of temporality as linear progress: "a nation made for adult citizens has been replaced by one imagined for fetuses and children" (Berlant 1). Sarah Palin and Michele Bachmann's maternal identities recentralize repronormative motherhood and perform the duty of conservative backlash to lesbian and gay families. She deployed five children and an anti-reproductive justice platform in 2008 and insisted that her identity as a mother qualified her to limit the rights women had over their own bodies, for "the children." Feminist antimilitarist rhetorical claims of "speaking for the voiceless" have a dangerous connection to the politics of conservatism that posit restrictions on others' rights in the name of the nation's future (Onses 82).

WOMEN'S BODIES AS PUBLIC SPACES

The contemporary American climate surrounding women's agency to determine whether or not to be mothers is another space of concern within this politicization of repronormative futurity. For example, in February 2011, Georgia State Representative Bobby Franklin introduced a bill that would make abortion illegal and criminalize miscarriages. The bill considered fetuses full human beings, carrying a sentence of murder for inducing miscarriages. Applying our standards of personhood to the zygote stage, the bill emphasized patriarchal political contempt for women's bodies.

Lauren Berlant's work (1997) shows how queer theoretical resources can help us understand what is at stake and in play in such legislation and its surrounding rhetoric. Berlant's analysis of the contemporary American political landscape centres on the transitioning nation, examining the reconstruction of cultural citizenship in a post-Reagan era in which neoconservatism has advanced the economic agenda of neoliberalism. Examining the failed promise of maternal value and social worth, which was supposedly extended to any woman, she challenges us to recognize maternal legitimacy as an exploitation of nationalist feminine imagery. In particular, she highlights the ways in which fetal motherhood, along with the nativist ideologies of the "pro-life" movement, have constructed a rhetoric where the "pregnant woman becomes the child to the fetus, becoming more minor and less politically represented than the fetus, which in turn is made more national" (Berlant 85). The pregnant body, which Berlant suggests is culturally read as the spatiality for future motherhood, becomes bound to the reproductive future of a repronormative citizenship and signifies "an identity machine for others, producing children in the name of the future, in service to a national culture whose explicit ideology of natural personhood she is also helping to generate" (Berlant 85). Both Edelman and Berlant argue that U.S. culture has been based on a future that obscures the perpetual nation-state and militarist violence through seemingly virtuous narratives of a future for Children. A queer politic against futurity destabilizes the naturalized politics of capitalist reproduction. As Edelman suggests, reproductive futurity is the mere repetition of the violent past, and we must instead insist "the future stops here" (31).

Nurit Peled-Elhanan, an Israeli feminist peace activist whose work has been associated in the broad network of Code Pink activism, spoke at the 2004 European Social Forum to address the impacts of imperial racism inherent in the occupation of Palestine. Her daughter's death by an act of terrorism in Jerusalem shapes her understanding of this imperialism: "It's time to make it clear that the death of one child, any child, be it Serbian, Albanian, Iraqi, or Jewish, is the death of the whole world, its past and its future" (Peled-Elhanan 104). Her remarks utilize the emotional appeal of children, but offer a stark contrast to the political motherhood of Palin, as her narrative and subsequent actions involve a material understanding of occupation. Furthermore, her statement troubles the commercial frameworks of time by posing temporality as a simultaneous operation of the past and future. The harrowing story surrounding her daughter's death is a site of resistance, giving it less traction in political discourse than Palin's neo-conservative narrative.

While I have argued to employ a queer temporality that refutes children as the markers of futurity, José Esteban Muñoz offers a potent critique of Edelman's insistence that "the future is kids stuff" (1-31) arguing: "the future is only the stuff of some kids. Racialized kids, queer kids, are not sovereign princes of futurity... [Edelman's] framing nonetheless accepts and reproduces this monolithic figure of the child that is indeed always already white" (95). His argument points the need for a transnational and antiracist component that recognizes time as racialized.

CONCLUSION: WHERE DO WE GO WITH NO FUTURE?

Activism mobilized around motherhood has to contend with three strains of problematic politics: colonialist and imperialist constructions of certain women as properly reproducing bodies, the concepts of repronormative futurity that privileges heterosexist reproduction and therefore denies some women's resistance and existence, and women's bodies as public spaces, rather than embodied political actors. As I have argued, anti-war motherhood methods have a historical importance in antimilitarist activism and continue in the critical work of such organizations as Code Pink and Mothers Acting Up. However, the contemporary context of maternal symbolism mitigates the efficacy of these efforts, as other forces advance maternal identities that support capitalism and nationalist violence.

Some antimilitarist actions articulate theorized critiques of the culture of neoliberal "momism." In 2012 prior to Mother's Day, Code Pink activist Laura Kacere confronted the commercialization of Mother's Day and demanded a return to Howe's feminist peace demand:

> We are also experiencing a still-rising commercialization of nearly every aspect of life; the exploitation of every possible human event and emotion at the benefit of corporations. Let's take this Mother's Day to excuse ourselves from the pressure to consume and remember its radical roots – that mothers, or rather all women, in fact, all people, have a stake in war and a responsibility as American citizens to protest the incredible violence that so many fellow citizens, here and abroad, must suffer through. (Kacere "Radical History of Mother's Day")

As I have shown in the course of this analysis, these important actions remain tied to our contemporary discourses surrounding the public spectacle of mothers.

Overwhelmingly, the highly visible examples of maternal politics in the United States such as pro-nationalist Republican women's actions reproduce the notions of neoliberalism embedded in the imperialist politics and ideologies of militarism. The multiplicity of maternal imageries reveals the limits of politicizing motherhood for anti-war organizing. As motherhood increasingly becomes a commercialized public discourse, less attention can be drawn from the strategic alliance of mothers against war and militarism.

Only certain motherhoods have been celebrated by the state, meaning that a transnational use of motherhood perpetuates material privileges for specific bodies. Repronormative time frames uphold capitalist heteropatriarchy in the production of a nation for "children and fetuses" (Berlant 1). Popular maternal politics, such as "Mamma Grizzlies" suggest that feminist activists need to remain attentive to neoliberal configurations of maternal imagery that occupy the national space. Edelman's argument that we stop the future is not the same as the end that seems near through destructive militarism, but this queer theoretical tool might offer valuable insight for activist temporalities to "Stop the Next War Now," as Code Pink has demanded.

NOTES

[1]The term "repronormative" was coined and theorized by Katherine Franke in her 2001 essay "Theorizing Yes: An Essay on Feminism, Law and Desire." It refers to the reduction of sex acts to reproductive imperative, especially in relation to female sexuality.

[2]Mothers Acting Up dismantled in 2011, but various coalitions and other maternal-activist engagements continue to thrive, such as World Pulse, CARE, ONEMoms, and The Motherhood (Mothers Acting Up. "Farewell." Web. 29 June 2011.)

WORKS CITED

Berlant, Lauren. *The Queen of America Goes to Washington City.* Durham, NC: Duke University Press, 1997. Print.

Briggs, Laura. *Reproducing Empire: Race, Sex, Science, and U.S. Imperialism in Puerto Rico.* University of California Press, 2003. Print.

Code Pink. "About Us." *Code Pink: Women for Peace.* 2003. Web. Accessed 30 September 2010.

Edelman, Lee. *No Future: Queer Theory and the Death Drive.* Duke University Press, 2004. Print.

Franke, Katherine. "Theorizing Yes: An Essay on Feminism, Law and Desire." *Columbia Law Review* 101 (2001): 181-208. Print.

Halberstam, Judith (Jack). *In a Queer Time and Place: Transgender Bodies, Sexual Subcultures.* New York: New York University Press, 2005. Print.

Howe, Julie Ward. "Mother's Day Proclamation." *Stop the Next War Now.* Eds. Medea Benjamin and Jodie Evans. Makawoa: Inner Ocean Publishing, Inc., 2005. 82-83. Print.

Kacere, Laura. "The Radical History of Mother's Day." *Code Pink,* N.p. 11 May 2012. Web. 10 Mar. 2013.

Leonardo, Micaela Di. "Morals, Mothers, and Militarism: Antimilitarism and Feminist Theory." *Feminist Studies*, 11:3, 1985:599-617. Print.

Muñoz, José Esteban. *Cruising Utopia: The Then and There of Queer Futurity*. New York City: New York University Press, 2009. Print.

Osnes, Beth. "Mothers of All the World's Children." *Stop the Next War Now.* Eds. Medea Benjamin and Jodie Evans. Makawoa: Inner Ocean Publishing, Inc., 2005. 80-82. Print.

Palin, Sarah. "Sarah PAC." 23 June 2010. Online Video Clip. YouTube. 30 September 2010.

Papanek, Hanna. "The Ideal Woman and the Ideal Society: Control and Autonomy in the Construction of Identity." *Gender and Society*. Vol. 7 No. 4, 1993. Print.

Peled-Elhanan, Nurit. "A Mother's Plea." *Stop the Next War Now.* Eds. Medea Benjamin and Jodie Evans. Makawoa: Inner Ocean Publishing, Inc., 2005. 100-105. Print.

Puar, Jasbir. *Terrorist Assemblages: Homonationalism in Queer Times.* Duke University Press, 2007. Print.

Rohrer, Judy. "'We Say Code Pink': Feminist Direct Action and the 'War on Terror'." *Feminism and War.* Eds. Robin Riley, Chandra Talpade Mohanty, and Minnie Bruce Pratt. Zed Press, 2008. Print.

Ruddick, Sara. *Maternal Thinking: Towards a Politics of Peace.* Beacon Press Books, 1989. Print.

"Sarah PAC." 23 June 2010. Online Video Clip. YouTube. 30 September 2010.

Sheehan, Cindy. "Matriotism." *Common Dreams.* 22 January 2006. Web. 19 August 2013.

Smith, Andrea. "Queer Theory and Native Studies: The Heteronormativity of Settler Colonialism." *GLQ: A Journal of Lesbian and Gay Studies*, 16:1-2. 2010: 42-68. Print.

Sturgeon, Noël. *Ecofeminist Natures: Race, Gender, Feminist Theory and Political Action.* NewYork: Routledge, 1997. Print.

Swerdlow, Amy. *Women Strike for Peace.* University of Chicago Press, 1993. Print.

15.

Towards a Collective and Materialist Approach to Queer Parenthood

A Conversation with Gary Kinsman

GARY KINSMAN AND MARGARET F. GIBSON

Gary Kinsman is a Canadian sociologist and longtime activist in queer and anti-poverty movements. He is the author of *The Regulation of Desire: Homo and Hetero Sexualities*, co-author (with Patrizia Gentile) of *The Canadian War on Queers: National Security as Sexual Regulation*, and editor of *Whose National Security?* and *Sociology for Changing the World.* Gary and Margaret met on a June morning to discuss queer parenting, class, race, the so-called War on Terror, queer theory, queer Marxism, schooling, and the "neoliberal queer."

M: So the first question is, can you tell me a bit about how queer parenting has figured in your life personally, academically, and politically?

G: I'll start with personally. My partner Patrick and I adopted our son when he was ten and a half. He's now 20. So the first thing I have to say is that it's a life-transformative experience adopting someone, and clearly a lot of people had already put labour into his life. Now he's also living with a learning disability so it's engaging with questions of parenting but also with questions of dealing with someone with a disability and having complex, intimate, sometimes passionate, sometimes angry relationships—all those ranges of experiences.

I think it's also raised a whole series of personal and political questions for me that I would not have encountered in the same way without having had this experience with our son of trying to nurture a young person. When he first came to live with us, I took adoption leave. I had that direct, personal care, nurturing relationship with him which I found quite transformative. Also I developed capacities that you wouldn't necessarily develop or encounter in other ways. A whole set of new questions were raised for me about having to engage with schools in a different way, with doctors in a different way, with a whole range of institutional relations. And certainly around my political perspectives and theorizing having to actually see the centrality of the concerns that young people face.

I can think back to the mid-'70s, when I was in Toronto and people would actually use the term "breeder" as a pejorative term against heterosexuals, which I always had anxieties about. I certainly understand where terms of derision were useful and necessary but that had a lot of political problems in terms of constructing the raising of kids as entirely separate and distinct from being queer and especially from being a queer man. Lesbians earlier on developed a different kind of relationship to this.

In terms of my academic, scholarly work, queer parenting is something I want to engage with but never really get around to. One of the things I really want to explore more is to develop a critique of the social form of schooling [see below]. Also, I've been doing some work on the emergence of autonomous Marxist and Marxist-Feminist forms of organizing in the 1970s. So that's also led me to re-encounter the development of Wages for Housework, and Wages Due Lesbians, but also the emergence of the Lesbian Mothers' Defence Fund which comes out of the work of Wages Due Lesbians. I'm beginning to appreciate that work far more profoundly than I ever did before.

I don't do an awful lot of queer activism in Sudbury. I'm mostly doing anti-poverty activism which brings you into contact with a lot of people parenting and raising kids, to pose things from a somewhat different perspective.

M: I'm going to shift here because you led into another question I had, which is, how do poverty and class come into your understanding of how queer parenting is talked about, practiced, and regulated?

G: The first thing is a general comment that doesn't necessarily directly relate to queer parenting. The way queer theory has impacted on theorizing around queer experiences is that it has largely led to the displacement of class and poverty from theorizing. There is something that it is focused on, that is 'queer,' but class and poverty get jettisoned as not being central. That happens practically in terms of what goes on with the emergence of new types of middle-class professional elites within queer communities, where questions of class and poverty get obliterated or fall off the radar screen in terms of having significance in queer politics. Obviously there is class politics going on all the time. There is a middle-class politics, and class struggles in queer communities, but they are not named as such. It's a much more general problem within queer theoretical work than simply around parenting and questions around mothering. But I think there are some specific problems this poses given the standard institutionalization and the discourses of parenting and mothering in particular.

The standard discourses of motherhood are based on middle-class, white notions. And these are also the notions that get privileged within queer communities in terms of what has been described as homonormativity and homonationalism. What that means is that queer people who are trying to raise kids in a context where they don't have the same access to material privilege, the same access to resources, the same access to social space, just don't have those types of benefits. It's a general problem in the capitalist, racist, patriarchal society we live in, the middle-class notions of how mothering is supposed to take place. And you can see it in curriculum guidelines for schooling. There's this assumption that there are going to be proper, middle-class parents, able to do all these things for their kids.[1] And someone who is on social assistance who is doing vital, socially necessary labour to support their kids in really materially difficult circumstances is not going to be able to access these resources in the same way. And many working-class people aren't going to have access to those either.

The unfortunate thing about the development of what I often describe as "the neo-liberal queer" is that there is an increasing acceptance within queer elites that neoliberal capitalism is the way forward, the way we're going to be able to secure our rights. Part of our movement got a bit confused when we thought we were winning against the moral conservative right wing, which was certainly a big part of the early emergence of neoliberalism. So when we won victories against Anita Bryant or Jerry Falwell we'd think we had won victories against neoliberalism more generally. And I think that's not at all the case, because there's also these less "moral conservative"-strands of neoliberalism that have been more successful in incorporating queer perspectives in a very middle-class, white fashion.

There are real problems in that queer theories, queer writing around parenting has not really raised fundamental questions about class and poverty. I think it's also related to how we've bought back into very individualized and privatized ways of doing parenting. So rather than sharing resources around parenting—which might actually begin to address some of the problems and concerns of parents living in poverty, queer parents living in poverty, or working-class parents—because parenting becomes individualized and privatized, it actually reinforces many of those problems. Queer middle-class people do have the resources to be able to participate in those relationships, when queer people living in poverty don't.

By not raising more fundamental critiques of the individualization and privatization of parenting, by not collectivizing it more, by not seeing it as a more fundamental part of what could become the queer commons, there are major problems. There's an intensification of how parenting gets increasingly defined as being white and middle class, and if you are not white and middle-class you are not living up to both broader social expectations, but also even queer middle-class expectations of what parenting is supposed to be like.

M: Where do you see the current, transnational "war on terror" influencing these sorts of neoliberal discourses of what queer parenting or queer parents should aspire to?

G. I think there are less direct and more clear and concrete ways to make these connections. One is the generation within the Northern, capitalist countries of certain forms of homonationalism, of queer identifications with their nation state.[2] In Canada this notion is that it's through the Charter of Rights and Freedoms, it's through the Canadian state, that we're going to achieve our rights. That's a very misguided notion but there's something to it because the Charter has allowed us to win certain types of victories, especially on the individual and formal level in terms of rights. But on the more substantive level of actually getting at the social roots of heterosexism and the two-gender binary system, it's been much less successful. What that's done, especially in the context of the so-called war on terror, and the new generation of Orientalist homonationalisms directed against people who are Arab or Muslim-identified, has been that you've got growing layers of white gay men (but this has an impact on lesbians and other queer people as well) with an identification with the Canadian nation state as the framework within which our liberation is going to be achieved.

It is also leading to a creation of the Canadian nation-state as the defender of 'us' against the so-called people in the Global South who are being constructed as our enemies, as being 'backward,' and constructed as 'homophobic.' There are lots of problems with that. It is a complete misunderstanding of the gender and sexual diversity among Arab and Muslim people[3] to begin with. And the other problem is that sometimes in the Western gay and lesbian movements, we participate in this problem in suggesting that indigenous gendered and erotic practices, whether it is three or four genders or various ways that eroticism is expressed, either do not exist or that they are somehow more 'primitive' or less 'advanced' than queer people are in the North now. So that's the general context and, I would say, it has led to this intensification of whiteness, of middle-classness within queer communities.[4] This of course raises all sorts of problems for people who are trying to raise kids in other contexts, in other material circumstances, who could never possibly "live up" to that.

The generation of homonationalism and what Lisa Duggan describes as "homonormativity" has major problems if we're trying to actually queer certain forms of parenting, or forms of motherhood.[5] Because what they lead to is the reinforcement of white, middle-class 'normality' around how kids are supposed to be raised, so they actually close down those possible queer critiques of the institutionalization of motherhood. They also close down alternative ways of doing it, more collective, more communal, more social ways of raising kids.

Clearly, for queer people of colour and indigenous queer people trying to raise kids, these generations of homonationalism create major difficulties and I think they create particular difficulties, also, for interracial couples trying to raise kids. If people of colour or people identified as Muslim are constructed as the 'enemy' in homonationalism then it really creates real problems for these people. Because not only are they being read out of being good citizens in the nation state, they are also being read out of, in this homonationalist sense, being good queer people and good parents.

In the context of neoliberalism there is also the "demand" that has been created by some queer parents for kids—not simply a demand coming from queer parents but demands from white, middle-class parents in the global North. You have the whole international adoption system, what some people refer to as the "traffic in babies." Patrick and I, when we thought about adopting, we just ruled out international adoption. I'm not uniformly trying to say that people shouldn't do this. For some people, there may be no alternative and I've seen some wonderful situations developing out of queer parents engaging in international adoptions.

But there is something about uneven development on a global scale, about racialization, about a whole series of problems that are often replicated in those types of relationships. So while neoliberalism has on the one hand led to the easier movement of capital around the world—and to some extent has created ways in which kids from the global south can be transferred here for parenting—it has created more barriers for everyone of the global south who is not highly educated in a formal sense or doesn't have the criteria that they want for immigrants to the Canadian state. For those queer parents, it creates even more difficulty for them, legally, coming into the Canadian state. There are problems around borders and boundaries that then get established that we have to deal with if we are going to establish a queer politics around parenting.

We really do need to engage with those questions. What are the consequences of white, middle-class, queer families adopting a kid from China, let's say? What does that mean about global economic and social pressures that create, in the world, real situations of desperation for parents either that they are giving up their kids or can't possibly support them? Is that the only thing we should be doing, or should we be talking about a global redistribution of wealth that means that people who want to be parents can actually keep their kids? And there are questions raised around indigenous children and the Children's Aid Society (CAS), because my understanding from talking to indigenous activists in northern Ontario is there are now more indigenous kids in CAS custody than there ever were in the residential school system. There are questions of race and racialization that have to be centrally addressed.

M: You've gotten a lot out of that question. I'm wondering if we're moving towards the question of what a queer materialist critique of parenting, queer parenting, and family formation might look like? You are bringing in, not just materialism, but critical race, transnational feminist perspectives, a whole bunch of things together. I guess I'm wondering where a Marxist analysis, or a queer materialism—which is an approach you have taken in your work—where that might take us?[6]

G: I'm sort of taken with the term "queer Marxism" of late.

M: Okay, we'll go with that then. What is "queer Marxism" to you?

G: Queer Marxism is an approach that both learns from queer critiques and the queer critique of Marxism, and is transformed by it, but avoids the limitations of the major strands of queer theory, which have tended to displace material social practices and replace them with rather ungrounded notions of discourse. For instance, Judith Butler's work—which is in some major ways quite wonderful, and I have an incredible respect for the way in which she has been engaging with questions around Israel and Palestine. But if you look at Judith Butler's work and you're looking for knowledge of class and poverty, you'll hardly ever find it.[7] It's just gone. Every once in a while in her work you'll see a reference to economically disadvantaged people, but class as a set of social relationships between people, or even poverty as a major set of social relationships between people, tends to disappear. It is not because Judith Butler is saying "I don't care about poor people, I don't care about working class people." It's that the theoretical perspective that she has adopted leads her to displace some of those material social practices and to focus on a certain notion of discourse that is uprooted from the material social practices in which it needs to be grounded.

What we need is a queer, materialist, Marxist-type approach that has a historical and social character to it, that can paint into the picture those material social practices. It needs to be able to learn from the queer critique and from queer theory, but to be able to resolve some of those questions in a different way, to be able to make visible the material social character of, for example, the discourses of motherhood, or the institutionalization of motherhood. And to not deal with it simply as a narrow discursive question, or a philosophical question, which is, to some extent, where a lot of queer theory ends up. And philosophy is great, but in a certain sense I do still think Marx's quote in *The Theses on Feuerbach* that "Philosophers have only interpreted the world. The point however is to change it" is really useful.[8] We need forms of knowledge that, in this particular context, queer parents, queer mothers, queer kids, 'queer spawn'[9] can use, that could actually make visible what's going on their lives in terms of how it's socially put together so they could collectively begin to act, to try to change it, but also can begin to develop collective, material solutions.

Where I would come back to is there was a real hope in some of the earlier discussions about queer parenting that 'we' would do it differently. That it would actually lead to a major social transformation about how children were being raised. And I think there's many great experiences that queer parents have had, and that lesbian mothers have had. And there are some really good support networks that have been constructed, some very useful programs and practices have been put in place. But by and large, we have been falling back into "we are just like other parents—except we're queer." We have the same types of notions of ownership of our kids, of our parental and individual responsibility. So I think the initial hope that was there was that we would do it differently, that we would transform what parenting was all about, that we would do it in an alternative way. Even though aspects of that hope live on, by and large in the material circumstances of neoliberal capitalism, it's actually led more people to be very individualized and privatized around it.

And I do know some other gay fathers, and it seems to me that that has affected them in even more profound ways, since there never were discussions that took place among gay men who wanted to be parents of how we could do it differently. There was never that same type of feminist political context for it.

M: Where are the lines around mothering and fathering here: is there something about queering those lines that could be personally and politically valuable? And do you think that's been happening?

G: I think one of the really important aspects of raising kids is that to raise kids requires certain kinds of nurturing, caring characteristics that are not your typical aspects of the hegemonic construction of masculinities. So I think the raising of kids, if men begin to engage in what I would describe as "mothering practices"—the nurturing types of relationships with a younger person—that actually develops skills and capacities among men, among queer men, or among any type of men, that are really important resources for us to build on in terms of challenging and transforming masculinities or perhaps getting rid of masculinity altogether. The development among men, whether they are queer men or not, of those nurturing, caring capacities is really important for any broader social transformation. So there is something really important about the development of the social practices of mothering among groups of men, and especially collectivizing that so that it doesn't just stay as an individual experience among some men. And I would like to see more gay men talking about these parenting experiences, and having that made more public and visible.

There is a difference in the institutionalization of mothering and the institutionalization of fathering in this society. I guess the more I think about fathering, the more I think that much of it is historical, patriarchal practices of ownership and control over women, over women's bodies, over the kids. I'm not sure what is so distinctly "good" that could be reclaimed or transformed out of fatherhood or the institutionalization of fatherhood. Obviously we want to challenge it, we want to transform it. There are some men who are not going to be able to articulate their experiences of being parents through "mothering," they're going to want to talk about it as "fathering." So there are ways that we have to engage with that, but I'm just not sure that there is something progressive and useful in transforming what fathering is about as opposed to developing the skills and capacities of mothering and nurturing among men.

For me, focusing on the social experiences of mothering, and how that moves far beyond the social relationships of physiological reproduction, is much more important. Now I still find the work of Adrienne Rich around mothering in *Of Woman Born*—where she makes this important distinction between mothering as a social experience which can be really liberating and empowering for women, versus the ways in which it's institutionalized as systematically subordinating women—to be very useful.[10] So part of what a critical queer politics of mothering and parenting needs to be about is how to expand those empowering social experiences while at the same time figuring out more profound ways in which to resist how mothering and parenting is institutionalized in ways that systematically disadvantages queer parents, women who are parents, lesbians who are parents. That to me is a very useful set of questions to think through in developing a critical queer politics around parenting that could be interrelated with the transformations of broader social and material circumstances. How can you build on the glimpses of liberated types of relationships we can sometimes see in parenting relationships and work against the systematic ways in which women have been regulated through the institutionalization of motherhood?

And a big part of that institutional regulation of mothers and other parents occurs through the systematic devaluation of the resources, the skills, and the capacities that you need to raise kids. This really impacts on people living in poverty. It's normalized that you are supposed to want to have kids, but in some ways it's really materially difficult. The whole social set of relationships is not constructed with nurturing at the centre. It's sort of an add-on, and it's only when you have a middle-class set of material circumstances that you can really do it.

M: I think you brought in other questions that I had there as well, which is great!

G: The socially necessary character of the labour that goes into parenting, and raising kids, is just not recognized. And it often leads me to think back to the theoretical acquisitions that occurred within feminism, and to some extent Marxism-feminism, and the theoretical work leading up to Wages for Housework.[11] Let's leave aside the actual campaign around Wages for Housework at this point in time. But it was an attempt within feminism and Marxism to develop a way of theorizing how socially necessary domestic labour and reproductive labour are. And it seems to me that the feminist movement and the left never adequately addressed that movement and what it made visible. Parenting and mothering is just not seen as "real work."

We need to begin to put in place the notion that at the centre of any real, healthy, living, vibrant society needs to be the nurturing and caring for kids and other people. And that gets us back to how queer critiques are not just about discourse but about transforming the material circumstances of people's lives, and about allowing people to have more control over the material circumstances of their lives.

M: That leads me to a more general question: what do you see queer activist movements having been very successful with? And if you were to provide an agenda for where you think they really need to go—in terms of family, in terms of parenting, in terms of equity—what would you suggest?

G: On the level of formal equality, people have celebrated important victories like those regarding 'same-sex marriage.' But it's on the level of formal, not substantive, equality. Marriage as a privileged relationship on the level of state and social policies is itself a practice of discrimination against all the other types of relationships that people construct. The equal rights and the human rights strategy that was developed out of the gay rights movements led us in one direction. And this is now on offer for other movements like the trans movements—people like Dean Spade offer important critiques about that and its relevance to trans experiences.[12] This 'rights' trajectory led us to wanting to be let in to a whole set of relationships. And there's something potentially transformative about that, but there's something that also can lead to our incorporation into the existing social forms of these relationships as they currently exist. Because what 'we' were looking to be let into were all of those established institutional relationships that made heterosexual people 'normal'. We wanted to be let in too.

I think at the beginning there was this notion that 'we' would transform what spousal relationships were about, that we would transform what family relationships were about. There was a demonstration around the time of the defeat of Bill 167 (on relationship and family recognition rights) in 1994, in Toronto, perhaps it was at the Pride Day march after the defeat of Bill 167 where thousands of people were chanting "We Are Family" at Queen's Park. There was a moment of possible transformation there. But with the legal rights strategy what we actually see is the incorporation of people into the already existing set of spousal relationships, the already existing set of family relationships. And so the moment of transformation gets subordinated to the moment of incorporation. I think that has become really clear around marriage. Again, marriage can make really important material differences in people's lives, so I'm not engaging in a moral critique of individuals who get married. Sometimes it makes complete sense in terms of safety and security for kids, for all sorts of reasons that people might want to get married. But that is not a queering of anything. It is actually a normalization of us into those sets of relationships.

What the Charter [the Canadian Charter of Rights and Freedoms] allowed for was that the movement itself was no longer deciding collectively and democratically what was going to happen. Individuals and their lawyers, particularly individuals who could get funding, whether it was from unions or from some other source, could figure out with their lawyers how they could win victories. There was no longer a participatory, democratic process of movement building. And of course, who has the ability to win legal victories? It's largely going to be white middle-class people, which means that other people fall behind and get excluded more and more. So the unfortunate thing is that the strategy of incorporation is at the very same time also a strategy of exclusion against all those queer people who can't possibly perform themselves in those forms of 'normality.'

In terms of queering parenting, are we actually learning from the alternatives that other people have tried to develop, about raising kids? Whether it's communally, whether it's more extended family situations that have existed in a lot of people of colour communities, whether it's some of the relationships around raising kids in some indigenous communities, that are maybe not 'queering' in the way in which we would describe it, but are trying to develop alternative and different ways of raising kids, often in a more collective fashion. So I think there's a white, middle-class narrowness that gets constructed around queerness that we have to challenge.

M: You mentioned schooling and changing the framework of schooling. Is there something in particular you would like to see us work on in terms of schooling queer kids, queer families, and also just a critique of schooling more generally?

G: Around schooling, part of why I started to think about this is in relationship to the "It Gets Better" campaign, which I had a lot of problems with.[13]

If you tell someone who is thirteen and gay in high school, "If you grin and bear it for three to four more years, it will get better and you'll actually be a stronger person because of it," it's not good news for them. It's not something that's going to provide an alternative. Obviously gay-straight alliances and curriculum changes are better than that. But what I think we need to move toward is challenging what I describe as "social forms." It's a Marxist expression,[14] allowing us to understand that there are particular social forms of family, particular social forms of schooling, that have their own historical conditions of existence.

So around schooling, some of us have learned certain skills as queer parents to go in and demand things for our kids, and to have them accept us in some ways as queer parents, even though we know that in the everyday of school life there is still this assumption that parents are a man and a woman. It's just written into the prevailing social fabric of schooling. If we really want to change it, we need to go so much further than just negotiating individual acceptance with the principal or the teacher, that "oh yeah, it's okay that their son has two dads." It's a much more generalized problem.

But if schooling is seen as a particular social form, that produces a normalized, hegemonic masculinity among young men with the ideology of "boys will be boys" that is used to justify hegemonic heterosexual masculinity, the challenge needs to be far more profound. We realize there is something fundamentally wrong with this social from of schooling, and it needs to be radically transformed. We need to figure out, how is gender a central organizing feature of schooling? What can we do to dislodge this notion that this active, aggressive, sexist, and heterosexist masculinity is supposed to be normal and natural in the schools? Because unless you engage with that, you're not getting at the fundamental social problems that young women are experiencing in the schools or that queer or trans people are experiencing in the schools.

These challenges raise a whole series of questions that we need to think about. How could we, in queer communities, think about more collective, more social notions of parenting? How can we also begin to recognize that the boundaries need to be challenged some more? What Rachel Epstein refers to as "queer spawn"—and to some extent our son would ambivalently identify with that term. He's gone to Pride Day marches, they are part of his culture, his community. So how can we begin to incorporate, into queer communities, people who are heterosexually-identified? It begins to really queer the boundaries of what queer communities are all about.

M: Was there anything more you wanted to say about more collective approaches to parenting? Anything you've tried or seen or have thought might be useful to explore?

G: Unfortunately I think I've had very limited experiences of that. I mean, there certainly are networks of lesbian parents in Sudbury that try to do it more collectively. Less so with gay men who have kids in Sudbury. But by and large, even if they do exist, and you participate in them partially, you still end up back in individualized parental practices. Well it's our son, it's our daughter—they are our property in some ways, that we have to protect and defend, but also that we can tell them what they should be doing and how they should be in some major ways. And I think it just falls back into those individualized and privatized parenting ways.

Now the one area we haven't addressed at all is sexuality. That's central here. There still is on a hegemonic level these notions that queer people are just trouble regarding sexuality, especially if you put queer people and kids at all in the same relationship. That contributes to some of the barriers to more collective practices since some of us (not necessarily on a conscious level) think that having a kid around a whole bunch of gay men might be seen by other people as a problem, and they might construct us as bad parents.

This means having much more frank discussions about eroticism and sexuality for young people, and recognizing that those discussions are going to be difficult. We have to begin to address those questions that have been quite displaced by what I would describe as the emergence of the neoliberal queer or the homonormative queer, which in some ways has led to desexualizing, to de-eroticizing the queer struggle so that we can be seen as being much more 'normal.' But I think we are going to have to get much more into those questions, and realize that we have to open up these discussions. There are still going to be people that continue to think that two men raising a kid together is sexually troubling, but even more troubling regarding gender. Where's the man? Where's the male role model? The thing is that when two men raise kids there are all sorts of sex-related questions that get raised.

M: That seems like one of those domains where the historical resonance might be different for women than for men.

G: Yes, I think the direct, sexual threat—especially given how the historical association of child sexual molestation and homosexuality was put in place in the 1950s and 60s[15]—that's there for gay men. But there are gendered aspects for lesbians that also can be regenerated. There was this media coverage, especially around alternative insemination, in Britain in the later 1970s, one of the newspapers used the expression about lesbians raising kids as "a manless horror world."[16] Even with all this acceptance of formal legal equality for lesbians and gay men, if you scratch the surface of the liberal tolerance, you still get incredible levels of violence. That's in part because the underlying social relationships haven't been altered. So you can change the legal procedures which have some real material impacts on people's lives, but you need to change an awful lot more than that.

This interview has been condensed and edited by the authors.

NOTES

[1]See Griffith and Smith *Mothering for Schooling* on the work expected of mothers by schools.
[2]See Jasbir Puar's *Terrorist Assemblages* (4) on homonationalism.
[3]See Joseph Massad, *Desiring Arabs* and Jasbir Puar, *Terrorist Assemblages* on this.
[4]On aspects of this see Kinsman "Challenging Canadian and Queer Nationalisms" and "Queerness Is Not In Our Genes."
[5]See Lisa Duggan, *The Twilight of Equality? Neoliberalism, Cultural Politics, and the Attack on Democracy.*

[6]See Kinsman and Gentile *The Canadian War on Queers,* and Kinsman *The Regulation of Desire*, "Challenging Canadian and Queer Nationalisms," and "Queerness Is Not In Our Genes."
[7]See Butler, *Gender Trouble* and *Undoing Gender.*
[8]See Marx *Theses on Feuerbach.*
[9] Epstein, Idems and Schwartz "Reading, Writing, and Resilience" and Evans "A Queer Spawn Manifesto."
[10]See Rich *Of Woman Born: Motherhood as Experience and Institution.*
[11] See Mariarosa Dalla Costa and Selma James, *The Power of Women and the Subversion of the Community* and Silvia Federici, *Wages Against Housework...*
[12]Dean Spade, *Normal Life: Administrative Violence, Critical Trans Politics, and the Limits of Law.*
[13]See Jasbir Puar, "In the Wake of It Gets Better."
[14] See Corrigan, *Social Forms-Human Capacities*, and Holloway, *How to Change the World Without Taking Power.*
[15]See Kinsman and Gentile, *The Canadian War on Queers* and Kinsman *The Regulation of Desire.*
[16]See Susan Hemmings, "Horrific Practices."

WORKS CITED

Butler, Judith. *Gender Trouble: Feminism and the Subversion of Identity.* London: Routledge, 1990. Print.

Bulter, Judith. *Undoing Gender.* London; Routledge, 2004. Print.

Corrigan, Philip. *Social Forms-Human Capacities: Essays in Authority and Difference.* London: Routledge, 1990. Print.

Dalla Costa, Mariarosa and Selma James, *The Power of Women and the Subversion of the Community.* Bristol: Falling Wall Press, 1972. Print.

Duggan, Lisa. *The Twilight of Equality? Neoliberalism, Cultural Politics, and the Attack on Democracy.* Boston: Beacon Press, 2003. Print.

Epstein, Rachel, Becky Idems, and Adinne Schwartz. "Reading, Writing, and Resilience: Queer Spawn Speak Out about School." *Who's Your Daddy? And Other Writings on Queer Parenting.* Ed. Rachel Epstein. Toronto: Sumach Press, 2009. 215-232. Print.

Evans, Jamie K. "A Queer Spawn Manifesto." *Who's Your Daddy? And Other Writings on Queer Parenting.* Ed. Rachel Epstein. Toronto: Sumach Press, 2009. 234-239. Print.

Federici, Silvia. *Wages Against Housework.* London: Power of Women Collective/ Falling Wall Press, 1975. Print.

Griffith, Alison I. and Dorothy E. Smith. *Mothering for Schooling.* New York: RoutledgeFalmer, 2005. Print.

Hemmings, Susan, "Horrific Practices: How Lesbians Were Presented in the Newspapers of 1978." *Homosexuality, Power and Politics.* Ed. Gay Left Collective. London and New York: Allison and Busby, 1980. 157-171. Print.

Holloway, John. *How to Change the World Without Taking Power: The Meaning of Revolution Today.* London: Pluto, 2005. Print.

Kinsman, Gary. *The Regulation of Desire: Homo and Heterosexualities (2nd ed.).* Montreal: Black Rose Books, 1996. Print.

Kinsman, Gary. "Challenging Canadian and Queer Nationalisms." *In a Queer Country: Gays and Lesbian Studies in the Canadian Context.* Ed. Terry Goldie. Vancouver: Pulp Arsenal Press, 2001. 209-234. Print.

Kinsman, Gary. "Queerness Is Not In Our Genes: Biological Determinism versus Social Liberation." *Making Normal: Social Regulation in Canada.* Ed. Deborah Brock. Toronto: Thomson Nelson, 2003. 262-284. Print.

Kinsman, Gary and Patrizia Gentile. *The Canadian War on Queers: National Security as Sexual Regulation.* Vancouver: UBC Press, 2010. Print.

Marx, Karl. "Theses on Feuerbach." *Karl Marx and Frederick Engels: Selected Works.* New York: International, 1968. Print.

Massad, Joseph. *Desiring Arabs.* Chicago: University of Chicago Press, 2007. Print.

Puar, Jasbir, K. *Terrorist Assemblages: Homonationalism in Queer Times.* Durham and London: Duke University Press, 2007. Print.

Puar, Jasbir. "In the Wake of It Gets Better." *theguardian.com*, Tuesday 16 November 2010, http://www.theguardian.com/commentisfree/cifamerica/2010/nov/16/wake-it-gets-better-campaign

Rich, Adrienne. *Of Woman Born: Motherhood as Experience and Institution (2nd ed.).* New York: W.W. Norton & Co., 1986. Print.

Spade, Dean. *Normal Life: Administrative Violence, Critical Trans Politics, and the Limits of Law.* Brooklyn, NY: South End Press, 2011. Print.

Contributors' Biographies

Tanya M. Cassidy is a Cochrane Fellow in the Department of Anthropology at the National University of Ireland, Maynooth (NUIM) and an adjunct Professor with the Department of Sociology, Anthropology and Criminology at the University of Windsor, Canada. Her doctoral research, from the Department of Sociology at the University of Chicago, USA, concerned a socio-cultural study of gender, family and alcohol in Ireland. In 2005 she took a career break that has resulted in a new research trajectory. She is now returning to full time research and adapting her work to issues related to the sociology of reproduction, in particular the feeding of the prematurely born.

Cary Gabriel Costello is an associate professor in the Department of Sociology and Coordinator of LGBT Studies at the University of Wisconsin-Milwaukee. He researches and teaches on sociology of the body, intersectional identity, science/medicine/technology, and social problems. He is an intersex person, assigned female at birth, now transitioned to male status, and is the birth parent of a teenaged daughter. He blogs about intersex issues at http://intersexroadshow.blogspot.com/.

Christa Craven is Chair of Women's, Gender, and Sexuality Studies (WGSS) and an Associate Professor of Anthropology and WGSS at The College of Wooster. She is the author of Pushing for Midwives: Homebirth Mothers and the Reproductive Rights Movement (2010) and co-editor of

Feminist Activist Ethnography: Counterpoints to Neoliberalism in North America (with Dána-Ain Davis, 2013). She is former co-chair of the Society of Lesbian and Gay Anthropologists (now the Association for Queer Anthropology). Her current project centers on the narratives of lesbian, gay, bisexual, trans*, and queer families about pregnancy, adoption, and loss.

Raine Dozier is a trans-identified queer mother of two daughters with a long history of activism, parenting, intellectual inquiry, and laundry. She is a sociologist and an associate professor in the Department of Human Services and Rehabilitation at Western Washington University. Raine is a gender theorist with research interests in inequality, gender, and race/ethnicity. Her article, "Beards, Breasts, & Bodies" was awarded the distinguished article in sex and gender by the American Sociological Association. She lives with her youngest daughter in Bellingham, Washington, a place of great beauty and few queers.

Rachel Epstein (MA, PhD) is a longtime LGBTQ parenting activist, educator and researcher and coordinates the LGBTQ Parenting Network at the Sherbourne Health Centre in Toronto, Canada. She has published on a wide range of issues, including assisted human reproduction, queer spawn in schools, butch pregnancy, and the tensions between queer sexuality, radicalism and parenting. Rachel is the editor of the 2009 anthology, Who's Your Daddy? And Other Writings on Queer Parenting (available from threeoclockpress.com) and recently published a chapter on queer parenting in Canada in Fitzgerald, M. and Rayter, S. (eds.) Queerly Canadian (Canadian Scholars' Press, 2012). Her doctoral dissertation was entitled "Married, Single or Gay?: Queerying and Trans-forming the Practices of Assisted Human Reproduction Services."

T. Garner is an instructor in the Department of Gender, Sexuality, and Women's Studies at Simon Fraser University and Community Organizer of the BC Poverty Reduction Coalition. Hir research is at the intersection of queer and transgender theory, critical studies of health and pathology, and new media studies. Recent works include "Chest Surgeries of a Different 'Nature' " (Annual Review of Critical Psychology, 2014) and "(De)Pathologization: Transsexuality, Gynecomastia, and the Negotiation of Mental Health Diagnoses in Online Communitions" (Critical Inquiries: Theories and Methodologies for Social Justice in Mental Health, forthcoming).

Margaret F. Gibson is a queer mother, social worker, and doctoral candidate in the Factor-Inwentash Faculty of Social Work at the University of Toronto. Her research interests include critical disability studies, queer theory, feminist research methods, and parenting studies. Margaret's work has been published in several book collections and journals including Culture, Health & Sexuality, The British Journal of Social Work, Disability Studies Quarterly, and Signs: A Journal of Women and Culture. Her current project is an ethnographic study of queer parents whose children have disabilities or 'special needs'.

Alisa Grigorovich is a post-doctorate fellow at University of Toronto. Her research interests include caregiving, aging, health care policy, sex/gender based analysis and LGBTQ health. Her PhD thesis was a feminist political economy analysis of older lesbian and bisexual women's experiences of using home care services in Ontario.

Barbara Gurr is currently an Assistant Professor in Residence in the Women's, Gender and Sexuality Studies Program at the University of Connecticut. Her research on reproductive healthcare for Native women has been published in the International Journal of Sociology of the Family and Sociology Compass among other places. Her current research examines family identity tasks for parents with affirmed transgender children.

Kelly Jeske is a queer femme, mama, and social work graduate student living in Portland, Oregon. Her essays have appeared in Who's Your Mama? The Unsung Voices of Women and Mothers, Storied Dishes: What Our Family Recipes Tell Us About Who We Are and Where We've Been, and The Adoption Constellation. Kelly reaches for time to write amidst the intensity of school, work, and parenting, and is excited about her recent steps into writing fiction.

Sujay Kentlyn is the LGBTI Elders' Wellbeing Project Officer for aged care service provider Evergreen Life Care. The project aims to deliver health and wellness capacity building programs to older lesbian, gay, bisexual, transgender and intersex people and service providers across NSW. Sujay is a sociologist whose work has focused on sex, gender and sexuality, as well as LGBTI ageing. Sujay has taught and researched at The University of

Queensland, conducted training in sexuality, sex and gender for health care and community sector workers throughout Queensland, and conducts training in providing culturally appropriate services to LGBTI older people.

Gary Kinsman and his partner Patrick live with their son who has transformed both their lives. Gary is the author of *The Regulation of Desire: Homo and Hetero Sexualities*, co-author (with Patrizia Gentile) of *The Canadian War on Queers: National Security as Sexual Regulation*, and editor of *Whose National Security?*, and *Sociology for Changing the World*. He is currently working on a new book called *The Making of the Neo-Liberal Queer* and is involved in the AIDS Activist History Project and the Sudbury Coalition Against Poverty. He has taken early retirement from teaching sociology at Laurentian University, on the territories of the Atikameksheng Anishnawbek nation.

Mary Jo Klinker is an Assistant Professor of Women's and Gender Studies at Winona State University. Her research focuses on the relation of queer activism and theory to feminist antimilitarist organizing and anti-imperialist critique. Mary Jo's teaching interests include LGBT/Queer politics and history, transnational feminism, and postfeminist media studies.

Katharina Miko is a sociologist who works as a post-doc researcher at the Center for Social Research Methods at the Vienna University of Economics and Business, Austria. Her main fields of research are gender studies, family research, security studies and sociological film. Recently she published her first sociological film "Queer feelings – Four love stories from Austria" (http://www.geyrhalterfilm.com/warme_gefuehle) which combines sociological research with film work within a queer studies approach. Her current main field of work is ethnographic and participatory research in security studies.

Joani Mortenson is queer momma social worker, a writer/blogger, a therapist and yoga teacher in private practice in White Rock, BC, Canada. She recently exited academia in order to avail herself fully of a more peaceful, wild-informed and artful life. Joani's scholarly life spanned 1 & ¾ graduate degrees and focused on research that examined queer-identified families who accessed midwifery services, and the roles of co-mothers in parenting.

With a passionate focus on diversity, inclusion and other social justice concerns, Joani now turns her skill set to working with diverse children and families who yearn for holistic, integrated and creative approaches to radiant health. Joani can be found at: http://jmty.ca

Luke Mortenson is an electrician living in the Okanagan (BC, Canada) with his wife and two beagles. He makes noise on weekends with his soul band. For whatever reason, Luke can't drink enough coffee or eat enough five cent candies. Luke loves his momma.

Elizabeth Peel is Professor of Psychology & Social Change at the University of Worcester, UK. She is a critical psychologist with research interests in health, sexualities and gender. She was an inaugural British Academy Mid-Career Fellow (2011). Her latest book *Lesbian, Gay, Bisexual, Trans & Queer Psychology: An Introduction* (Cambridge University Press, 2010, with Victoria Clarke, Sonja J. Ellis and Damien W. Riggs) won the British Psychological Society book award 2013.

Damien Riggs is an Australian Research Council Future Fellow and senior lecturer in social work at Flinders University, where he teaches and researches in the areas of gender/sexuality, family studies, and mental health. He is the author of over 100 publications in these areas including *What about the Children! Masculinities, Sexualities and Children* (Cambridge Scholars Press, 2010), and in 2013 was the winner (with Victoria Clarke, Sonja Ellis and Elizabeth Peel) of the British Psychological Society book prize for the text *Lesbian, Gay, Bisexual, Trans and Queer Psychology: An Introduction* (Cambridge University Press, 2010).

Karin Sardadvar is a sociologist who works as a senior researcher at the Working Life Research Centre (FORBA) in Vienna, Austria, and teaches sociology at the University of Vienna. Her main fields of research and teaching are sociological theory, gender studies, family studies, and work research. She has received several scientific awards for her Master's thesis on gender and parental leave, her Ph.D thesis on older mothers, and her teaching in the field of family research. She is currently working in research projects on parenthood and employment and on gender equality in companies.